T0302278

The Digital Disruption of Financial Services

This book contributes to the present state of knowledge, offering the reader broad evidence on how new digital technologies impact financial systems. It focuses on both macro- and micro-perspectives of ICT influence on financial markets.

The book demonstrates how ICT can impact trading systems or information systems, which are crucial for financial systems to work effectively. It also shows how individuals can benefit from the adoption of digital technologies for everyday financial (e.g., banking) systems usage. The book provides empirical evidence of how digital technologies revolutionize the banking sector and stock exchange trading system and explores the associations between technology and various aspects of firms' functioning. Furthermore, it raises elements of financial inclusion, ICT-based microfinance service and finance-related gender issues.

The principal audience of the book will be scholars and academic professionals from a wide variety of disciplines, particularly in the fields of finance and economics. It will be especially useful for those who are addressing the issues of new technologies and the financial markets, FinTech, financial innovations, stock markets, and the role of technological progress in a broadly defined socio-economic system. It will be a valuable source of knowledge for graduate and postgraduate students in economic and social development, information and technology, worldwide studies, social policy or comparative economics.

Ewa Lechman is Professor of Economics at the Faculty of Management and Economics at Gdańsk University of Technology, Poland.

Adam Marszk is Assistant Professor at the Faculty of Management and Economics at Gdańsk University of Technology, Poland.

Banking, Money and International Finance

The Digital Disruption of Financial Services

International Perspectives

Edited by
Ewa Lechman and Adam Marszk

Routledge
Taylor & Francis Group

LONDON AND NEW YORK

First published 2021
by Routledge
2 Park Square, Milton Park, Abingdon, Oxon OX14 4RN

and by Routledge
605 Third Avenue, New York, NY 10158

Routledge is an imprint of the Taylor & Francis Group, an informa business

British Library Cataloguing-in-Publication Data
A catalogue record for this book is available from the British Library

Library of Congress Cataloging-in-Publication Data
Names: Lechman, Ewa, editor. | Marszk, Adam, editor.
Title: The digital disruption of financial services : international
perspectives / edited by Ewa Lechman and Adam Marszk.
Description: 1 Edition. | New York, NY : Routledge, 2022. | Series:
Banking, money and international finance | Includes bibliographical
references and index.
Identifiers: LCCN 2021027247 (print) | LCCN 2021027248 (ebook) |
ISBN 9781032057699 (hardback) | ISBN 9781032057682 (paperback) |
ISBN 9781003199076 (ebook)
Subjects: LCSH: Financial services industry–Technological
innovations. | Capital market–Technological innovations. | Information
technology–Management. | Digital media–Economic aspects.
Classification: LCC HG4515.5 .D54 2022 (print) | LCC HG4515.5
(ebook) | DDC 332/.04150285–dc23
LC record available at https://lccn.loc.gov/2021027247
LC ebook record available at https://lccn.loc.gov/2021027248

ISBN: 978-1-032-05769-9 (hbk)
ISBN: 978-1-032-05768-2 (pbk)
ISBN: 978-1-003-19907-6 (ebk)

DOI: 10.4324/9781003199076

Typeset in Times New Roman
by KnowledgeWorks Global Ltd.

Contents

Figures

Tables

Authors short bios

Fernando Lera-Lopez is Professor of Applied Economy at Public University of Navarra and senior researcher at the Institute for Advanced Research in Business and Economics. His research interests include Information and Communication Technologies (ICT) diffusion, their economic impacts, the digital divide and economic development, and ICT adoption among firms and households. His work has been published in international refereed journals, such as Telematics and Informatics, Telecommunications Policy, Review of World Economics, Tecnovation, International Journal of Human Resource Management, Industrial Management & Data Systems, Growth and Change, International Journal of Manpower, European Planning Studies, Empirical Economics, Information Technology and People, Information Development, and Journal of Global Information Technology Management, among others. He has been visiting professor in several universities and institutions, such as Sheffield Hallam University and Loughborough University, in the UK. He has continuously participated in research projects with the financial support of the Spanish Ministry of Science and Innovation. Also, he has enjoyed several national and international research grants.

Rocío Marco is Associate Professor of Applied Economy at Autonomous University of Madrid (Spain). Her research interests include the Information and Communication Technologies (ICT) diffusion and the digital divide, gender, and economic performance. She has published articles in various refereed journals, including International Journal of Hospitality Management, Empirical Economics, Information Technology and People, Journal of Finance & Economics, Business Ethics-A European Review, Telecommunications Policy, and Review of World Economics, among others.

Margarita Billon is Associate professor at the School of Economics and Business at Autonomous University of Madrid (Spain) where she also got her Ph.D. in Economics. Her current research focuses primarily on the economic impacts of Information and Communication Technologies (ICT) and the digital divide, digital innovation, ICT and economic development. Her work has been published in international refereed journals, such as Telematics and Informatics, Research Evaluation, Telecommunications Policy, Review of World Economics, Growth and Change, International Journal of Manpower, European Planning Studies, Empirical Economics, Information Technology and People, Journal of Global Information Technology Management, among others. She has been visiting professor in several universities and institutions, such as University of Essex, University of Amsterdam, and Dickinson College, Pennsylvania (USA). She received a Fulbright scholarship from the US State Department for university teachers and also enjoyed many other research grants. She has been the director of the Research Group CONOCYTEC at UAM until 2015. She is Academic Advisor and Board member for the PhD and MBA programs in Economics and Management of UAM-Accenture Chair in Economics and Innovation Management. She participates in several international programmes and collaborates with the Jean Monet network, "The European Union, Mediterranean and Africa integration in the Global Age" (AMENET).

Oskar Kowalewski is Professor of Finance at the Department of Finance at the IESEG School of Management (Campus Paris), member of LEM-CNRS 9221 and Associate Professor at the Institute of Economics, Polish Academy of Sciences. He is Fellow of the Wharton Financial Institutions Center at the University of Pennsylvania. He received his habilitation in Finance from the Warsaw School of Economics. He holds a Ph.D. and MS degree from the Kozminski University and LLM degree from the Maria Curie-Sklodowska University. His research focuses on financial system development, financial innovations and financial intermediaries' performance, in particular on the banking industry.

Paweł Pisany is economist and lawyer, Ph.D. in finance, Assistant Professor at the Institute of Economics, Polish Academy of Sciences. He completed a Ph.D. program at the Warsaw School of Economics, holds Master's degree in finance and accounting from the Warsaw School of Economics and a Master's degree in law from the University of Warsaw. He is most active in the research areas of the development and stability of financial systems, in particular in the context of the ownership structure in developed and emerging economies, as well the impact of technological innovations on the financial system and the financial intermediaries.

Joanna Wolszczak-Derlacz is an Associate Professor at Gdańsk University of Technology, Faculty of Management and Economics, Poland. Her scientific interests focus on the theory and empirics of economic convergence, productivity and efficiency analyzes, economics of education and labour markets. In 2015, she obtained habilitation based on the two series of publications: "Efficiency and productivity of higher education institutions" and "Convergence of wages and prices" for which she received Awards of the Prime Minister and Minister of Science and Higher Education. She was a visiting scholar at University of Rome "La Sapienza" (September 2019–January 2020), University of California, Berkeley (September 2013–May 2014), European University Institute in Florence (2007–2008), Katholieke Universitei Leuven (September 2005–February 2006), and Glasgow University (March–June 2004). She has been a principal investigator of various research projects, among others funded by Ernst & Young under the Better Government Program, National Science Centre, Polish Ministry of Science and Higher Education and Center for Economic Research and Graduate Education of Charles University (CERGE). In the period: 2016–2019 she was holding Jean Monnet Chair in Economics. Currently, she is Principal Investigator of project: "Effects of global production networks on employment, earnings and factor allocation in the presence of workers, firms and tasks heterogeneity," funded by National Science Centre, Poland. She is a member of the Science of Science Committee of the Polish Academy of Science. In December 2018, she has been appointed to a member of the Council of the National Science Centre (NCN).

Amar Nath Das has been teaching Commerce at the Department of Commerce, Nabagram Hiralal Paul College since the last 4 years. He has also been served as guest faculty in post graduate section at Department of Commerce, The University of Calcutta since 2012. Dr. Das received Doctorate degree from the University of Burdwan. His areas of research interest include Financial Inclusion, Financial Literacy, and Human Development. He has published a number of research articles in Scopus listed national and internationally reputed journals of Social Science, as also in an edited volume published by *Springer Nature publishers.*

Arindam Laha has been teaching Economics at the Department of Commerce, The University of Burdwan, West Bengal since the last 11 years. Gold-medalist in Post-graduation from the University of Burdwan and State Funded Research Fellow, The University of Burdwan, Dr. Laha received Doctorate degree from the University of Burdwan. His areas of research interest include Agrarian Institutions, Financial Inclusion, Financial Literacy, Human Development, and Social and Solidarity Economy. He has written one book and has published a number of research articles in Web of Science and Scopus listed national and internationally reputed journals of Social Science, as also in various edited volumes published by Routledge Publication, Cambridge Scholars Publishing, *IGI Global, Emerald, Springer Nature, and Taylor and Francis publishers.* He also actively engaged in executing research projects of various funding agencies, UGC and ICSSR. He has also co-authored chapter in District Human Development Report (UNDP and Govt. of West Bengal) and District Gazetteer Report (Govt. of West Bengal). He has been awarded ILO's South-South

Triangular Cooperation (SSTC) scholarship to participate in the 8th Social and Solidarity Economy Academy at Seoul, South Korea.

Tomasz Korol, Ph.D. in economics obtained in June 2004, and the degree of habilitated doctor in March 2015 at Gdansk University of Technology (GUT). Principal investigator of two research grants obtained at the National Science Center (NCN) in Poland. He also participated in panel meetings of experts reviewing research applications submitted to the NCN. In 2015–2016, he was a member of accreditation committee at SKVC – Center for Quality Assessment in Higher Education in Lithuania, evaluating four economic universities. In 2015–2020, he was the Chairman of the Faculty Committee for Education Quality Assurance, and since September 2020, he is the Vice-Dean for Science and the Chairman of the Social Sciences Council at the GUT. Author of seven papers published in journals from the JCR list (the total Impact Factor is 14.08). According to the Google Scholar database, his publications have been cited 710 times, and the Hirsch Index is 12. The reviewer of papers for such JCR journals as Economic Modeling, European Journal of Operational Research, Knowledge-Based Systems. He won the international competition for the position of "associate professor" twice – at Tecnologico de Monterrey in Mexico (2008–2009) and I-Shou University in Taiwan (2012–2013). Both universities are listed in high positions in the international TOP 500 university rankings in the world. In 2002–2007, he was also a visiting lecturer at the University of Applied Science Stralsund in Germany.

Rashmi Umesh Arora is a senior lecturer in development economics at University of Bradford, United Kingdom. Prior to joining Bradford as a lecturer, she was Research Fellow in the Department of Accounting, Finance and Economics, Griffith Business School, Griffith University, Australia. In 2007 she was also a Postdoctoral Research Fellow at the Centre for Asia Pacific Social Transformation Studies, University of Wollongong, Australia. She has also worked as Assistant Adviser and Research Officer in the Reserve Bank of India (India's central bank) in its economic policy department for several years. Her current teaching and research areas are finance for development, economic growth and developing economies and development economics. She has published in several well-known international journals including World Development, Applied Economics, Journal of Developing Areas, Third World Quarterly among others.

Błażej Prusak works as an Associate Professor of Economics in the Management and Economics Faculty of Gdansk University of Technology, Poland. He is Head of the Finance Department. His main research interests are corporate bankruptcy prediction, institutional aspects of corporate bankruptcy, business valuation, investment projects, financial analysis, risk management, and stock recommendations. Currently, he is a representative of the Editorial Board of the Intellectual Economics Journal, as well as a member of the Reviewer Board of the Journal of Risk and Financial Management. He is the author or co-author of several monographs about corporate bankruptcy, financial analysis, stock recommendations and market ratios. He has also published in several international journals.

Marcin Potrykus is an Assistant Professor at the Faculty of Management and Economics, Gdansk University of Technology, Poland. His scientific interests mainly concern the construction of the investment portfolio using not only traditional investments but also less known alternative investments. His other scientific interests are connected with event studies and hedonic regression. He is a member of the Polish Finance and Banking Association since 2013. He was an organizer of the conference "The First Million" together with Kronenberg Foundation. He is a supervisor for the team in the CFA Research Challenge and a mentor in the "School of Eagles" program of Ministry of Science and Higher Education.

Oluwafemi Michael Olagunju, FCA, is a Fellow of the Institute of Chartered Accountants of Nigeria (ICAN). He is currently a staff of the Bursary Department of the University of Ibadan, Nigeria. He bagged his Bachelor and Master degrees in Accounting from the Olabisi Onabanjo University, Nigeria. He has several years of working experience in the Nigerian commercial banking sector and other private sectors organizations as a chartered accountant. He also runs and teaches in a school dedicated to training and preparing students for the ICAN professional examination. Currently he works at the Investment and Endowment Unit of the Department of Bursary, University of Ibadan, Nigeria.

Samuel C. Avemaria Utulu, Ph.D., is an Assistant Professor at the Department of Information Systems, School of Information Technology and Computing, American University of Nigeria, Yola, Nigeria. He backed Master degrees in Information Science at the Africa Regional Center for Information and Data Sciences, University of Ibadan, Nigeria and his doctoral degree at the University of Cape Town, South Africa. He won the Research Associate Award of the University of Cape Town, South Africa, in 2014. The award is given by the university's Vice-Chancellor to Postgraduate students with good records of scholarly publishing. He has over ten years working experience as Systems Librarian and Lecturer at Bells University of Technology, Nigeria, Redeemer's University, Nigeria and Afe Babalola University, Nigeria. He has also taught at the Information Science Unit of the Department of Library and Information Science, Faculty of Business and Social Sciences, Adeleke University, Nigeria. Dr. Utulu has attended several international conferences around the world and has about thirty publications in journals, conference proceedings and chapters in book of readings. His research interests include development informatics and adoption and implementation of information systems for education.

Acknowledgements

This work was supported by the National Science Centre in Poland under Grant no. 2015/19/B/HS4/03220.

Foreword

The digital disruption of financial services:
International perspectives

Digital disruption is a term that describes changes to established operating models or functions under specific circumstances due to digitalization. The areas of digital destruction can be industry, organization, and society. Digital disruption often affects all three levels. The concept of digital disruption is based on two different foundations: digital innovation and disruptive innovation. Disruptive innovations are innovations that disrupt other entities (such as a product, company, or industry). Usually, they start attacking the market's periphery, but they gradually grow to replace the market's current operator position. The business model will change. The field of digital disruptions is not well studied. Therefore, we welcome this book to tackle the challenges of digital disruptions in financial services. It can be beneficial in terms of analysis, and especially in terms of vision and directions in the short medium term. Bill Gates stated that "Banking is necessary, banks are not." This statement applies to financial services in general. Traditional and new financial services still exist. To stay relevant, they need to innovate, take advantage of the digital revolution, and completely rethink financial services' role to add value to the customers. This change in cultural concepts can be a significant challenge in implementing new business models. Some people may think that digitalization alone can bring revolutionary innovations to the financial industry. This statement is not true. Fintech organizations are one of the leading proponents of digital destruction. The suffix "tech" in the word fintech may mislead people into thinking that fintech organizations are merely technical financial services applications. Not so. Many fintech organizations do not limit innovation to technology. Fintech organizations can introduce new digital technologies but successful fintech organizations also introduce new business models that disrupt existing financial services models. The papers in this book discuss the main determinants of digital disruptions: digital innovation and disruptive innovations such as sustainability and inclusiveness. Recently, another factor of disruptive innovation has emerged: the pandemic and the vision of a new normal. This factor has become a powerful accelerating force for digital disruption of financial services with business model innovation. This book recognizes that disruptive innovation will vary from culture to culture. Globalization is certainly relevant, but more people and countries are discovering each economy and each country characteristics. Examples of digital disruptions are coming from emerging parts of the world: like Mpesa in Africa or Ant Financials in Asia.

This book reminds Darwin's words: "It is neither the strongest species nor the brightest. The things that survive are the ones that are most adaptable to change." The dilemma in digital disruptions is not "if" but "when." The answer is now.

Bernardo Nicoletti
Professor of Management Science at Temple University

A note from the editors

Rationale

Digital technologies are claimed General Purpose Technologies; hence they generate path-breaking innovations and are recognized as fundamental factors in long-run technological progress and deep-going structural and qualitative shifts in economy and society (Bresnahan, 2010; Coccia, 2017; Sahal, 1981). As argued in Rosenberg and Trajtenberg (2001), digital technologies are *epochal innovations* as they demonstrate the capacity to radically reshape the contours of the world economy, ways of doing business, enforce the emergence of new industries, services *et alia* (Cheng et al., 2021). Digital technologies are also widely acknowledged as critical drivers for knowledge and information acquiring, labour and capital productivity, social, political, and economic empowerment (Fernández-Portillo et al., 2020; Graham, 2019). Digital technologies, due to the strong network effects (Katz & Shapiro, 1985) that they generate, they enable the emergence of various networks reshaping the way that businesses are run, trading and consumption patterns, economic and social behaviours, social norms and attitudes (Graham & Dutton, 2019).

Financial systems are not digitally neutral; it is widely acknowledged that digital technologies fundamentally reshape financial systems (Comin & Nanda, 2019; Kauffman et al., 2015). Technological progress is a disruptive process that alters financial system structures, stimulating the emergence of a new *status quo*. Digital technologies by creating effective and cheap ways for information flows, they define how the financial system functions (Coccia, 2018; Nambisan et al., 2019). The crucial impact of digital technologies on financial systems is demonstrated through the emergence of cutting-edge changes, but above all, the generation and emergence of various networks, eliminating information asymmetries (Farboodi & Veldkamp, 2020). Fast and unlimited flows of information among geographically separated agents effectively boost both the volume and value of financial markets transactions; the broad adoption of ICT enhances the emergence of the unique financial system network, which links agents facilitating the exchange of information among them and – to some point – links financial institutions and legal frameworks that seem to influence one another. ICT contribute to the emergence of new, tech-based financial products, trading techniques, and information systems, which – in the longer time perspective, change the way the financial systems work and economic agents behave. Financial systems may be claimed as information systems (Henrique et al., 2019; Wilhelm, 2001), and the emergence of such system due to ICT deployment network connectivity effectively strengthens, it makes it work more effectively, and thus increases the profits it generates. Fast spread of various types of information may lead to gradual eradication of information inequalities and hence to the elimination of one of the market failures that hinders the system's effectiveness. ICT introduction effects in the financial system are not limited to the eradication of information asymmetries, but above all new technologies bring new opportunities to the financial systems. These new opportunities are, in the first place, demonstrated through the development and diffusion of new financial products and pricing systems (Gomber et al., 2018; Wong et al., 2017).

Financial markets shaped by the adoption of new technologies can be labelled *digital financial markets* (Eholzer & Roth, 2017; Moşteanu, 2019). Despite the economy broad profound changes inflicted by the diffusion of ICT, the existence of dynamic links between technological progress and various aspects of financial markets cannot be neglected. Digital technologies also influence the infrastructure of financial systems (Essendorfer et al., 2015), like, e.g., financial markets facilitate trading, processing, and settlement of securities, commodities, and currencies between counterparties as well as the provision of other supportive services such as aggregation of data and information from multiple sources. Adoption of digital technologies means that the position of floor-based exchanges diminishes as market participants begin to opt for exchanges with electronic trading systems due to their time and cost efficiency, processes that were labelled by Hendershott and Madhavan (2015) as "voice to electronic." It also means that competition among trading venues becomes more intensive as incumbents are challenged by new entrants due to lowered entry barriers – the most noticeable area is derivatives trading (e.g., futures and options), where the linked effect is the introduction of new types of contracts, unfeasible to trade on conventional exchanges (Ernkvist, 2015; Lee et al., 2010), yet it applies to all types of dematerialized securities, i.e., held in the form of digital records at depositary institution (Kauffman et al., 2015); the benefit of the dematerialization, which does not require physical exchange of the transacted stocks, is reduction of the transactions' costs and duration.

Structure and content

This book contributes to the present state of knowledge, offering the reader broad evidence on how digital technologies impact financial systems. The authors take a broad perspective and show how ICT can impact trading systems or information systems that are crucial for financial systems to work effectively, but they also show how individuals can benefit from the broad adoption of digital technologies for everyday financial (e.g., banking) systems usage. Consistent with the foregoing, which will allow providing broad theoretical and empirical evidence on the role of digital technologies for financial market development, this volume includes eight chapters. First six chapters presents broad macroeconomic and micro perspectives on how and why digital technologies may affect the functioning of financial markets, while the remaining two present country-based evidence.

Chapter 1 *Internet banking in European regions: Evolution and regional patterns and differences* develops a regional approach for studying internet banking use rates in Europe and analyses internet banking use in 244 European regions in 2019, considering the role played by technological, economic, social, and demographic factors. These findings contribute to a better understanding of the European regional internet baking divides and the variety of socioeconomic factors that may explain them. Next, Chapter 2 *Different faces of digital financial inclusion across countries* investigates banks – financial technology sector (fintech) relationships as well as digital financial inclusion mechanisms in emerging and developed economies and the roles that banks and fintechs play in it. It claims that banks are often not able to fill the financial exclusion gap in low-income economies, while independent fintech ventures, owing to their unique business and technology competences, are providing these services instead of banks. It concentrates on the discrimination between developed and low-income counties regarding the digitalization of financial systems and the opportunities it offers. This chapter also raises the issues of financial inclusion and potentially arising discrimination. In the consecutive Chapter 3 entitled *ICT, financial markets and their impact on firms' performance and internationalisation* the author examines the nexuses between ICT, finance, and growth. It intends to test the linkages between ICT usage and finance constraints and firms' internationalisation decisions. The study uses cross-section of firm-level data from the World Bank Enterprise Survey and covers 139 economies over the period from 2006 to 2019. The major findings are that firms' performance is positively correlated to ICT usage and negatively to financial constraints, and that enterprises operating in foreign markets generally use ICT more intensively. In Chapter 4 *Determinants of the Sustainability of MFIs: Delineating the role of digitization of Micro Finance Services* we find developments on microfinance ideas as a panacea of channelizing small finance in the backdrop of credit market failure of commercial banks. It is claimed that MFIs are highly dependable on donors' funds coupled with lower margin of investment, but also they are recognized as an effective tool for financial inclusion. Information and Communication Technology (ICT) plays an imperative role in scaling down operating expenses, delivering better customer experience, extending outreach, operations etc. It aims to measure the magnitude of sustainability of selected MFIs across the world regions and delineate the role of ICT in explaining the sustainability of MFIs. Chapter 5 *Impact of ICT on the reliability of risk forecasting models – case study of enterprises in three global financial market regions* focuses on the evaluation of the impact of digital technologies on the reliability of financial risk forecasting models; it is shown that the development of ICT can improve the effectiveness of such models. Using five traditional statistical and five soft computing models for enterprises in Far-East Asia, Europe, and Latin America, it identifies the most effective method for predicting the financial failure of enterprises in the short-, medium-, and long-term for firms in each region. Finally, the last three chapters present a more country-based and regional perspectives. Chapter 6 *Digital financial services, gendered digital divide and financial inclusion: Evidence from South Asia* examines the extent of the digital divide in access to digital financial services to women and its role in financial inclusion. The region of interest is South Asia as gender inequality is pervasive in the South Asian countries; it raises elements of women's access to digital financial services in South Asia, the barriers women face in accessing digital financial services. In this chapter, the analysis is run for selected South Asian countries using data from World Bank's Global Findex database. In Chapter 7 *Intraday price reaction to filing bankruptcy and restructuring proceedings – the evidence from Poland* we find why digital technologies maybe useful for analysing stock exchange behaviour. More specifically, it focuses on the price reaction of shares listed on the Warsaw Stock Exchange to filing, bankruptcy and/or restructuring applications. Using event study, the authors run the analysis at ten, five, and one-minute intervals. The analysis results show that ICT allows fast reacting as it takes 1–2 minutes after the information on bankruptcy and restructuring applications was made public. Lastly, Chapter 8 *Money Market Digitization Consequences on Financial Inclusion of Businesses at the Base of the Pyramid in Nigeria* aims to explain why microfinance bank digitization has not promoted financial inclusion at the base of the pyramid economy in Nigeria. It adopts unstructured interviews run in six rural settlements in Oyo State (Moniya, Idi-Ose, and Ajibode) and Osun State (Ede, Ode-Omu, and Gbongan) in Nigeria. Major findings show that microfinance bank digitization promotes financial inclusion at the base of the pyramid economy in Nigeria, and it demonstrates the need to promote microfinance banks digitization and financial inclusion at the base of the pyramid economy in Nigeria.

References

Bresnahan, T. (2010). General purpose technologies. *Handbook of the Economics of Innovation*, *2*, 761–791.

Cheng, C. Y., Chien, M. S., & Lee, C. C. (2021). ICT diffusion, financial development, and economic growth: An international cross-country analysis. *Economic Modelling*, *94*, 662–671.

Coccia, M. (2017). Sources of technological innovation: Radical and incremental innovation problem-driven to support competitive advantage of firms. *Technology Analysis & Strategic Management*, *29*(9), 1048–1061.

Coccia, M. (2018). A theory of the general causes of long waves: War, general purpose technologies, and economic change. *Technological Forecasting and Social Change*, *128*, 287–295.

Comin, D., & Nanda, R. (2019). Financial development and technology diffusion. *IMF Economic Review*, *67*(2), 395–419.

Eholzer, W., & Roth, R. (2017). The role of high-frequency trading in modern financial markets. In *Equity markets in transition* (pp. 337–361). Springer.

Ernkvist, M. (2015). The double knot of technology and business-model innovation in the era of ferment of digital exchanges: The case of OM, a pioneer in electronic options exchanges. *Technological Forecasting & Social Change*, *99*, 285–299.

Essendorfer, S., Diaz-Rainey, I., & Falta, M. (2015). Creative destruction in Wall Street's technological arms race: Evidence from patent data. *Technological Forecasting & Social Change*, *99*, 300–316.

Farboodi, M., & Veldkamp, L. (2020). Long-run growth of financial data technology. *American Economic Review*, *110*(8), 2485–2523.

Fernández-Portillo, A., Almodóvar-González, M., & Hernández-Mogollón, R. (2020). Impact of ICT development on economic growth. A study of OECD European union countries. *Technology in Society*, *63*, 101420.

Gomber, P., Kauffman, R. J., Parker, C., & Weber, B. W. (2018). On the fintech revolution: Interpreting the forces of innovation, disruption, and transformation in financial services. *Journal of Management Information Systems*, *35*(1), 220–265.

Graham, M., & Dutton, W. H. (Eds.). (2019). *Society and the internet: How networks of information and communication are changing our lives*. Oxford University Press.

Hendershott, T., & Madhavan, A. (2015). Click or call? Auction versus search in the over-the-counter market. The Journal of Finance, 70(1), 419–447.

Henrique, B. M., Sobreiro, V. A., & Kimura, H. (2019). Literature review: Machine learning techniques applied to financial market prediction. *Expert Systems with Applications*, *124*, 226–251.

Katz, M. L., & Shapiro, C. (1985). Network externalities, competition, and compatibility. *The American Economic Review*, *75*(3), 424–440.

Kauffman, R. J., Liu, J., & Ma, D. (2015). Innovations in financial IS and technology ecosystems: High-frequency trading in the equity market. *Technological Forecasting and Social Change*, *99*, 339–354.

Lee, M., Kim, K., & Cho, Y. (2010). A study on the relationship between technology diffusion and new product diffusion. *Technological Forecasting and Social Change*, *77*(5), 796–802.

Moşteanu, N. R. (2019). International financial markets face to face with artificial intelligence and digital era. *Theoretical & Applied Economics*, *26*(3).

Nambisan, S., Wright, M., & Feldman, M. (2019). The digital transformation of innovation and entrepreneurship: Progress, challenges and key themes. *Research Policy*, *48*(8), 103773.

Rosenberg, N., & Trajtenberg, M. (2001). *A general purpose technology at work: The corliss steam engine in the late 19th century US (no. w8485)*. National Bureau of Economic Research.

Sahal, D. (1981). Alternative conceptions of technology. *Research policy, 10*(1), 2–24.

Wilhelm, W. J. Jr (2001). The internet and financial market structure. *Oxford Review of Economic Policy, 17*(2), 235–247.

Wong, V. W., Schober, R., Ng, D. W. K., & Wang, L. C. (Eds.). (2017). *Key technologies for 5G wireless systems*. Cambridge University Press.

1   Internet banking

A new digital divide between the European regions?

Fernando Lera-Lopez, Rocío Marco, and Margarita Billon

1.1 Introduction

Information and Communication Technologies (ICT) has become a key determinant in the recent evolution of the financial system, favouring the development of digital innovations that have changed the landscape of the global financial environment (Asongu & Nwachukwu, 2019; Dumičić et al., 2015; Lechman & Marszk, 2019). The increasing penetration of the internet has boosted the adoption of electronic systems and the emergence of innovative financial products and services (Marszk & Lechman, 2019; Sadigov et al., 2020) that have led to important transformations in the relationship between financial agents. In a context of intense and increasing competition, banks and other financial institutions are forced to develop digital innovations as a key strategy, not only to boost efficiency and reduce costs, but also to augment profitability and expand their activities to gain market share (Aktan et al., 2009; Mahmoodi & Naderi, 2016; Nazaritehrani & Mashali, 2020).

In the banking system, digital innovations such as the development of e-banking have transformed financial services, impacting the relationships between banks and customers (European Banking Authority, 2019). In addition to these effects at the micro level, the adoption of internet banking may have important socio-economic impacts at higher levels of analysis, such as regional or country ones. In fact, the development of digital innovations in the financial sector may have an impact on economic growth (Sadigov et al., 2020). In turn, its effects on the socio-economic context could lead to new socio-economic inequalities at regional and macro levels (Lucendo-Monedero et al., 2019; Takieddine & Sun, 2015) that may be considered as new sources of digital divides and that deserve attention academically.

From this point of view and within the framework of the Digital Agenda for Europe, research on the use of internet banking at the regional level in the EU may be understood as a key topic that can help to identify possible existing disparities and divides within the European regions. Moreover, the European Commission (2020) is currently preparing a new Digital Finance Strategy oriented to guarantee that the European consumers and

DOI: 10.4324/9781003199076-1

the financial industry can benefit from the potential advantages of the digital transformation while reducing the possible new risks associated with the digital revolution. According to the European Commission, it is essential to overcome the fragmentation of the Single Market for digital financial services, in particular in the context of the COVID-19 pandemic. The coronavirus emergency that has led to lockdowns suffered by a great part of the population in Europe has evidenced the relevance of the digitalization process of financial products and services.

In this context, the analysis of internet banking in Europe could contribute to a better understanding of digital finance implementation in this geographical area. Although internet banking is on the rise in the European Union and more than half of the EU population is using online banking (European Banking Authority, 2019), there are still important divides among countries and regions (Eurostat, 2020). Nevertheless, the available academic evidence on internet banking in Europe is mainly at the country level (Blagoev & Shustova, 2019; Dumičić et al., 2015; Takieddine & Sun, 2015) and is mostly devoted to explaining the cultural determinants of internet banking use (IBU). To our knowledge, there are only very few studies exploring internet banking adoption at the regional level in Europe (Lucendo-Monedero et al., 2019). The analysis of internet banking diffusion at the regional level could provide interesting insights into the usage of digital financial services in Europe from a comparative perspective.

The present research aims to fill this gap. In particular, the chapter analyses the situation of IBU in the European Union at the regional level from a geographical and socio-economic perspective. Following this approach, the main purpose of this chapter is twofold. First, we aim to classify the European regions into differentiated groups to create a taxonomy of regions according to their levels of IBU. Second, we are interested in defining the main regional technological and socio-economic characteristics that explain the regional classification obtained by identifying the decisive regional characteristics that might explain the use of internet banking among European regions. We contribute to the literature in various ways. First, our research provides a characterization of the European regions in terms of internet banking adoption. Second, the study identifies the regional determinants that explain this taxonomy. Finally, the findings may contribute to a better understanding of the existent regional e-banking divides and the variety of technological and socio-economic factors that may explain them in the case of the European regions.

1.2 Literature review and conceptual framework

Internet banking can be defined as a banking channel that allows customers to perform financial and non-financial services through a bank's website at a place and time of their choosing (Hoehle et al., 2012; Sharma et al., 2020). Following Takieddine and Sun (2015), online banking saves up to 40% of operational costs in comparison with offline banking. At the same time, banks may increase revenue not only by reducing operational costs but also by retaining actual customers and attracting new ones, while increasing customers' satisfaction and loyalty. Also, it could represent a source of competitive advantage throughout the differentiation of e-banking services. For customers, internet banking provides them flexible access to their latest financial information and aids with conducting financial transactions, making and scheduling payments, saving and investing money, checking account balances, printing statements, and finding other information related to accounts anytime, etc. But internet banking could cause some concern, too, mainly associated with security issues and the potential fast obsolescence of some e-banking tools and systems (ISPO, European Commission, 2001).

Given the importance of internet banking for both banks and customers, the academic literature has been mainly focused on the analysis of the determinants of IBU from the perspective of banks and consumers' acceptance, usually using data for specific countries and world regions. Takieddine and Sun (2015) and Keskar and Pandey (2018) provide useful reviews of the available empirical evidence at this level of analysis.

However, while these studies provide a better understanding of internet banking development at an individual level (a specific banking system or country), they do not provide a general picture at the regional or macro levels. The huge disparities in internet banking adoption in different contexts, such as those between developed versus developing countries (Takieddine & Sun, 2015; Yuen et al., 2010) motivate the interest to analyse the factors that explain those differences. This type of analysis would allow researchers to gain knowledge about internet banking diffusion and about the factors that may be associated with the disparities between countries and regions and, therefore, would help to identify the factors behind the e-banking use divide.

At the country level, very few studies analyse the situation in Europe. Dumičić et al. (2015) investigate the determinants of IBU for a sample of 28 European countries in 2011–2012. Their results point to the role played by ICT infrastructure, mainly broadband and internet access. In a similar vein, Takieddine and Sun (2015) demonstrate for a group of 33 European countries in 2013 the role played by technological factors, especially internet access, to explain IBU. Internet access mediates, in turn, the impacts of socio-economic factors on internet banking usage. Blagoev and Shustova (2019), using a sample of 30 European countries in 2018, show the relevance of national culture differences in explaining internet banking diffusion. At the regional level, the available empirical evidence is even more scarce. Druhov et al. (2019) investigate financial innovation in Europe. To our knowledge, at the regional level in Europe, only Lucendo-Monedero et al. (2019) take into account e-banking use to create an index to measure access and use of ICT in the European regions.

Following the analysis of the literature developed by Hoehle et al. (2012), we can find different theoretical approaches that have been used to frame internet banking diffusion, although all of them focus on customers' adoption. These approaches are the Technology Acceptance Model (TAM) (Davis, 1989), the Unified Theory of Acceptance and Use of Technology (UTAUT) (Venkatesh et al., 2003), and the Theory of Planned Behaviour (TPB) (Ajzen, 1991). Among the theories that are not limited to the individual level of adoption, the Diffusion of Innovations (DOI) (Rogers, 2003) is the most known and applied at the national and regional levels. As this research refers to the regional level, and we cannot measure individuals' attitudes and behaviours or customers' satisfaction, we argue that the best theoretical framework for understanding the differences in internet banking at the regional level is the DOI and heterogeneity models (Rosenberg, 1972).

According to Rogers (2003), social interactions affect an individual's perception of any technology use, including IBU. These social interactions are developed in a specific socio-economic context where the individual lives. In this framework, heterogeneity models (Rosenberg, 1972) highlight the relevance of differences in social and economic features of users and countries to explain ICT diffusion (Kondo & Ishida, 2014). In this vein, empirical evidence about ICT diffusion has emphasized the relevance of economic and demographic regional features in internet diffusion (Lera-Lopez et al., 2010; Vicente & López, 2006). Moreover, some authors argue that the process of technology diffusion is constrained by the economic structure and the country's economic development (Comín & Mestieri, 2014; Karshenas & Stoneman, 1995). These arguments justify the inclusion of some economic variables such as Gross Domestic Product (GDP), unemployment, and economic activity rates as well as the importance of the main economic sectors at the regional level. Besides, as a way to consider potential income limitations in the population within regions, we have included in our analysis a particular indicator of economic and social poverty.

The literature review has also shown that the adoption of new technology is mainly constrained by appropriate infrastructure. In this case, the adoption of internet banking in Europe is closely associated with ICT infrastructure, mainly internet accessibility and internet speed (Dumičić et al., 2015; Takieddine & Sun, 2015). Following this previous evidence, we include internet use (IU) in our analysis because it is necessary for conducting internet banking.

Also, the DOI argues that the individual's degree of willingness to adopt innovations, in this case, internet banking, is mainly constrained by the individual's prior knowledge about this technology and its risk aversion. In this sense, because education level could play a significant role in internet banking diffusion, we take this variable into account in our empirical analysis. Similarly, young people have been more disposed to adopting new technologies than older people. Consequently, we have included two variables associated with the age groups of the population.

Last but not least, the academic evidence has shown that technology diffusion may be developed to a greater extent in urban areas that exhibit higher population density, where ICT infrastructure is expected to be high, and where technology knowledge could be more easily expanded (Schleife, 2010). We have included the population density variable to check these arguments.

To sum up, following the DOI theory, we develop a framework based on four types of variables (economic variables, economic specialization in the main sectors, demographic variables, and education level) to explain IBU at the regional level in European countries. We also include IU as a preliminary condition for using internet banking.

1.3 Data and methodology

Our variable of analysis is IBU in Europe. This variable is defined as the percentage of individuals between the ages of 16 and 74 using the internet for internet banking in the last 12 months. Unfortunately, there is no information about the frequency of IBU. The data related to IBU in our analysis correspond to regional information provided by Eurostat in its website's regional statistics category (Eurostat, 2020), specifically, the 2nd level of Eurostat Nomenclature d'Unité Territoriales Statistiques (NUTS2), excluding data from the UK, Polish, Greek, and German regions because no information about the NUTS2 level is provided. In these countries, regional data correspond to the NUTS1 level. The territory examined is finally composed of a total of 244 European regions belonging to 36 countries: the 27 EU countries plus Albania, Iceland, Montenegro, North Macedonia, Norway, Serbia, Switzerland, United Kingdom, and Turkey. We will focus the analysis in 2019, the last year with available regional data for IBU, although we also analyse the evolution of IBU overtime at the country level from 2006, the first year with available IBU data.

In line with the aim of the research, we first create a taxonomy of the European regions according to their levels of IBU. Based on the frequency distribution of the variable, we cluster the European regions into three groups: regions with low, middle, and high penetration of IBU. The regional group membership is the qualitative outcome that is subsequently modelled by applying a multinomial logistic regression (MLR). Using the battery of variables described in the previous section, the econometric model allows us to identify the factors influencing the probability of belonging to one of the clusters. The probabilities in a multinomial logit model (Greene, 2012) are:

$$Prob(Y_i = j) = P_{ij} = \frac{\exp(x'_i \beta_j)}{1 + \sum_{g=1}^{J} \exp(x'_i \beta_g)} \tag{1.1}$$

where Y_i represents the value that indicates the qualitative response for the ith region and takes a discrete set of values reflecting J categories, x_i

represents the vector that characterizes the ith region, and β_j is the coefficient vector for the jth category of the dependent variable. The log-odds can be computed between any pair of alternatives. Taking h as the baseline category, the model consists of J-1 logits for the response variable to compare each categorical level to the reference category:

$$ln\left[\frac{P_{ij}}{P_{ih}}\right] = x'_i\beta_j \qquad \text{when} \quad j \neq h \tag{1.2}$$

Therefore, the odds ratio for alternative j, P_{ij}/P_{ih}, will also depend on the h alternative used as the baseline category. The maximum-likelihood method was used to estimate the parameters of the model.

Regarding the potential variables influencing the probability of belonging to one of the clusters, and considering both the available academic literature and conceptual framework, we include the GDP at current market prices purchasing power standard per inhabitant at the regional level. GDP explains to a great extent the variation in IBU within European countries (Dumičić et al., 2015). Since we aim to develop a detailed analysis of the regional economic situation, we have considered other variables such as unemployment, economic activity rates, and the percentage of the regional population at risk of poverty or social exclusion (AROPE). The second group of variables captures regional economic specialization, including regional percentages of employment in agriculture (agriculture, forestry, and fishing), industry (industry and construction), and services (Billon et al., 2017). Since demographic features and education levels are key determinants of IBU (see Zagalaz Jiménez & Aguiar Díaz, 2019 for a recent literature review), we consider population density, the young-age dependency ratio (population aged 0–14 to population 15–64 years), the old-age dependency ratio (population 65 and over to population 15–64 years), and population with tertiary education. Finally, we have included IU, which measures the frequency of people who access the internet at least once a week. ICT use is a necessary condition for e-banking. All variables are taken from Eurostat for the year 2019 (Eurostat, 2020), with population density, GDP, and AROPE corresponding to 2018 due to a lack of 2019 data. Table 1.1 shows the main descriptive statistics for IBU and the set of demographic, educational, structural, economic, and internet-use indicators of regional ICT infrastructure.

1.4 Exploratory analysis

In order to explore the relationship between IBU and ICT infrastructure, described in the literature review section, first we analyse the relationship between IBU and IU in the period 2006–2019. This will show a parallel evolution, denoting a positive relationship. In a second step, we will consider the situation of IBU in the year 2019 at the regional level by country in

Table 1.1 Main descriptive statistics

Variable	obs	Minimum	Maximum	Mean	Median	Std. Dev.	Variable description
Internet banking use	244	2.000	97.000	56.529	60.000	23.544	Internet banking use. Users per 100 people (% of individuals aged 16–74).
Internet use	244	53.000	100.000	83.902	85.000	9.719	Frequency of internet access: once a week (including every day). Users per 100 people (% of individuals aged 16–74).
Education	243	11.700	59.600	31.842	31.700	10.500	Tertiary education (levels 5–8) (in %), age from 25 to 64 years. Percentage of individuals.
Density	244	3.400	7471.500	374.133	117.750	927.180	Population density. People per square kilometre.
Young dependency	243	17.200	57.600	24.762	24.100	4.839	Young-age dependency ratio. Population aged 0–14 to population 15–64 years.
Old dependency	243	8.100	47.200	30.387	30.700	7.005	Old-age dependency ratio. Population 65 and over to population 15–64 years.
GDP	236	8.000	80.900	28.542	26.450	11.473	Gross domestic product at current market prices, purchasing power standard per inhabitant. Thousands of Euros.
Unemployment	243	1.300	27.000	7.144	5.600	4.980	Unemployment rate, age 15 years or over, in %.
Economic Activity	243	39.800	81.200	58.068	58.100	6.349	Economic activity rate, age 15 years or over, in %.
AROPE	241	7.900	53.600	22.484	20.000	8.963	People at risk of poverty or social exclusion, in %.
Agriculture	243	0.000	45.428	5.490	3.087	7.395	People working in agriculture, forestry and fishing, percentage of individuals (over total employment).
Industry	243	0.000	48.463	23.386	22.525	8.167	People working in Industry and Construction, percentage of individuals (over total employment).
Services	243	34.003	91.873	69.808	71.105	10.596	People working in Service, percentage of individuals (over total employment).

Note: All variables correspond to 2019, except for Density, GDP and AROPE that correspond to 2018.

Europe as a preliminary stage to establish a taxonomy of regions in 2019 according to their IBU.

1.4.1 Relationship between internet use and internet banking use

Figure 1.1 depicts the time evolution of the internet and internet banking penetration in Europe based on country-level data (NUTS0). Specifically, the sample corresponds to the 33 countries with data over the whole 2006–2019 period. Regional data for IBU is not available until 2011. The lines correspond to the European averages, while the shaded areas represent the gap of IU (left side) and IBU (right side) across countries over time. The gap depicts the difference between the countries with the largest and lowest use. An increasing, parallel evolution of IU and IBU is observed, which denotes a positive relationship between both variables. The results confirm the existing digital divide among European countries observed for other indicators, such as general IU. Internet penetration has evolved towards convergence across countries: the divide evolves from 66 users in 2006 to 31 users in 2019. However, the IBU divide has only grown during the same period: from 67 users in 2006 to 87 users in 2019, confirming previous empirical evidence about the heterogeneity in internet banking adoption in European countries and regions (Dumičić et al., 2015; Lucendo-Monedero et al., 2019).

Next, we divide the 33 countries into three groups according to their IBU level in 2019: bottom, middle, and top countries. The time evolution by group is depicted in Figure 1.2. The risen digital divide noticed in Figure 1.1 is mainly due to the bottom countries, the countries with the lowest IBU levels. For this group of countries, the gap has increased since 2006.

The positive relationship between IU and IBU over time observed in Figure 1.1 is also noticed from a cross-section perspective. The scatterplot in Figure 1.3 depicts the 244 European regions with available data in 2019. There is a large, positive linear relationship between IBU and IU (correlation coefficient equal to 0.897). There are some bivariate outliers, mostly located in regions with low IBU: Romania, Bulgaria, Macedonia, and

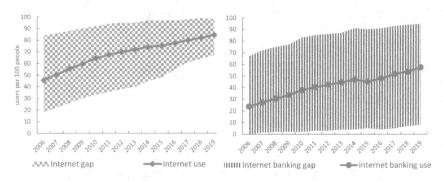

Figure 1.1 Evolution of internet and internet banking use, 2006–2019.

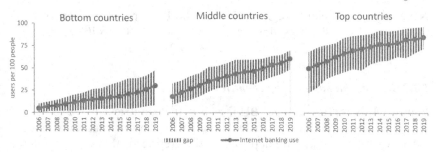

Figure 1.2 Internet banking use by levels.

Serbia show an IBU level below expected values given their internet penetration. Conversely, some Turkish regions have a relatively large level of IBU compared to that of IU.

Like Figure 1.1, the scatterplot in Figure 1.3 also denotes the larger divide in IBU compared to IU: from two IBU users in Albania to 97 users in the

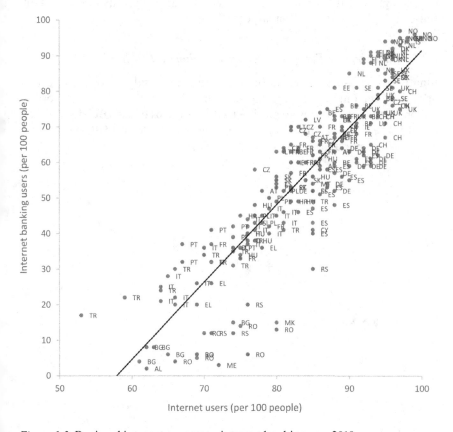

Figure 1.3 Regional internet use versus internet banking use, 2019.

Norwegian Nord-Norge region (NO07). The IU gap is narrower: from 53 users in the Turkish Güneydogu Anadolu region (TRC) to 100 users in the Norwegian Agder og Rogaland region (NO04).

1.4.2 Internet banking use by countries

Figure 1.4 shows the average IBU level and the countries' divide for the 36 countries with available data in 2019. The maximum and minimum regional values within a country are depicted by the grey vertical bar, the country's average IBU is represented by the cross, and the "x" depicts the region where the country's capital is located. In most cases, the IBU level in the capital region is above the country's average, except for the case of Belgium and Croatia.

Again, it is noticeable that the IBU level observed in Europe practically covers all the potential 0–100 range: from two users in Albania to 97 users in the Norwegian Nord-Norge region (NO07). The length of the grey bar depicts the within-country IBU gap. The countries' divide seems related to their geographical extensions. The largest countries, such as France, Spain, Italy, or Turkey, show in turn larger IBU diversity.

1.4.3 Clustering the European regions according to IBU level

Finally, in this section, we develop the regional analysis to create a taxonomy of regions by considering rates of IBU. We cluster the European regions into three groups according to the quartiles of the IBU distribution in 2019. The first quartile groups the regions with the lowest IBU, where 40% or less of the population use e-banking. This cluster is named the low-IBU

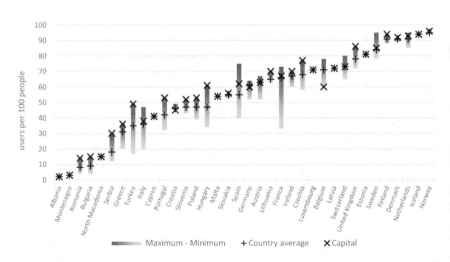

Figure 1.4 Internet banking use, European countries, 2019.

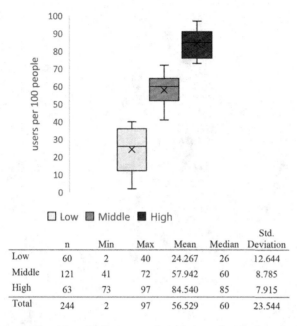

	n	Min	Max	Mean	Median	Std. Deviation
Low	60	2	40	24.267	26	12.644
Middle	121	41	72	57.942	60	8.785
High	63	73	97	84.540	85	7.915
Total	244	2	97	56.529	60	23.544

Figure 1.5 Internet banking use by groups: boxplots and main descriptive statistics.

group. In contrast, the fourth quartile clusters the top-IBU regions, those where more than 72% of people using internet banking. Finally, the regions with e-banking users ranging between 40% and 72% are grouped in the middle-IBU cluster, which captures the 50% central observations.

Figure 1.5 shows the boxplots and main descriptives for both the overall sample and by group. As in Figure 1.3, the lower the level of IBU, the larger their variability: the low-IBU group shows the largest standard deviation.

Figure 1.6 depicts the map of the European regions according to their IBU level. This map suggests east-west and north-south gaps in terms of IBU level, showing the highest level of IBU in the northern regions. The corresponding list of regions included in each cluster is available in Table 1.A1 in the Appendix.

To explore the socio-economic differences across the three clusters defined by IBU level, Figure 1.7 depicts the cluster mean values for each indicator. Standardized values of the indicators are here represented to avoid the problem of comparison due to different units. As shown in Figure 1.7, the differences between means across clusters seem remarkable in the case of IU, education, GDP, unemployment, economic activity rate, AROPE, agriculture, and service sectors.

Next, one-way analyses of variance (ANOVA) are carried out in order to statistically assess the differences of the demographic and socio-economic indicators across clusters that have been previously identified. In this

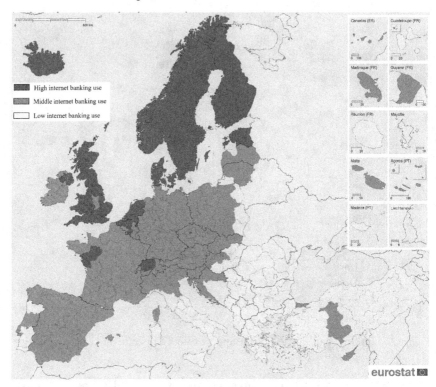

Figure 1.6 Map of European NUTs2 regions according to the level of internet banking use.

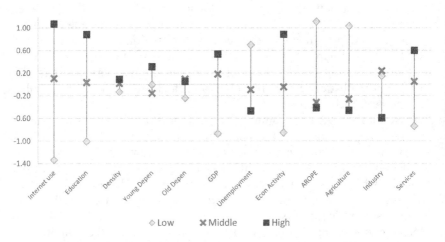

Figure 1.7 Average values of (standardized) socio-economic indicators by IBU cluster.

Table 1.2 One-way ANOVA results

Variables	F	p-value	Post hoc multiple comparisons
Internet users[a]	346.708	0.000	L ≠ M ≠ H
Education	98.329	0.000	L ≠ M ≠ H
Density	1.820	0.442	–
Young dependency[a]	4.209	0.018	M ≠ H
Old dependency[a]	2.301	0.104	–
GDP[a]	55.369	0.000	L ≠ M ≠ H
Unemployment[a]	24.517	0.000	L ≠ M ≠ H
Economic activity[a]	67.019	0.000	L ≠ M ≠ H
AROPE[a]	69.748	0.000	L ≠ M ≠ H
Agriculture[a]	44.616	0.000	L ≠ M ≠ H
Industry[a]	17.508	0.000	L, M ≠ H
Services[a]	31.623	0.000	L ≠ M ≠ H

Notes: F reports the F-ratio statistic testing the null hypothesis of equal means.

[a] F statistic reports the Brown-Forsythe robust test of equality of means for the indicators where the assumption of variance homoscedasticity is not accepted according to the Levene's statistic test ($\alpha = 5\%$).

Pairwise multiple comparisons report the clusters pairs with significant mean differences at 5% significance level using the Bonferroni procedure. Tamhane's T2 procedure is used for those indicators ([a]) where variance homoscedasticity is not accepted.

bivariate analysis, the categorical factor is the three-cluster grouping that classifies the European regions into low, middle, and high IBU. The null hypothesis stands for no differences across the population group means. The ANOVA results are shown in Table 1.2.

Regarding the ANOVA outcomes, the regional level of IBU is related to all the considered indicators at the usual 5% significance level, except for population density and old dependency rate. Pairwise multiple comparisons point to the rejection of the null hypothesis due to significant differences between all pair groups in most indicators.

1.5 Explicative analysis with multinomial logistic regression

After developing a taxonomy of European regions according to IBU, we determine the potential variables that explain this taxonomy of regions, considering the set of indicators described in our conceptual framework. We apply a MLR where we have as dependent variable the regions' membership to one of the three clusters. The MLR model predicts the IBU cluster that a region is likely to belong to given the socio-economic indicators used to characterize it. Table 1.3 shows the parameter estimates for the MLR model. Regarding the explanatory variables, agriculture is removed

Table 1.3 Multinomial logistic regression: parameter estimates

				95% CI for Exp(b)	
Variables	b	Std. error	Exp(b)	Lower bound	Upper bound
Middle- versus low-banking use					
Education	0.152	(0.048)***	1.164	1.060	1.278
Density	0.001	(0.000)	1.000	0.999	1.000
Young dependency	0.120	(0.076)	1.128	0.971	1.310
Old dependency	0.023	(0.053)	1.024	0.923	1.136
GDP	0.093	(0.049)*	1.097	0.996	1.208
Unemployment	0.061	(0.080)	1.062	0.908	1.243
Economic activity	0.184	(0.083)**	1.202	1.022	1.415
AROPE	−0.079	(0.043)*	0.924	0.850	1.006
Industry[a]	0.149	(0.067)**	1.149	1.007	1.310
Services[a]	0.063	(0.064)	1.065	0.940	1.207
Intercept	−25.655	(9.176)***			
High- versus low-banking use					
Education	0.235	(0.061)***	1.264	1.121	1.426
Density	0.001	(0.000)	1.000	0.999	1.000
Young dependency	0.462	(0.117)***	1.587	1.261	1.998
Old dependency	0.232	(0.081)***	1.261	1.076	1.478
GDP	0.040	(0.059)	1.040	0.927	1.168
Unemployment	−0.254	(0.146)*	0.776	0.582	1.034
Economic activity	0.436	(0.113)***	1.547	1.240	1.930
AROPE	−0.030	(0.073)	0.970	0.841	1.119
Industry[a]	−0.142	(0.090)	0.867	0.727	1.035
Services[a]	0.005	(0.075)	1.005	0.868	1.163
Intercept	−46.804	(13.040)***			

Notes: $-2LL$ model change $\chi^2_{20} = 277.010$, $p < 0.001$; Pseudo $R^2 = 0.695$ (Cox & Snell), 0.796 (Nagelkerke).

[a] Agriculture is the reference variable for the economic sectors set (Industry, Service, and Agriculture).
***, **, and * denote significance at 1% ($p < 0.01$), 5% ($p < 0.05$), and 10% ($p < 0.10$), respectively.

from the explanatory set to avoid perfect multicollinearity in the model. Therefore, agriculture is the variable acting as a reference for the subset of economic sector weights: industry (including construction), services, and agriculture.

Concerning the model fitting, the Cox & Snell's and Nagelkerke's pseudo-R^2 values (0.695 and 0.796, respectively) point to the substantive significance of the model, as does the change in −2 Log-Likelihood ($-2LL$) that compares the model with only the intercept to the final model ($\chi^2_{20} = 277.01$, $p < 0.001$). The low-IBU cluster is acting as the baseline category for the pair-comparisons in the multinomial model.

Tertiary education, economic activity, economic structure, GDP *per capita* and AROPE rate help to predict whether a region belongs to the middle-banking or low-banking group (top panel, Table 1.3). An odds ratio, *Exp(b)*, statistically greater than 1 means that as the indicator increases, the odds of a region having middle-banking (rather than low-banking) use increase. Specifically, a 1 percentage rise in the proportion of tertiary edu-cated people increases by 1.164 the odds of being a middle-banking rather than low-banking region. Raising the weight of industry-construction sec-tor by 1 percentage point (to the detriment of agriculture sector, its base variable) also increases the odds of being a middle-banking region (odds rate 1.149). The same applies to the economic activity rate (odds rate 1.202) and GDP *per capita* (odds rate 1.097). However, a larger AROPE rate decreases the chance to be a middle-banking region (odds rate 0.924). In short, the larger the tertiary education rate, the economic activity rate, the industry weight, the GDP *per capita*, and the lower the AROPE rate, the more likely a region is to be classified as a middle-banking rather than a low-banking region.

The second panel of Table 1.3 shows the odds between the high and the low IBU groups. An increase in tertiary education (odds rate 1.264), young dependency rate (1.587), old dependency rate (1.261), and economic activity (1.547) helps to generate a switch from the low-baking to the high-bank-ing cluster, while a rise in unemployment would decrease the odds of being a high e-banking in favour of low e-banking region (odds rates 0.776). Population density and size of services, although with the expected sign, are not statistically significant to explain the probability of belonging to any of the IBU clusters in the MLR model.

Figure 1.8 summarizes these results and highlights the heterogeneity of European regions regarding the determinants of IBU.

Finally, we introduce IU as explanatory variable in the MLR model together with the previous explanatory set of variables (economic level and structure specialization, demographic variables, and education level).

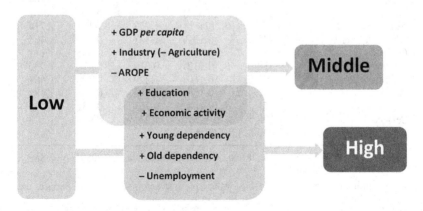

Figure 1.8 Summary of results.

Table 1.4 shows these new results. The IU variable is strongly significant in explaining the region's membership to the high- and the middle-banking clusters. Nevertheless, the presence of IU in the model diminishes the influence of some of the variables that were previously statistically significant (model in Table 1.3). For example, the inclusion of IU reduces the direct influence that education, GDP, economic activity, or unemployment would exert on IBU. These variables would be partially absorbing the influence of IU when this variable is not considered directly under the analysis.

Table 1.4 Multinomial logistic regression including internet users

Variables	b	Std. error	Exp(b)	95% CI for Exp(b) Lower bound	Upper bound
Middle- versus low-banking use					
Internet users	0.604	(0.137)***	1.830	1.400	2.393
Education	0.018	(0.059)	1.018	0.907	1.143
Density	0.001	(0.000)	1.000	0.999	1.000
Young dependency	0.110	(0.149)	1.117	0.834	1.495
Old dependency	0.018	(0.090)	1.019	0.854	1.215
GDP	0.095	(0.062)	1.099	0.974	1.241
Unemployment	0.033	(0.117)	1.033	0.821	1.301
Economic activity	0.124	(0.114)	1.132	0.905	1.415
AROPE	−0.130	(0.071)*	0.878	0.764	1.009
Industry[a]	−0.029	(0.109)	0.972	0.785	1.203
Services[a]	−0.079	(0.108)	0.924	0.749	1.141
Intercept	−54.858	(17.344)***			
High- versus low-banking use					
Internet users	1.465	(0.250)***	4.326	2.653	7.056
Education	0.126	(0.094)	1.134	0.944	1.364
Density	0.001	(0.001)	1.000	0.998	1.001
Young dependency	0.573	(0.217)***	1.773	1.159	2.714
Old dependency	0.123	(0.131)	1.131	0.875	1.462
GDP	−0.016	(0.078)	0.984	0.845	1.147
Unemployment	−0.330	(0.212)	0.719	0.474	1.090
Economic activity	0.206	(0.160)	1.229	0.898	1.681
AROPE	0.131	(0.134)	1.140	0.877	1.482
Industry[a]	−0.271	(0.184)	0.763	0.532	1.093
Services[a]	0.208	(0.125)*	1.231	0.964	1.573
Intercept	−130.39	(29.207)***			

Notes: $-2LL$ model change $\chi^2_{22} = 381.003$, $p < 0.001$; Pseudo $R^2 = 0.805$ (Cox & Snell), 0.921 (Nagelkerke).

[a] Agriculture is the reference variable for the economic sectors set (Industry, Service, and Agriculture).
***, **, and * denote significance at 1% ($p < 0.01$), 5% ($p < 0.05$), and 10% ($p < 0.10$), respectively.

1.6 Conclusions and discussion

This research analyses IBU in the European Union at the regional level from a geographical and socio-economic perspective. First, we have classified European regions into three different groups to create a taxonomy of regions according to their levels of IBU. At first glance, the results show a great disparity in IBU at the regional level, confirming previous evidence at the national and regional levels among EU countries (e.g., Dumičić et al., 2015; Lucendo-Monedero et al., 2019). Particularly, these disparities are higher among the regions with a lower adoption rate than in the other two groups of EU regions. This low-banking group of regions is composed of 60 regions, mainly belonging to Eastern countries, such as Bulgaria, Romania, Hungary, Turkey, and some southern countries like Portugal, Greece, and Italy. In contrast, the regions with the highest use of internet banking are 63 regions, mainly belonging to the North of Europe (Norway, Finland, Denmark, and Sweden), The Netherlands, Belgium, and the UK. Our results also suggest east-west and north-south gaps in terms of the IBU level, showing the highest level of IBU in the northern regions.

Second, we have defined the main socio-economic characteristics that explain the previous regional classification obtained by identifying the decisive regional features that might explain the different levels of e-banking use among European regions. We have found that education and economic variables such as economic activity rate are the main factors associated with more intense use of internet banking in European regions, confirming previous empirical evidence of adoption of internet banking among EU countries (Dumičić et al., 2015; Zagalaz Jiménez & Aguiar Díaz, 2019). For example, increasing GDP *per capita* and reducing the AROPE rate or the size of agriculture in favour of the industry sector are factors that might help low-internet banking regions to become middle-banking regions. Meanwhile, larger young and old dependency rate (demographic variables) and less unemployment are the key factors that support a "big jump" from the low- to the high-banking group. Finally, IU plays a key role in explaining IBU among European regions, also confirming the previous evidence in Europe (Dumičić et al., 2015; Takieddine & Sun, 2015). Accounting for IU leads to diminished direct influence of some indicators such as the economic ones and education levels.

Our empirical results can be put into the context of the DOI theory and heterogeneity models, emphasizing the relevance of a set of economic, demographic, and social features to explain IBU at the regional level in European countries. Also, this research shows how the adoption of internet banking in Europe is closely associated with IU.

The results of this research can lead to important implications for policy-makers in order to reduce the heterogeneity in IBU by European citizens at the regional level. In order to facilitate and develop IBU in Europe, emphasis should be put on promoting education and internet skills among the population and boosting economic development. In that way, by providing an economically favourable environment for IBU, the banking sector and financial development should be enhanced. This might be positively affected by rising ICT adoption, which seems to have a positive impact on economic development and structural shifts in European economies (Lechman & Marszk, 2019). Also, any progress in IU seems to have a direct and positive impact on IBU. At the same time, any increase in internet banking adoption, in a context of a multi-channel strategy, could boost a greater share from the market (Nazaritehrani & Mashali, 2020) and improve the efficiency and effectiveness of financial services (Mahmoodi & Naderi, 2016). In this way, a reduction of heterogeneity in IBU at the regional level, shown in our results, could be useful to overcome the fragmentation of the European Single Market in digital financial services.

This research presents some limitations; one of the main ones is the lack of information at the regional level in Eurostat. Information about the frequency of IBU and some aspects of ICT infrastructure, such as internet speed or internet security, is not available at the regional level in the EU. In addition, financial services literature has mainly focused on internet banking. In the future, it should be of interest to apply a multi-focus approach to consider different online channels (internet, mobile apps, etc.) to explain digital banking diffusion in Europe. This approach might offer interesting and useful implications in the context of the new digital finance strategy in Europe.

Appendix

Table A1. Regional classification according to the Internet banking use

Cluster 1: Low internet-banking use

AL - Albania	RO11 - Nord-Vest	ITG1 - Sicilia	ITI2 - Umbria
ME - Montenegro	RO32 - Bucuresti - Ilfov	ITF2 - Molise	PT20 - Região Autónoma dos Açores (PT)
BG42 - Yuzhen tsentralen	BG41 - Yugozapaden	RS11 - Beogradski region SERBIA	FRY4 - La Réunion
RO22 - Sud-Est	MK - North Macedonia	TR8 - Bati Karadeniz	ITI3 - Marche
RO31 - Sud - Muntenia	TRC - Güneydogu Anadolu	TR7 - Orta Anadolu	PT11 - Norte
BG32 - Severen tsentralen	EL6 - Kentriki Ellada	ITF1 - Abruzzo	HU23 - Dél-Dunántúl
BG33 - Severoiztochen	ITF5 - Basilicata	PT18 - Alentejo	ITI4 - Lazio
RO21 - Nord-Est	RS12 - Region Vojvodine	TR6 - Akdeniz	TR4 - Dogu Marmara
RO41 - Sud-Vest Oltenia	ITF6 - Calabria	FRY1 - Guadeloupe	PL8 - Makroregion Wschodni

Table A1. Continued

RO42 - Vest	ITF3 - Campania	HU31 - Észak-Magyarország	PT15 - Algarve
BG31 - Severozapaden	TRA - Kuzeydogu Anadolu	TR2 - Bati Marmara	ES64 - Ciudad Autónoma de Melilla (ES)
BG34 - Yugoiztochen	TRB - Ortadogu Anadolu	TR3 - Ege	HU32 - Észak-Alföld
RO12 - Centru	TR9 - Dogu Karadeniz	EL3 - Attiki	HU33 - Dél-Alföld
RS21 - Region Sumadije i Zapadne Srbije	ITF4 - Puglia	EL5 - Voreia Ellada	ITC3 - Liguria
RS22 - Region Juzne i Istocne Srbije	EL4 - Nisia Aigaiou, Kriti	ITG2 - Sardegna	ITI1 - Toscana

Cluster 2: Middle internet-banking use

CY00 - Kypros	ES12 - Principado de Asturias	DE3 - Berlin	FRE1 - Nord-Pas-de-Calais
ITC1 - Piemonte	ES23 - La Rioja	ES51 - Cataluña	FRI2 - Limousin
PT16 - Centro (PT)	PL5 - Makroregion Poludniowo-Zachodni	FRD2 - Haute-Normandie	CZ03 - Jihozápad
TR5 - Bati Anadolu	SI04 - Zahodna Slovenija	FRF1 - Alsace	FRE2 - Picardie
FRY3 - Guyane	ES52 - Comunidad Valenciana	FRJ1 - Languedoc-Roussillon	FRL0 - Provence-Alpes-Côte d'Azur
ITH3 - Veneto	PL9 - Makroregion Województwo Mazowieckie	IE04 - Northern and Western	AT31 - Oberösterreich
PT30 - Região Autónoma da Madeira (PT)	PT17 - Área Metropolitana de Lisboa	DE7 - Hessen	AT33 - Tirol
ES43 - Extremadura	SK04 - Východné Slovensko	ES22 - Comunidad Foral de Navarra	CH01 - Région lémanique
ITH5 - Emilia-Romagna	DED - Sachsen	HU11 - Budapest	FR10 - Île de France
PL7 - Makroregion Centralny	ES11 - Galicia	DE9 - Niedersachsen	IE05 - Southern
SI03 - Vzhodna Slovenija	MT00 - Malta	ES30 - Comunidad de Madrid	BE33 - Prov. Liège
ITC2 - Valle d'Aosta/Vallée d'Aoste	ES53 - Illes Balears	FRB0 - Centre - Val de Loire	BE34 - Prov. Luxembourg (BE)
HR04 - Kontinentalna Hrvatska	SK02 - Západné Slovensko	AT12 - Niederösterreich	CZ08 - Moravskoslezsko

(*Continued*)

Table A1. Continued

Cluster 2: Middle internet-banking use

ITH1 - Provincia Autonoma di Bolzano/Bozen	SK03 - Stredné Slovensko	AT13 - Wien	FRH0 - Bretagne
ITH4 - Friuli-Venezia Giulia	ES24 - Aragón	AT34 - Vorarlberg	CZ02 - Strední Cechy
PL4 - Makroregion Pólnocno-Zachodni	HU21 - Közép-Dunántúl	BE32 - Prov. Hainaut	CZ06 - Jihovýchod
ES42 - Castilla-la Mancha	SK01 - Bratislavský kraj	DEA - Nordrhein-Westfalen	FRK2 - Rhône-Alpes
ITH2 - Provincia Autonoma di Trento	DEG - Thüringen	DEB - Rheinland-Pfalz	CZ05 - Severovýchod
ES41 - Castilla y León	FRD1 - Basse-Normandie	DEE - Sachsen-Anhalt	FRI3 - Poitou-Charentes
ITC4 - Lombardia	FRY2 - Martinique	DEF - Schleswig-Holstein	FRJ2 - Midi-Pyrénées
ES62 - Región de Murcia	CZ04 - Severozápad	FRC2 - Franche-Comté	IE06 - Eastern and Midland
HU22 - Nyugat-Dunántúl	ES13 - Cantabria	FRF3 - Lorraine	LT01 - Sostines regionas
HR03 - Jadranska Hrvatska	ES70 - Canarias (ES)	FRK1 - Auvergne	BE22 - Prov. Limburg (BE)
HU12 - Pest	AT32 - Salzburg	FRM0 - Corse	CH05 - Ostschweiz
PL6 - Makroregion Pólnocny	DE1 - Baden-Württemberg	LT02 - Vidurio ir vakaru Lietuvos regionas	LU - Luxembourg
TR1 - Istanbul	DE5 - Bremen	CZ07 - Strední Morava	FRI1 - Aquitaine
PL2 - Makroregion Poludniowy	DE6 - Hamburg	DE2 - Bayern	LV - Latvia
ES61 - Andalucía	ES21 - País Vasco	DEC - Saarland	UKF - East Midlands (UK)
AT11 - Burgenland (AT)	AT21 - Kärnten	FRF2 - Champagne-Ardenne	
DE4 - Brandenburg	AT22 - Steiermark	CH07 - Ticino	
DE8 - Mecklenburg-Vorpommern	BE10 - Région de Bruxelles-Capitale / Brussels Hoofdstedelijk Gewest	FRC1 - Bourgogne	

Table A1. Continued

Cluster 3: High internet-banking use

BE23 - Prov. Oost-Vlaanderen	UKC - North East (UK)	NL12 - Friesland (NL)	NL33 - Zuid-Holland
BE31 - Prov. Brabant wallon	CZ01 - Praha	UKI - London	DK01 - Hovedstaden
CH02 - Espace Mittelland	BE24 - Prov. Vlaams-Brabant	FI1D - Pohjois- ja Itä-Suomi	DK04 - Midtjylland
CH06 - Zentralschweiz	SE32 - Mellersta Norrland	NL34 - Zeeland	NL32 - Noord-Holland
FRG0 - Pays-de-la-Loire	UKM - Scotland	DK03 - Syddanmark	FI1B - Helsinki-Uusimaa
UKL - Wales	CH04 - Zürich	FI19 - Länsi-Suomi	IS - Iceland
BE35 - Prov. Namur	EE00 - Eesti	NL41 - Noord-Brabant	NO06 - Trøndelag
UKD - North West (UK)	SE22 - Sydsverige	DK02 - Sjælland	NL31 - Utrecht
UKE - Yorkshire and The Humber	SE31 - Norra Mellansverige	FI1C - Etelä-Suomi	NO02 - Hedmark og Oppland
UKG - West Midlands (UK)	UKK - South West (UK)	NL21 - Overijssel	NO03 - Sør-Østlandet
ES63 - Ciudad Autónoma de Ceuta (ES)	SE21 - Småland med öarna	NL22 - Gelderland	NO04 - Agder og Rogaland
UKJ - South East (UK)	SE23 - Västsverige	NL23 - Flevoland	NO05 - Vestlandet
UKN - Northern Ireland (UK)	UKH - East of England	NL42 - Limburg (NL)	SE33 - Övre Norrland
BE21 - Prov. Antwerpen	NL11 - Groningen	DK05 - Nordjylland	NO01 - Oslo og Akershus
BE25 - Prov. West-Vlaanderen	SE11 - Stockholm	FI20 - Åland	NO07 - Nord-Norge
CH03 - Nordwestschweiz	SE12 - Östra Mellansverige	NL13 - Drenthe	

References

Ajzen, I. (1991). The theory of planned behavior. *Organizational Behavior and Human Decision Processes, 50*, 170–211.

Aktan, B., Teker, E., & Ersoy, P. (2009). Changing face of banks and the evaluation of internet banking in Turkey. *Journal of Internet Banking and Commerce, 14*, 1–11.

Asongu, S., & Nwachukwu, J. (2019). ICT, financial sector development and financial access. *Journal of the Knowledge Economy, 10*, 465–490.

Billon, M., Marco, R., & Lera-Lopez, F. (2017). Innovation and ICT use by firms and households in the EU: A multivariate analysis of regional disparities. *Information Technology & People, 30*, 424–448.

Blagoev, V., & Shustova, E. (2019). The national culture effect on the adoption of internet-banking. *Economic Studies Journal, 28*(6), 19–38.

Comín, D., & Mestieri, M. (2014). Technology diffusion: Measurement, causes and consequences. In P. Aghion, & S. Durlauf (Eds.), *Handbook of economic growth* (Vol. 2, Chapter 2, pp. 565–622). Elsevier.

Davis, F. D. (1989). Perceived usefulness, perceived ease of use, and user acceptance of information technology. *MIS Quarterly, 13*(3), 319–339.

Dumičić, K., Časni, A.Č, & Palić, I. (2015). Multivariate analysis of determinants of internet banking use in European union countries. *Central European Journal of Operations Research, 23*(3), 563–578.

Druhov, O., Druhova, V., & Pakhnenko, O. (2019). The influence of financial innovations on EU countries banking systems development. *Marketing and Management of Innovations*, 3, 167–177.

European Banking Authority (2019). *Consumer Trend Report 2018–2019.* Retrieved 18th August 2020 from https://eba.europa.eu/eba-publishes-consumer-trends-report-for-2018-19.

European Commission (2020). *Consultation on a New Digital Finance Strategy for Europe.* Retrieved 15th September 2020 from https://ec.europa.eu/info/consultations/finance-2020-digital-finance-strategy_en

Eurostat (2020). *Database.* Retrieved 22nd May 2020 from https://ec.europa.eu/eurostat/data/database.

Greene, W. H. (2012). *Econometric analysis* (7th ed.). Prentice Hall.

Hoehle, H., Scornavacca, E., & Huff, S. (2012). Three decades of research on consumer adoption and utilization of electronic banking channels: A literature analysis. *Decision Support Systems*, 54, 122–132.

ISPO, European Commission (2001). Internet banking in Europe. In SCN Education BV- (Ed.). *Electronic Banking*, pp. 53–65. Springer.

Karshenas, M., & Stoneman, P. (1995). Technological diffusion. In P. Stonemann (Ed.), *Handbook of the economics of innovation and technological change* (pp. 265–297). Blackwell.

Keskar, M., & Pandey, N. (2018). Internet banking: A review (2002–2016. *Journal of Internet Commerce, 17*(3), 310–323.

Kondo, F., & Ishida, H. (2014). A cross-national analysis of intention to use multiple mobile entertainment services. *Journal of Global Information Technology Management, 17*, 45–60.

Lechman, E., & Marszk, A. (2019). *ICT-driven economic and financial development.* In *Analyses of European countries.* Academic Press.

Lera-Lopez, F., Billon, M., & Gil, M. (2010). Determinants of internet use in Spain. *Economics of Innovation and New Technology, 20*, 127–152.

Lucendo-Monedero, A. L., Ruiz-Rodríguez, F., & González-Relaño, R. (2019). Measuring the digital divide at regional level. A spatial analysis of the inequalities in digital development of households and individuals in Europe. *Telematics and Informatics, 41*, 197–217.

Mahmoodi, S., & Naderi, H. (2016). Assessment of modern banking services to achieve and realization of e-commerce and its impact on the profitability of banks listed on the Tehran stock exchange. *Modern Applied Science, 10*(9), 263–273

Marszk, A., & Lechman, E. (2019). New technologies and diffusion of innovative financial products: Evidence on exchange-traded funds in selected emerging and developed countries. *Journal of Macroeconomics, 62*, 1–29.

Nazaritehrani, A., & Mashali, B. (2020). Development of e-banking channels and market share in developing countries. *Financial Innovation, 6*(12), 1–19

Rogers, E. (2003). *Diffusion of innovations* (5th ed.). The Free Press.

Rosenberg, N. (1972). Factors affecting the diffusion of technology. *Explorations in Economic History, 10*, 3–33.

Sadigov, S., Vasilyeva, T., & Rubanov, P. (2020). Fintech in economic growth: Cross-country analysis. *Economic and Social Development: Book of Proceedings*, 729–739.

Schleife, K. (2010). What really matters: Regional versus individual determinants of the digital. *Research Policy, 39*, 173–185.

Sharma, R., Singh, G., & Sharma, S. (2020). Modelling internet banking adoption in Fiji: A developing country perspective. *International Journal of Information Management, 53*, 102116.

Takieddine, S., & Sun, J. (2015). Internet banking diffusion: A country-level analysis. *Electronic Commerce Research and Applications, 14*, 361–371.

Venkatesh, V., Morris, M. G., Davis, G. B., & Davis, F. D. (2003). User acceptance of information technology: Toward a unified view. *MIS Quarterly, 27*(3), 425–478.

Vicente, M. R., & López, A. J. (2006). Patterns of ICT diffusion across the European union. *Economic Letters, 93*, 45–51.

Yuen, Y., Yeow, P., Lim, N., & Saylani, N. (2010). Internet banking adoption: Comparing developed and developing countries. *Journal of Computer Information Systems, 51*(1), 52–61.

Zagalaz Jiménez, J. R., & Aguiar Díaz, I. (2019). Educational level and internet banking. *Journal of Behavioral and Experimental Finance, 22*, 31–40.

2 Different faces of digital financial inclusion across countries

Oskar Kowalewski and Paweł Pisany

2.1 Introduction

Rapid information and communications technology (ICT) advancement is reshaping the environment for provisioning financial services worldwide. Financial technology (fintech) is nowadays seen as a vital tool for financial inclusion, especially in emerging economies. Moreover, bank–fintech relationship is an important context of economic research and debate on fintech.

Fintech is a sophisticated phenomenon and even defining it remains a challenge. In our study, we follow the definition presented by Financial Stability Board (FSB). It states that fintech *is technology-enabled innovation in financial services that could result in new business models, applications, processes, or products, with an associated material effect on the provision of financial services* (FSB, 2017). It is a broad definition and, in our opinion, accurate, as it includes both new alternative technology-driven financial business models, as well as innovative ventures aimed at improving the efficiency of well-established and regulated financial institutions, particularly banks. The broad approach towards fintech is also reflected in a categorisation prepared by the Basel Committee on Banking Supervision (BCBS, 2018). The framework by BCBS depicts three fintech product sectors:

- credit, deposit, and capital-raising services (e.g., crowdfunding, lending marketplaces, mobile banks)
- payments, clearing, and settlements services (e.g., mobile wallets, peer-to-peer transfers, or digital exchange platforms)
- investment management services (e.g., high-frequency trading, copy-trading, and robo-advisors).

The BCBS framework also encompasses the so-called market support services, which include, among others, big data analytics, machine learning algorithms application, cloud computing, distributed ledger technology applications (e.g., smart contracts), and artificial intelligence applications (e.g., bots and advanced customer identification and authentication tools).

DOI: 10.4324/9781003199076-2

Against this background, the aim of this chapter is to shed some light on fintech emergence, and, on the mechanisms that are behind fintech-driven financial inclusion in emerging and developed markets. We claim that inter-links between the financial innovation sector and banks, as well as the role of fintech in financial inclusion, differ significantly in emerging and developed markets. That leads to a set of problems that needs to be addressed by legislators and supervisors across countries.

The rest of the chapter is organized as follows. Section 2.2 presents the empirical research on interlinks between the fintech start-up formation process and the banking sector, both in emerging and developed financial systems. Section 2.3 shows the different faces of digital financial inclusion. Section 2.4 focuses on the upcoming challenges and risks in that field. Section 2.5 provides a summary of our research findings.

2.2 Bank–fintech relationships – empirical study

2.2.1 Relevant literature

Fintech is a relatively new topic in research agendas and consequently the literature is relatively scarce, despite the growing interest in the topic. A comprehensive literature review on the fintech sector emergence as well as on banks–fintech relationships is provided by Thakor (2020) and Allen et al. (2020). Below, we refer to the literature focused on the determinants of fin-tech formations, as in our model, we associate the number of new fintech ventures created in a given economy with the condition and structure of the banking sector.

Haddad and Hornuf (2019) underline the importance of technology determinants in explaining the diversity of fintech development between countries. They find that the presence of venture capital, as well as number of secure Internet servers, mobile telephone subscriptions, and an avail-able labour force, are positively associated with the formation of fintech companies. Overall, Haddad and Hornuf (2019) confirm that a set of eco-nomic and technology factors plays a vital role in the formation of fintech ventures. Lacasse et al. (2016) underline the potentially disruptive power of the fintech sector and describe it as a competitive threat against banks. In contrast, Holotiuk et al. (2018) show the potential gains from bank–fintech company cooperation. In another study, Jagtiani and Lemieux (2018) prove that wide access to alternative data can foster the creation of fintech com-panies. Buchak et al. (2017) discuss the positive role of light regulations or lack of regulations imposed on fintech business models for the development of this sector. The forms of collaboration between fintechs and banks in selected developed economies have been the subject of empirical research by Hornuf et al. (2020). Moreover, fintech is starting to be an issue of super-visory policy, which focuses on the implications of fintech emergence for banks, including financial system stability (Navaretti et al., 2018).

2.2.2 Data and method

To empirically verify the thesis referring to various relationships between fintech ventures and banking sectors in different regions of the world, we construct a model with the number of fintech companies established in a country in a given year as the dependent variable.

Similar to Haddad and Hornuf (2019), the dependent variable was retrieved from Crunchbase – a market information platform developed mostly for investment professionals who are looking to pursue new opportunities in the sector of innovative start-ups. Crunchbase provided us with data on the creation of 4,708 fintech start-ups in the period 2005–2017 in 50 selected economies for our study. Our database includes markets from all three main groups from the MSCI[1] classification – developed markets (23 countries), emerging markets (18 countries), and frontier markets (6 countries). Additionally, three markets that are not included in the main MSCI classification, namely, Cyprus, Latvia, and Luxembourg, were added to the database.

Stock market classification seems to be a good proxy for the development of a country's financial system. It is adequate for our study, as we aim to understand the interactions between fintech companies and well-established financial intermediaries across different countries. Finally, in the regressions, we use the full sample, as well as two subsamples, representing developed (24) and developing (26) financial systems. The detailed composition of countries in our sample is presented in the Appendix Table 2.1A. As Figure 2.1 shows, we can observe a growing number of active fintech ventures across the globe in the last decade. However, we also observe that the increase is uneven across regions and countries.

We follow Haddad and Hornuf (2019) and choose a random effects negative binomial (RENB) model as our estimation method. A negative binomial model is a type of generalized linear model, in which the dependent variable is a count of the number and follows the negative binomial distribution. This means that the values of the independent variable are the non-negative integers (Zwilling, 2013). In our model, the dependent variable is the number of fintech companies established in country i in year t.

As our main aim is to analyse the bank-fintech interlinks, we employ three variables to proxy for the condition in the banking sector. We use Return On Equity (*ROE*), which reflects the profitability of the banks; we assume it will have a negative impact on the number of fintech formations. On the other hand, high profitability of banks may attract fintech companies. Henceforth, we are ambiguous about the impact of banks' profitability on fintech start-ups. One advantage of fintech companies over traditional banks are their low cost. We proxy the banks' overhead costs using the variable cost to income (*C/I*), which we assume will be positively related to the creation of fintech ventures. The last variable shows the ratio of non-performing loans (*NPL*) to gross loans in the banking sector (*NPL*), and proxy for the quality

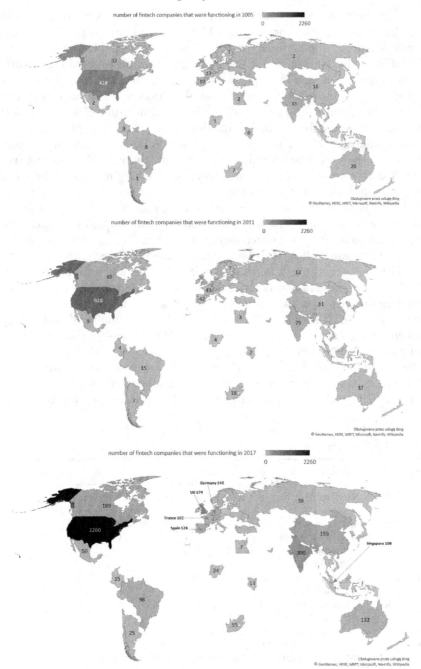

Figure 2.1 Active fintech companies cumulatively included in the years 2005–2011.
Note: countries for which data is missing are marked in white.

Source: Crunchbase.

of borrowers. We may assume that fintechs are more likely to expand in markets that are risky for traditional lenders. Consequently, we assume a positive relationship between the NPL ratio and fintech formation.

Additionally, we control for the structure of countries' banking sectors, using three variables. The first variable is *CR5* that measures the cumulated share of the assets of the five largest banks in those countries. The second measure is the *Lerner* index, which is a measure of market power in the banking sector, defined as the difference between output prices and marginal costs (relative to prices). Both higher concentration and higher values of the Lerner index indicate lesser competition in the banking sector. We assume that the less competitive the banking market is, the more difficult and/or costly it is to obtain a loan. In fact, our last variable, *access* to loans, is an index that reflects the ability of individuals or companies to obtain debt financing. The index is based on a survey, and the higher the index, the easier it is to obtain a loan in a country. As mentioned before, we assume financial inclusion to be strongly related to fintech, and therefore, we assume a negative relationship between the index and fintech formation.

We follow Haddad and Hornuf (2019) and Claessens et al. (2018) in controlling for the countries' economic development using the countries' GDP per capita (*GDPpc*). Moreover, we control for the countries' technology advancements using three variables: *Fixed, Mobiles,* and *Internet.* All three of these variables reflect technological development and infrastructure. We assume that the better the infrastructure, the more likely is the fintech formation in the country. The definitions of all the regressors are presented in Table 2.1. In the regressions, the independent variables are lagged by one

Table 2.1 Variables descriptions

Variable	Description	Source
Fintech	Number of companies founded in a given year	Crunchbase
Mobile	Mobile-cellular telephone subscriptions per 100 inhabitants	International Communication Union
Internet	Individuals using the Internet per 100 inhabitants	
Fixed	Fixed broadband subscriptions per 100 inhabitants	
GDPpc	Gross Domestic Product per capita (constant 2010 US$)	World Bank
ROE	Bank return on equity (%, after tax)	
C/I	Bank cost to income ratio (%)	
NPL	Bank nonperforming loans to gross loans (%)	
Lerner	Lerner index for the banking sector	
CR5	Five-bank asset concentration	
Access	Ease of access to loans, one to seven (best)	

period to address the potential problem of reverse causality (Dushnitsky et al., 2016), and because relationships between variables are not expected to be immediate.

2.2.3 Results

In Table 2.2, we present the results of RENB estimation. In columns (1)–(3), we show the results for all the countries in our sample and find that the level of the countries' economic development is not a positive determinant of fintech formation process. The coefficients of GDP per capita are negative and highly significant in columns (2)–(3). Thus, the results indicate that fintech formation is more likely in poorer economies where the need of fostering financial inclusion is more present than in developed countries. As our results confirm that economic development determines the development of fintech companies, we divide our sample into two subsamples based on the development of the financial sector. In columns (4)–(6) and (7)–(9), we present the results for the subsample consisting of emerging markets and developed financial markets, respectively. Once again, we find that the coefficient *GDPpc* is negative but statistically significant for the emerging countries in two of the three specifications. By contrast, for the developed countries, the coefficient is significant in only one of the specifications. This, in our opinion, confirms that fintech is more likely to play a role for financial inclusion in emerging markets.

In line with Haddad and Hornuf (2019), we find that the technology infrastructure is an important determinant for the creation of fintech companies. The coefficients of variables representing this dimension, that is, *Internet, Mobile,* and *Fixed* (included in separate estimations due to high multicollinearity) are positive and statistically significant at the 1% level in all the specifications, including the sub-samples for emerging and developed markets.

More importantly, as expected our results show different fintech *vs.* banking sector interlinks, depending on the development level of the financial system in the host country. This indirectly, yet quite convincingly, suggests varied fintech-driven financial inclusion paths within developed and emerging financial systems. To begin with, we see that *NPL* is a statistically significant determinant for fintech companies' formations, both in developed and emerging markets but the coefficients have opposite signs in those sub-samples. In developed markets, the sign is positive.

Banks that are facing increasing numbers of NPLs have potentially more difficulties in expanding lending, facilitating young fintechs (providing alternative financing) to fill the gap. Thus, one can assume that fintech lending ventures provide financing for clients in developed markets when NPLs are piling up in banks' balance sheets. Technology-based financial business models in developed markets can potentially stand for alternative and spare sources of financing for households. However, doubt remains as to whether fintechs can provide sufficient financing volumes to effectively fulfil

Table 2.2 Fintech formations and banking sector

	All markets			Emerging markets			Developed markets		
	(1)	*(2)*	*(3)*	*(4)*	*(5)*	*(6)*	*(7)*	*(8)*	*(9)*
ROE	-0.01*** (0.004)			0.002 (0.008)			-0.013*** (0.004)		
C/I			-0.002 (0.005)			-0.0173 (0.0123)			-0.002 (0.006)
NPL		-0.014 (0.012)			-0.041*** (0.015)			0.032* (0.019)	
CR5		-0.025*** (0.004)			-0.0267*** (0.007)			-0.020*** (0.006)	
Lerner	2.804*** (0.651)			1.251 (1.086)			3.513*** (0.783)		
Access			-0.365*** (0.0905)			-0.0493 (0.166)			-0.405*** (0.108)
GDPpc	-0.000 (0.000)	-0.000*** (0.000)	-0.000*** (0.000)	-0.000** (0.000)	-0.000*** (0.000)	-0.000 (0.000)	-0.000 (0.000)	-0.000** (0.000)	0.000 (0.000)
Fixed			0.141*** (0.0186)			0.233*** (0.033)			0.165*** (0.020)
Internet		0.059*** (0.004)			0.055*** (0.005)			0.088*** (0.0071)	
Mobile	0.0217*** (0.003)			0.027*** (0.004)			0.0217*** (0.0045)		
Constant	-2.069*** (0.341)	0.683* (0.361)	1.227*** (0.444)	-1.151** (0.489)	1.991*** (0.507)	1.563 (0.989)	-3.371*** (0.788)	-2.766*** (0.777)	-1.270 (1.045)
Observations	461	568	397	238	295	207	223	273	190
Countries	50	50	50	26	26	26	24	24	24

Note: This table reports the RENB regression results. The dependent variable is the number of created fintech companies in a given year in a given country over the years 2007–2017. Independent variables are one-period-lagged and their definitions are presented in Table 2.1. In columns (1)–(3) all 50 markets are included, (4)–(6) only emerging markets and (7)–(9) only developed markets. Robust standard errors are in parentheses. ***, **, and * denote statistical this function. Another explanation of our results may be just the intensification of banks activities aimed at improving the business model, in cooperation with some newly established innovative technology enterprises, as an answer to the deteriorating quality of loan portfolios.

Taking into account the diversification of fintech sector product structures in developed markets, the mix of the two interpretations probably describes the situation most accurately. In line with those outcomes, the coefficient for access to loans in developed markets is negative and highly significant. Conversely, in emerging markets, rising NPLs are just a symptom of a weakening economy, which in general, impedes business, particularly innovations.

However, as the concentration in the banking sector is negatively associated with fintech formations, the estimated coefficient of the Lerner index (a more accurate measure of market power in the banking market) reveals some interesting results. The coefficient for the sub-sample of developed markets is highly significant and positive, while the coefficient for emerging markets is insignificant.

The estimation results for the Lerner index suggest that banking sectors with high market power in advanced economies foster the formation of fintechs, among others by accelerators' initiatives. Those banks indeed may treat fintech ventures not as competition, but rather as a source of fresh, innovative business ideas and technology solutions. Indeed, one can assume that banks in most developed financial markets have substantial and well-established advantages over relatively young, independent fintech companies.

We also see that the ROE in the banking sector is negatively associated with the number of fintech ventures, but only in the case of estimations performed on the full sample of developed markets, which is in line with the previously-described interpretation of coefficients of NPL and access loans.

Our empirical studies on fintech start-ups and the condition of the banking sector confirm different links between financial innovation ventures and well-established financial intermediaries, depending on whether we are talking about a developed or an emerging financial system. This is associated to the different characteristics and perspectives of digital financial inclusion, which we will deal with later in this chapter.

2.3 Digital financial inclusion

2.3.1 Financial inclusion in emerging markets

Financial inclusion is strongly related to social inclusion. Both of them are on the agenda of many governments, as existing research indicates that they may accelerate long-term economic growth, as well as inequality and poverty reduction (Čihák & Sahay, 2020; Mushtaq & Bruneau, 2019; Sahay et al., 2015). Thus, not surprisingly, financial inclusion is also on the agenda of the World Bank (WB). WB defines financial inclusion as the state where "... *individuals and businesses have access to useful and affordable financial products and services that meet their needs – transactions, payments, savings, credit and insurance – delivered in a responsible and sustainable way ...*"[2]. WB is involved in fostering financial inclusion through its many projects under the label "Universal Financial Access by 2020" and "Global Partnership for Financial Inclusion." In a recent study, Sahay et al. (2020) also use the term "digital financial inclusion/fintech-enabled financial inclusion," which includes financial services provisioned both by fintech companies and banks through digital channels, such as mobile phones (smartphones and non-smartphones), and computers with Internet access.

This is to emphasize that financial exclusion has declined in the last decade. According to the Findex database by Demirgüç-Kunt et al. (2017), financial institutions' account access, which is a financial inclusion indicator that measures the percentage of people aged 15+ with access to traditional finance, increased from 51% in 2011 to 67% in 2017 worldwide. As per the Global Findex Report framework, financial institution access refers to the percentage of respondents who report having an account (individual or joint accounts) at a bank or another type of financial institution.

In the same period, this indicator grew from 13% to 24% for low income countries, and from 29% to 56% for lower middle income economies. The Figure 2.2 shows the regions with the highest financial institution account access in 2011 and 2017. The map shows significant variation in availability of financial institutions' services across regions and countries. Moreover, we find that financial exclusion remains a significant issue in many countries, in particular in Africa.

Account access[3], which is a broader financial inclusion indicator and includes, among others mobile money accounts[4], increased from 51% in 2011 to 69% in 2017 worldwide (Demirgüç-Kunt et al., 2017; Scharwatt et al., 2014). Most of the growth in access can be observed in poorer countries of

Figure 2.2 Financial institution account in 2011 and 2017 (% of people age 15+) in a grey scale. Note: countries for which data is missing are marked in white.

Source: Findex database.

Figure 2.3 Mobile money accounts[5] in emerging markets in 2014 and 2017 (% of people age 15+) in a grey scale. Note: countries for which data is missing are marked in white.

Source: Findex database.

the world. According to Findex, account access in low income countries grew from 13% in 2011 to 36% in 2017, and in Sub-Saharan Africa (SSA) from 23% in 2011 to 43% in 2017. On one hand, we may observe a significant increase in access to finance and accounts in developing economies. We attribute this development mainly to new technologies, particularly, mobile phones and the Internet. On the other hand, the data clearly show that financial exclusion remains a significant economic problem in emerging and developing countries.

Figure 2.3 provides a general view of the increase in mobile money account access in emerging economies between 2014 and 2017. SSA is the best example of this market, where fintech solutions (i.e. mobile money services) plays a vital role in improving the financial inclusion process; it is the only developing region where the mobile money access indicator is actually above 20%; it increased from 12% in 2014 to 21% in 2017. To assess the role of basic mobile money accounts in SSA, it should be considered that financial account access among adults (15+) was 33% in 2017, while mobile money access amounted to 21%, and account access (the broadest measure) to 43%. As can be seen from the numbers above, some customers are using both financial and mobile money services, or some mixed offer. Blakstad and Allen (2018) argue, by the example of the enterprise M-Pesa, that fintech offers may ultimately encourage and empower people to open traditional bank accounts.

Bazarbash (2019) and Manyika et al. (2016) consider fintech as a vital driver for financial inclusion, but the importance of ICT as a tool for developing affordable and widely available financial services gained momentum during the COVID-19 crisis (Boakye-Adje, 2020; Sahay et al., 2020). Sahay et al. (2020) also show that in all 52 emerging markets and developing economies, digital financial inclusion increased between 2014 and 2017, especially in Asia and Africa, including countries where "traditional" financial inclusion decreased or stayed stagnant in the last decade.

Although financial inclusion is rising, the challenge of providing basic financing services to more people still remains, especially in low income countries. The latest available edition of the Global Findex Report by Demirgüç-Kunt et al. (2017) show that the number of unbanked people amounted to 1.7 bn worldwide, which means that 31% of all adults do not have a basic transaction account.

Figure 2.4 shows the reasons financial institutions' offers do not represent an effective solution for extending financial inclusion in emerging markets. The graphs below present the most important declared reasons for not having a financial institution account in four parts of the world, excluding high income countries in each case. The following regions are included: Latin America and Caribbean (where the financial institution account access reaches 53.5% of adult people); SSA (financial institution access at the level of 32.8%); Europe and Central Asia (accordingly 65.1%); and East Asia and Pacific (70.4%). As can be seen, financial inclusion differs substantially among poorer countries across regions, but the reported reasons for not having a financial institution account are quite similar.

The most serious factor in all the above-mentioned regions is the lack of sufficient funds. This cannot be directly addressed by the actions of the financial sector alone. However, offers of mobile money services are potentially widely available for people with minimal savings, as it is a low marginal cost business. Interestingly, the significance of other factors seems to be similar in poorer economies in all four regions. The price of financial services is the second-most important determinant, while excessive physical distance to financial institutions' branches is indicated as a third-most crucial issue, followed by the lack of trust in financial institutions in general. Moreover, in some countries, a large portion of inhabitants is not provided with the official documentation usually required by banks to open a traditional account, such as an identity card or a wage slip. For example, due to varied reasons, possession of an identity card issued by the authorities is available to only 15.7% of adults in Malawi; 21.4% adults in South Sudan; 37.3% of population in Chad; 38.2% in Armenia; and 40.7% in Lao PDR (Demirgüç-Kunt et al., 2017).

The analysis of reasons for not having a financial institution account leads, in our opinion, to a significant conclusion – technology-driven solutions are indeed the answer. They can solve cost and distance-related obstacles, and help the financial system to leap-frog the *brick-and-mortar* infrastructure barriers and employ the modern digital finance framework. Moreover, fintech ventures are rarely perceived as "untrustworthy and greedy," especially by younger people. Finally, fintechs usually bear light regulatory burdens and do not have strict internal business procedures as international banking groups do. They can sell their services to a wide public, including people without the set of traditionally required documents.

The last issue is however quite ambiguous, as banks have a very good justification for detailed and accurate customer identification, namely

Figure 2.4 Reasons for not having a financial institution account. Note: % of people
without a financial institution account, age 15+, excluding high income
economies.

Source: Findex database.

preventing both money laundering and funding for illegal and vicious activities. Thus, the optimal strategy would be rather to work on advanced digital ID programs, as in the cases of Argentina, Nigeria, or India (White et al., 2019).

2.3.2 *Financial inclusion in developed markets*

Though financial inclusion should be perceived as both a task and a challenge, especially for low income countries and emerging markets, there is also a space for improvement in some high-income countries. The Findex database reports that the account access indicator amounted to 94% in high income countries (and *nota bene,* the same value is reported for financial institution account access). Thus, in general, the problem of financial exclusion in rich parts of world does not exist. Still, it seems that some developed countries are facing, just as in emerging economies, challenges related to the *men-women gap* and the *rich-poor gap* for financial inclusion (defined by account access). Demirgüç-Kunt et al. (2017) document that in the Czech Republic in 2017, the *men-women gap* was 5 percentage points (pp.) and the *rich-poor gap* amounted to 17 pp., while in Hungary, these figures are, 6 and 12 pp., respectively. As far as the *rich-poor gap* is concerned, it is worth mentioning that this indicator is 10 pp. in Slovak Republic, 8 pp. in Portugal and 12 pp. even in Israel.

In developed markets, looking at the problem only from the perspective of basic transaction account access is inadequate, as financial exclusion may be more sophisticated and related, for example, to the practical erasure of young people from the credit market due to their short credit history or unprivileged legal form of labour contract. In the case of entrepreneurs, if credit policy is mechanically strict, one previous business failure and bankruptcy may result in effective exclusion from the debt financial market. Furthermore, digital competences may also become the reason for exclusion, if digitalisation develops quickly. However, fintech seems to be a promising tool for developed countries with the above-mentioned challenges, though it may, at the same time, pose serious risks, such as discrimination and unfair distribution of financing. We discuss this issue in more detail in the third part of this chapter, in the context of both emerging as well as advanced economies.

The need of financial inclusion creates different challenges in emerging and advanced economies. Moreover, banks and non-bank fintech ventures play different roles in financial inclusion, depending on the income level of the country in which they are operating.

In emerging economies, fintech ventures are focused on providing financial services directly to customers where banking services do not reach. In this way, fintech significantly contributes to basic financial inclusion in low income countries and emerging economies.

On the other hand, financial inclusion in developed markets is associated with widely available financial services provisioned with banks. Moreover, independent fintech ventures are often focused on cooperation with well-established financial institutions and contribute to the improvement in financial inclusion through joint projects. Thus, banks in developed economies do not treat fintech companies as competitors, but rather as technologically advanced solution-suppliers, as well as sources of new fresh business ideas, which has been indicated by our model in Section 2.2.

2.4 Risks and challenges in further fostering financial inclusion

2.4.1 Bank–fintech relationships as a challenge both in emerging and advanced economies

In Section 2.3, our study shows that the traditional banking sector is not able to become the driver of financial inclusion in the poorest countries on a scale required. Fintech seems to be a solution to the obstacles identified in those countries. Probably to some extent, banks can introduce technology-driven solutions and contribute to financial inclusion, through transforming and extending their business models. However, some barriers for traditional intermediaries at emerging markets will remain. As Demirgüç-Kunt et al. (2017) show, those obstacles are related to a lack of trust in banks, or underdeveloped official procedures and legal environments in some poorer countries. Finally, banks may find providing services in some parts of the world unprofitable, especially when regulatory burdens and costs are combined with the tiny scale of transactions that need to be serviced in some low-income countries. This is probably the reason we do not see much competition between banks and fintechs in low-income countries and emerging economies.

One can assume that, for the time being, fintech companies and banks offer their products to slightly different customer segments in less developed markets. The more advanced economies and financial systems in poorer countries become, the more potentially profitable market segments for banks arise. On the one hand, this may be good, as banks are strictly regulated entities and, at least in theory, they are prepared to serve the economy when markets become more sophisticated and new risks emerge. On the other hand, smaller technology-oriented financial companies (for example, the Kenyan *Farm Drive*, an advanced analytics company that fosters financial inclusion of smallholder farmers, or *Branch*, a mobile lending application with a machine-learning tool for automated credit scoring, that is offering debt products in Kenya, Nigeria, Tanzania, Mexico, and India) will surely be still very beneficial for social and financial inclusion (Biallas & O'Neill, 2020). They simply have unique know-how in relation to the poorest and most underserved groups of people.

In advanced economies, bank–fintech relationships are more sophisticated. Banks fosters fintech formations, as they usually have a substantial market advantage and perceive their position as safe. Fintechs, with their truly entrepreneurial spirit, can be suppliers but more importantly also sources of business inspiration. This applies to smaller companies (labelled as fintechs) that are functioning in areas of client experience improvement, cybersecurity, data analytics, advanced algorithms in sales optimizations or risk management, and effective payment systems, or in other words, those fintech enterprises that are working on products that can be easily incorporated into banks' businesses. We assume that these mechanisms are the ones that we catch in our empirical study in Section 2.2. Among the most important challenges concerning the relationship between banks and fintech suppliers – both smaller ones as well as tech-giants – are high cybersecurity and outsourcing standards.

The fintech landscape is, however, much more complex in developed economies, in particular where there is a substantial number of enterprises that are offering alternative finance directly to customers via Internet or mobile channels. To illustrate, the latest available edition of comprehensive reporting on alternative finance markets by the Cambridge Center for Alternative Finance (CCAF, 2020) indicates that the biggest online alternative finance models in Europe (excluding Great Britain) in 2018 are *Peer-to-Peer Marketplace Consumer lending* (USD 2.9 bn), *Balance Sheet Property Lending* (USD 1.4 bn), and *Peer-to-Peer Marketplace Business lending* (USD 997 mn). On a global scale, the structure is similar. In 2018, the largest online alternative finance model was *P2P/Marketplace Consumer Lending* (USD 195.29 bn), followed by the second largest segment, *P2P/Marketplace Business Lending* (USD 50.3 bn). Peer-to-peer business models, as well as so-called *marketplaces* that are essentially brokerage businesses, can create the risk of regulatory arbitrage. However, their services may be in some cases very similar to ones offered by regulated financial entities, such as banks, they are usually created outside the banking system without licensing processes. It may be not easy to properly assess whether an alternative finance company is essentially providing banking or investment-advisory regulated services, while hiding behind a currently trendy label – financial innovation. Thus, it seems crucial for legislators and particularly supervisors to have in mind the risk of regulatory arbitrage, while dealing with technological innovation on financial markets.

2.4.2 Unintended potential consequences of digitalization for financial inclusion

The impact of modern innovative technology solutions on financial inclusion level may be ambiguous, even in advanced economies. First, we need to keep in mind that digital competences in societies are distributed unevenly, and that, elderly or simply tech-unaware people, for example, may face social and financial exclusion in an increasingly digitalized environment. Second, the greater the advancement in digital financial inclusion is, the more critical ICT infrastructure becomes. The proximity of a bank branch is no longer a problem but computers, mobile phones and the Internet are essential. The more complex financial services and products are becoming, the faster and more expensive is the Internet service needed (prospective broadband connection).

Figure 2.5 presents the basic indicator of ICT infrastructure quality. Low income countries and emerging economies were unsurprisingly underdeveloped in comparison to richer parts of the world in 2017. It applies, in particular, to African countries and is reflected by the composite measure

IDI 2017 Value

0.96　　　　　8.98

Figure 2.5 The ICT development index (IDI)[6] in 2017, scale: Min (0.96) – Max (8.98).

Note: countries for which data is missing are marked in white.

Source: International Telecommunication Union.

by the International Telecommunication Union (ITU), which includes, among other measures, Internet access or mobile cellular telecommunication subscriptions.

Interestingly, we find that mobile telecommunication is a more effective channel for digital financial inclusion than the Internet in low-income countries. The value of indicator *Mobile cellular subscriptions* for low income countries stands at 52% of the index value for the whole world, while the value of indicator *Individuals using the Internet* for low income economies is only 33% of global value of the latter index.

Another area where the unintended effects of digitalisation may occur is in the algorithmic automation of risk management in finance. The quality of credit scoring determines the actual quality of financial inclusion. If consumers or small entrepreneurs that were provided with financing for the first time (in a way included into the credit market) are not able to pay the debt, then the risk of falling into a debt spiral arises.

More importantly, modern fintech credit risk assessment is based on big data analysis and machine-learning algorithms. Currently, one can gather unprecedented amounts of data on potential debtors, both financial data as well as so called alternative data from social media, e-commerce activities, and mobile phone usage (Aitken, 2017). Though machine learning algorithms applied for alternative data seems to be quite an effective way to assess creditworthiness (Frost et al., 2019; Gambacorta et al., 2020), they may also result in some unintended and even unethical outcomes. Algorithm-based decisions may be biased and lead to unfairness and discrimination, and consequently, to the exclusion of some groups of people (Gikay, 2020). Moreover, these decisions, which are often fully automated, may be opaque to customers (Desai & Kroll, 2017). This creates a set of challenges, both in emerging as well as advanced markets. For the time being, the European Union is working on establishing a framework for the effective development of ethical and trustworthy artificial intelligence (European Commission, 2020; European Parliament, 2020).

2.4.3 Fintech in the pandemic era

Lastly, some reflections on digital financial inclusion in the pandemic era seem justified. Though the current economic crisis caused by the COVID-19 pandemic may boost the evolution of customer preferences towards remote financial services, there are also at least two important factors that may hamper fintech development and digital financial inclusion as a consequence. First, as we are facing a full-fledged economic crisis, the economic activity and demand will fall, and it will hit all companies, including the financial innovation sector.

Second, one can expect that the resilience of fintech start-ups will be seriously challenged during the pandemic crisis, as they usually do not possess reserves and a liquidity cushion. Furthermore, they often lack the chance to fully establish their business models and reach a break-even point. We do not have access to comprehensive and complete data on financing for the financial innovation sector. However, the disclosed information (Figure 2.6) does not confirm any serious difficulties among young start-up ventures. One can assume that this is the result of the potential attractiveness of some fintech business models in the difficult time of COVID-19, as they provide financial services through mobile/remote channels, without the necessity of physical contact. The Klarna e-payment and e-shopping service is a good example. With its broad range of services such as extending consumer credit opportunities by introducing

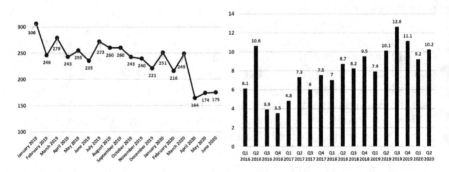

Figure 2.6 Number of global deals to fintech companies January 2019–June 2020 (left-hand panel) and global disclosed funding to fintech companies Q1 2016–Q2 2020 (bn USD) (right-hand panel).

Source: https://www.cbinsights.com/research/coronavirus-fintech-financing-impact/

advanced machine-learning analytics for deferred payment solutions, the company is benefitting from the preference of the current market to switch to online shopping. In September 2020, Klarna announced a USD 650 mn equity funding round that translates to a valuation of 10.65 USD bn[7].

2.5 Conclusions

Digitalisation of finance is inevitable and the COVID-19 pandemic is bound to accelerate this phenomenon. Digital financial inclusion means a possibility to offer basic financial products to financially excluded people in low income countries through mobile channels and to create new ways of extending the customer base in developed markets as well.

In low income economies, such as in many African countries, this represents a chance to boost social inclusion and to foster economic development. Light business models of newly-created independent fintech ventures in low income countries make them quite different entities than banks. Cooperation is possible, but in the long run, when financial business in the poorest countries become more profitable, more competition from banks and international banking groups may arise. It has both potential pros and cons for financial systems in low income countries.

In developed markets, as well as in some more advanced emerging economies where banking business is well-established, interlinks between fintechs and banks are more sophisticated, mostly because the fintech sector is heterogeneous. On the one hand, some fintech ventures are focused on providing traditional financial intermediaries with new technology-based solutions, as in the area of customer experience in digital service channels, cybersecurity, and data analytics. In this way, fintech contributes to banks' business model transformation, but does not create competition. On the other hand, there are also so-called online alternative finance business models that are focused on offering financial products directly to customers or enterprises. All in all, the sophistication of the fintech sector in developed markets requires public policy that includes, among other factors, high outsourcing standards, cybersecurity issues, and careful market monitoring, especially from the perspective of regulatory arbitrage risk.

However, some challenges are common in emerging and developed economies, they are likely to be felt first in more advanced financial systems. Using artificial intelligence and machine-learning in assessing credit risk is a good example. It is a chance to offer credit to people with short credit histories after performing credit scoring based on alternative data analysis. This may be an effective solution, both in low income countries as well as in some particular customer segments in high income countries. Still one cannot ignore that ethical problems connected with the risk of *algorithmic discrimination* arise. Finally, the necessity of acknowledging the rise in financial and technological awareness in societies is crucial, both in emerging and developed markets.

Finally, it is worth underlining some limitations of our study. We are trying to emphasize on economic mechanisms and do not consider the countries' legal environments in detail. Moreover, we have concentrated mainly on purely fintech ventures and their relationships to banks. However, BigTechs (large technology enterprises such as Google, Amazon, Facebook, and Apple from the US, or the Alibaba Group from China) are also shaping the future of finance and are determining financial inclusion both in emerging and developed economies. Including this issue is essential in presenting a more complex view of the impact of technological innovations on financial intermediaries. We leave these aspects for future research.

Funding

This work was supported by the National Science Center (NCN), Poland, under grant no. 2019/33/B/HS4/00369.

Appendix

Table 2.1A List of countries included in estimations –
classification by MSCI

Developed markets	Emerging markets
Australia	Argentina
Austria	Brazil
Belgium	Chile
Canada	China
Denmark	Colombia
Finland	Czech Republic
France	Cyprus
Germany	Estonia[a]
Hong Kong	Egypt
Ireland	India
Israel	Indonesia
Italy	Kenya[a]
Japan	Latvia
Luxembourg	Lithuania[a]
New Zealand	Malaysia
Norway	Mexico
Portugal	Nigeria[a]
Singapore	Poland
Spain	Russian Federation
Sweden	South Africa
Switzerland	South Korea
The Netherlands	Thailand
United Kingdom	Turkey
United States	Ukraine[a]
	United Arab Emirates
	Vietnam[a]

[a] Countries classified as frontier countries.

Notes

1. https://www.msci.com/market-classification
2. https://www.worldbank.org/en/topic/financialinclusion/overview
3. The percentage of respondents who report having an account (by themselves or together with someone else) at a bank or another type of financial institution, or report personally using a mobile money service in the past 12 months (from Findex database).
4. Data on adults with a mobile money account include respondents who reported personally using services included in the GSM Association's Mobile Money for the Unbanked (GSMA MMU) database to pay bills or to send or receive money in the past 12 months. The data also include an additional 0.60% of respondents in 2017 who reported receiving wages, government transfers, a public sector pension (included in 2017 data), or payments for agricultural products through a mobile phone in the past 12 months (from Findex database).
5. Mobile money account (e-money) – account that is primarily accessed using a mobile phone and that is held with the e-money issuer. In some jurisdictions, e-money accounts may resemble conventional bank accounts, but are treated differently under the regulatory framework because they are used for different purposes (for example, as a surrogate for cash or a stored value that is used to facilitate transactional services). An active mobile money account is a mobile money account that has been used to conduct at least one transaction during a certain period of time (usually 90 days or 30 days) (from GSMA).
6. Composite indicator details: https://www.itu.int/en/ITU-D/Statistics/Pages/publications/mis/methodology.aspx
7. https://www.klarna.com/international/press/klarna-announces-650m-funding-round-to-further-accelerate-global-growth/

References

Aitken, R. (2017). All data is credit data: Constituting the unbanked. *Competition & Change, 21*(4), 274–300.

Allen, F., Gu, X., & Jagtiani, J. A. (2020). *A Survey of Fintech Research and Policy Discussion*. FRB of Philadelphia Working Paper No. 20–21.

Thakor, A. V. (2020). Fintech and banking: What do we know? *Journal of Financial Intermediation, 41*, 100833.

Basel Committee on Banking Supervision (BCBS) (2018). *Sound practices: Implications of fintech developments for banks and bank supervisors.*

Bazarbash, M. (2019). *FinTech in Financial Inclusion: Machine Learning Applications in Assessing Credit Risk*. IMF Working Paper No. 19/109. International Monetary Fund.

Biallas, M., & O'Neill, F. (2020). Artificial intelligence innovation in financial services. In *Emerging markets compass 85/2020*. International Finance Corporation.

Blakstad, S., & Allen R. (2018). *FinTech Revolution*, https://doi.org/10.1007/978-3-319-76014-8_7

Boakye-Adje, N. Y. (2020). *Covid-19: Boon and bane for digital payments and financial inclusion.* Financial Stability Institute Briefs 9. Bank for International Settlement.

Buchak, G., Matvos, G., Piskorski, T., & Seru, A. (2017). Fintech, Regulatory Arbitrage, and the Rise of Shadow Banks. NBER Working Papers, No. 23288.

CCAF. (2020). The global alternative finance market benchmarking report trends, opportunities and challenges for lending, equity, and non-investment alternative finance models. Vol. 35. The Cambridge Centre for Alternative Finance.

Claessens, S., Frost, J., Turner, G., & Zhu, F. (2018). *Fintech credit markets around the world: Size, drivers and policy issues.* BIS Quarterly Review September.

Čihák, M., & Sahay, R. (2020). *Finance and inequality. IMF staff discussion note no. 20/02.* International Monetary Fund.

Demirgüç-Kunt, A., Klapper, L., Singer, D., Ansar, S., & Hess, J. (2017). *The global findex database. Measuring financial inclusion and fintech revolution.* World Bank Group.

Desai, D. R., & Kroll, J. A. (2017). Trust but verify: A guide to algorithms and the law. *Harvard Journal of Law & Technology*, Available at SSRN: https://ssrn.com/abstract=2959472

Dushnitsky, G., Guerini, M., Piva, E., & Rossi-Lamastra, C. (2016). Crowdfunding in Europe: Determinants of platform creation. *California Management Review*, *58*, 44–71.

European Commission (2020). White paper. On Artificial Intelligence – A European Approach to Excellence and Trust. COM(2020) 65 Final.

European Parliament (2020). European Parliament Resolution With Recommendations to the Commission on a Framework of Ethical Aspects of Artificial Intelligence, Robotics and Related Technologies. 2020/2012(INL).

Financial Stability Board. (2017). Financial Stability Implications From FinTech. https://www.fsb.org/wp-content/uploads/R270617.pdf

Frost, J., Gambacorta, L., Huang, Y., Shin, H. S., & Zbinden, P. (2019) BigTech and the Changing Structure of Financial Intermediation. BIS Working Paper No. 779.

Gambacorta, L., Huang, Y., Qiu, H., & Wang, J. (2020). How Do Machine Learning and Non-Traditional Data Affect Credit Scoring? New Evidence From a Chinese Fintech Firm. BIS Working Paper No. 834.

Gikay, A. A. (2020). The American Way – Until machine learning algorithm beats the law? algorithmic consumer credit scoring in the EU and US. *Case Western Reserve Journal of Law, Technology & the Internet.* doi: forthcoming, https://dx.doi.org/10.2139/ssrn.3671488.

Greene, W. (2007). *Fixed and random effects models for count data.* New York: Department of Economics, Stern School of Business, New York University.

Haddad, C., & Hornuf, L. (2019). The emergence of the global fintech market: Economic and technological determinants. *Small Business Economics*, *53*(1), 81–105

Hornuf, L., Klus, M., Lohwasser, T., & Schwienbacher, A. (2020). How Do Banks Interact With Fintech Startups? CESifo Working Paper Series No. 7170.

Holotiuk, F., Klus, M. F., Lohwasser, T. S., & Moormann, J. (2018). *Motives to form alliances for digital innovation: The case of banks and fintechs.* Vol. 22. BLED Proceedings.

Jagtiani, J., & Lemieux, C. (2018). The Roles of Alternative Data and Machine Learning in Fintech Lending: Evidence From the Lending Club Consumer Platform. Federal Reserve Bank of Philadelphia Working Paper, no. 18–15.

Lacasse, R. M., Lambert, B., Osmani, E., Couture, C., Roy, N., Sylvain, J., & Nadeau, F. (2016). *A digital tsunami: FinTech and crowdfunding.* Quebec City, Canada: International Scientific Conference on Digital Intelligence.

Manyika, J., Lund, S., Singer, M., White, O., & Berry, C. (2016). *Digital finance for all: Powering inclusive growth in emerging economies.* McKinsey Global Institute.

Mushtaq, R., & Bruneau, C. (2019). Microfinance, financial inclusion and ICT: Implications for poverty and inequality. *Technology in Society, 59,* 101154.

Navaretti, B. G., Calzolari, G., Mansilla-Fernandez, J. M., & Pozzolo, A. F. (2018). *Fintech and Banking. Friends or Foes?* Available at SSRN: https://ssrn.com/abstract=3099337

Sahay, R., Eriksson von Allmen, U., Lahreche, A., Khera, P., Ogawa, S., Bazarbash, M., & Beaton, K. (2020). The promise of fintech; Financial inclusion in the post COVID-19 era. *IMF Departmental Papers Policy Papers 20/09.* International Monetary Fund.

Sahay, R., Čihák, M., N'Diaye, P., Barajas, A., Mitra, S., Kyobe, A. ... Reza Yousefi, S. (2015). Financial Inclusion: Can It Meet Multiple Macroeconomic Goals? IMF Staff Discussion Note No. 15/17, International Monetary Fund.

Scharwatt, C., Katakam, A., Frydrych, J., Murphy, A., & Naghavi, N. (2014). *State of the industry 2014: Mobile financial services for the unbanked.* New York: GSMA.

White, O., Madgavkar, A., Mumbai Manyika, J., Mahajan, D., Bughin, J., McCarthy, M., & Sperling, O. (2019). *Digital identification a key to inclusive growth.* McKinsey Global Institute.

Zwilling, M. L. (2013). Negative binomial regression. *The Mathematica Journal, 15,* 1–18.

3 ICT, financial markets and their impact on firms' performance and internationalisation

Joanna Wolszczak-Derlacz[1]

3.1 Introduction

The effects of information and communication technology (ICT) and financial development on growth are highly debated in the literature. While from the theoretical perspective they are considered key drivers of economic growth, the empirical studies produce a mixed picture (Sassi and Goaied, 2013; Vu, 2011). Empirical analyses are either conducted at the aggregate level in which country statistics are employed (surveyed, e.g., by Stanley et al., 2018) or at the firm level (reviewed, e.g., by Pilat, 2005 and Polák, 2017). Furthermore, the methodology and the measurements of the phenomenon differ, so, in the end, divergent and inconclusive conclusions should not be a surprise. Interestingly, Polák (2017) in a meta-analysis of firm-level studies dedicated to ICT-growth nexus found only a weak effect, while Stanley et al. (2018), in their review of studies conducted at the country level, provide evidence that ICT has contributed positively to economic growth, at least on average. Finally, Vu et al. (2020), based on a comprehensive literature survey of 208 studies (carried either at the level of a country, industry, or firm), dedicated to the link between ICT and growth, confirms that ICT has a positive effect on growth.

From the historical perspective, it was noticed that investments in ICT do not have to necessarily contribute to higher growth. This lack of productivity gains from ICT advancements is referred to in the literature as the productivity paradox[2] (Attewell, 1994; Brynjolfsson, 1993). Numbers of explanations have been proposed; most of them refer to measurement issues – where ICT inputs and outputs are not properly measured and growth accounting also is a challenge, time delay – the growth effects of ICT need time to materialise, redistribution – when gains from ICT are not distributed equally, and mismanagement – poor management can make the ICT investment unbeneficial for growth, e.g., through the wrong choice of ICT applications, lack of support, and limited service after ICT implementation (Brynjolfsson and Yang, 1996; Brynjolfsson et al., 2019; Schweikl and Obermaier, 2020). Similarly, the development of financial markets (also through digitalisation) is not essentially accompanied by higher growth, which is referred to in the

DOI: 10.4324/9781003199076-3

literature as the finance-growth puzzle (Sassi & Goaied, 2013). Theoretically, finance development and digitalisation of financial markets should improve the efficiency of resource allocation and stimulate technological innovation. Practically, however, the outcomes may depend on some additional macro or micro conditions (e.g., financial literacy).

From the micro perspective, the advantages of ICT may depend on some crucial characteristics and capabilities of firms, such as worker capabilities, organisational structure, job training, and business process redesign (Dedrick et al., 2003). Brynjolfsson and Hitt (2003) underline the need for complementary investments in organisational changes for the company to benefit fully from ICT.

Additionally, the usage of ICT and the development of digital financial markets (with different digital services accessed and delivered through digital channels) are not limited to banking services only. What is more, they can enhance the growth of a firm and provoke its opening to foreign markets (internationalisation). With the usage of ICT and easier access to financial markets, firms may be more anxious to take part in international markets, either through export, import, or involvement in global value chains (GVC). Luo and Bu (2016) show that especially in the case of emerging economies, the ICT-growth channel is materialised through the internationalisation process.

Thanks to the digitalisation of financial markets, some of the sources of market failure, e.g., information asymmetry, can be overcome. For example, Head and Mayer (2013) find that among other impediments to trade, imperfect information and information friction have the same properties as physical distance. From the macro perspective, Meijers (2014) shows that Internet use does not explain economic growth directly, however, its impact on growth is indirect through the stimulation of international trade.

Motivated by previous studies and their mixed results, in this study, we propose an analysis to re-examine the ICT-finance puzzle. We go beyond country-specific or sector-specific studies and conduct cross-country analysis with firm-level data. It enables obtaining a broad picture of the ICT-finance-growth nexus. Importantly, our analysis takes into account enterprises from emerging and transformation economies.

This study aims threefold. First, we want to answer the question whether the usage of ICT and easier access to financial resources (lower finance constraints) are among the crucial determinants of firms' performance (labour productivity).

The second aim is to examine what the main determinants of firms' involvement in internationalisation processes are and to what extent the usage of ICT and access to financial resources determine a company's decision to enter foreign markets. This part of the analysis is rooted in Melitz (2003) model where firms' heterogeneity is taken into account. Finally, we look more closely at the performance of enterprises during coronavirus disease of 2019 (COVID-19).

The main analysis is based on the cross-section of firm-level data from the World Bank Enterprise Survey (February 2021 update) covering 139 countries over the period from 2006 to 2019. The survey covers a broad range of business environment topics, including access to finance, corruption, infrastructure, crime, competition, and performance measures. Additionally, we avail of ES follow-up surveys dedicated to studying the impact of the COVID-19 pandemic on businesses. The collected information refers to changes in operation status (temporary or permanent closures), changes in sales, employment, and finance, along with policy responses and expectations.

The structure of the chapter is as follows. In section 3.2, a short review of the previous studies on the nexus between ICT, finance, growth, and internationalisation is presented. Section 3.3 presents the data with basic descriptive statistics. The empirical analysis is conducted in Section 3.4. Section 3.5 contains conclusions. The main findings show that firms' performance (labour productivity) is positively correlated to ICT usage and negatively to financial constraints. Some of the ICT proxies are conditioned on worker qualifications: firms with a higher share of non-production and skilled workers gain more from the ICT employed. Additionally, enterprises present in foreign markets are on average characterised by higher ICT usage. Some ambiguous results are found in this aspect as far as financial conditions and firms' internationalisation processes are considered. Finally, the firms' adjustment to COVID-19 is reported.

3.2 Literature review

In terms of theoretical background[3], it is shown that the spread of ICT and digitalisation of financial services are important for the performance of firms. For example, Cooley and Quadrini (2001) derived a theoretical model, which yields that both financial factors and technological differences are important for the dynamics of firms. Interestingly, based on this model, the authors conclude that financial factors are more vital for the size of a firm, while the technological differences are more relevant for the age of the company. Albeit the consensus about the growth effects of ICT, the exact linkage between ICT and firm performance remains ambiguous (Stoel & Muhanna, 2009).

At the micro-level, when firms' performance is analysed, it is stressed that productivity gains from ICT and digitalisation of financial services can be obtained when some initial conditions are fulfilled. Such conditions are related to essential competencies of workers, which are not limited to technical skills only but also refer to broader capabilities: educational, organisational, and even cultural ones (Díaz-Chao et al., 2015). Díaz-Chao et al. (2015), in their study of small and medium-sized enterprises (SMEs) in Spain, observe an indirect relationship between co-innovation and productivity in firms that initiate international expansion. Dedrick et al. (2003), based on the review of 50 empirical studies dedicated to the topic, argue that the productivity paradox can be no longer confirmed. However, they emphasise that the gains in productivity growth due to ICT investments depend on the complementary investments dedicated to the decision-making system training and business process restructure. Aral and Weill (2007) put forward two organisational explanations for the variation in productivity gains from ICT investments: differences in firms' IT investment allocations and their IT capabilities. Luo and Bu (2016) show that the ICT-growth nexus is conditioned on additional macro- and micro-level requirements. The link between ICT and productivity is more pronounced in less economically developed economies, and when a firm is present in foreign markets or has superior quality control and assurance.

Additionally, Nwankpa and Roumani (2016), based on a survey of 167 chief information officers (CIOs) from firms across the United States, conclude that IT capability positively influences digital transformation. Abbasi and Weigand (2017) examined 39 relevant studies dedicated to the topic concerning the impact of digital financial services on a firm's performance. The results of different studies depend on econometric techniques; however, the majority of studies (82%) confirm that digital financial services improve the performance and profitability of a firm. The authors underline that most of the studies they surveyed were limited to the banking sector, and this sector restriction should be overcome in future analysis. The same is confirmed by Singh et al. (2021); there is a need to analyse firms not only from the banking sector since financial services can be an additional source of revenue generation for firms from different industries.

Interestingly, one of the channels through that ICT and digitalisation of financial services can enhance the overall productivity is through international trade. For example, Meijers (2014) finds that the use of the Internet does not explain economic growth directly, but its impact on growth is indirect through the stimulation of international trade. Head and Mayer (2013) stress that among other impediments to trade, imperfect information and information friction have the same properties as physical distance, and ICT can be a tool to overcome it. In this context, ICT can serve to reduce trade barriers, lower transaction and transportation costs, and reduces the international market uncertainty of exporters and importers. Traditionally, productivity was considered the main determinant of firms' presence in foreign markets. Melitz (2003) in his seminal work underlines that only the most productive firms decide to enter foreign markets since they have to cover additional fixed costs, so there is self-selection by exporters. This hypothesis was tested in many previous studies confirming the theoretical background usually taking into account such determinants of exporters as size, age, and ownership (reviewed, e.g., by Wagner, 2007). However, ICT and better access to financial services can serve to reduce the initial fixed costs connected with entering foreign markets. Hagsten and Kotnik (2017) show that ICT can act as a facilitator of internationalisation for small and medium-sized enterprises, Berman and Héricourt (2010) highlight the impact of firms' access to finance on their decision to enter the export market.

3.3 Data and descriptive statistics

Our empirical analysis is based on firm-level data coming from the World Bank Enterprise Survey (February 2021 update). The survey is limited to private enterprises from non-agriculture sectors with a minimum of five employees. The questionnaire is answered by business owners and top managers and consists of broad topics covering a firm's characteristics (year of foundation, size, sales), financial situation, international relations (trade indicators), infrastructure, innovation and technology, performance measures, major obstacles, etc. The sampling method is based on stratified random sampling where strata are defined based on firm size, business sector, and geographic region within a country. The detailed information on the methodology of data collection, questionnaires, and manuals are available on the web page of Enterprise Surveys (ES) World Bank.[4]

Our analysis is based on the most recent release of ES World Bank (February 2021), which covers 139[5] developing and transition economies from the period 2006–2019. Data are pooled from all available waves based on a standardised methodology with harmonised questions common to companies from different countries where the intervals between waves are three or four years. Thanks to the individual firm's identification number, it is possible to merge data from the original survey with ES indicators and total factor productivity (TFP) estimates. Cross-section samples were obtained, so the conclusions about time trends should be made with caution since the panel data characteristic of the sample is limited.

In the final sample, information concerning almost 170,000 enterprises, including 55% from the manufacturing sector and 45% from the services sector, are collected. Some of the questions are limited only to the companies from the manufacturing sector. The surveyed enterprises come from 139 countries representing six regions: 30% of all companies are from Europe and Central Asia (ECA), 20%, respectively, from Sub-Saharan Africa (AFR) and Latin America & Caribbean (LAC), 11% from East Asia & Pacific (EAP) and South Asia (SAR) and 8% from the Middle East & North Africa (MNA).

The focus of our interest is variables describing the usage of ICT and financial conditions (to be employed in further empirical analysis). Table 3.1 shows the distribution of companies across different regions according to the usage of different forms of ICT. ICTs are proxied by different variables. *Cert* shows whether a firm possesses internationally recognised quality certification. Generally, 22% of all enterprises have such a certificate, with the highest percentage in South Asian and European & Central Asian countries. Around 15% of companies use technology licensed from foreign companies (*Tech foreign*) and ECA countries are

Table 3.1 Proportion of companies characterized by ICT usage, by region

Variable (ICT)	AFR	EAP	ECA	LAC	MNA	SAR	Total
Cert	0.139	0.244	0.257	0.202	0.193	0.326	0.222
Tech foreign	0.153	0.176	0.196	0.141	0.13	0.104	0.155
Web	0.275	0.426	0.608	0.567	0.496	0.421	0.480
Email	0.512	0.672	0.829	0.87	0.616	0.682	0.712
New prod	0.468	0.292	0.269	0.588	0.196	0.418	0.376
New prodmarket	0.68	0.726	0.675	0.624	0.698	0.674	0.669
Inn process	0.478	0.407	0.193	0.488	0.198	0.596	0.371
RD	0.197	0.199	0.110	0.341	0.105	0.287	0.199

Notes: East Asia & Pacific (EAP), Europe & Central Asia (ECA), Latin America & Caribbean (LAC), Middle East & North Africa (MNA), South Asia (SAR), Sub-Saharan Africa (AFR). *Cert* – possessing internationally recognised quality certifications; *Tech foreign* – using technology licensed from foreign companies (excluding office software), *Web* – having own web page, *Email* – using email to communicate with clients/suppliers,

New prod – introduction of new or significantly improved products or services over the last three years, *New prodmarket* – introduction of new products/services over the last three years that were also new to the main market, *Inn process* – introduction process innovations, *RD* – expenditure on formal research and development activities, either in-house or contracted with other companies, excluding market research surveys.

Source: Own compilation based on data from ES World Bank (February 2021 release).

again characterised by a percentage of companies with foreign technology higher than the average. Most of the companies use email (*Email*) to communicate with clients/suppliers (71%), and around 50% have their own web page (*Web*): 60% in ECA countries. Approximately one-third of enterprises introduced a new product/service (*New_prod*) and more than 60% of companies introduced a new product/service, it was also new to the main market (*New_prodmarket*). The process innovation[6] (*Inn_process*) is introduced in 37% of surveyed companies, with the highest share in LAC countries (almost 50%). Finally, the last variable describing the ICT capability is whether the firm is spending money on R&D: from 10% in the MNA to 29% in countries from SAR. Based on these descriptive statistics, regional variability of ICT usage among enterprises can be observed. Similarly, the size of the company is relevant in regard to the use of ICT by an enterprise. Among large companies with over 100 employees (Table 3.2), the usage of all listed different ICT proxies is more frequent than in small (less than 20 employees) and medium-size (from 20 to 99 employees) enterprises.

The companies' financial conditions are also surveyed. Among all companies, 25% of firms identify access to finance as a major constraint (among other obstacles, they list access to land, business licensing and permits, taxes, corruption, etc.). Additionally, 43% of the firms indicated that they do not need a loan and 8% reported that their recent loan applications were rejected. There is also information available on the proportion of investments and working capital financing from different sources: internal funds,

Table 3.2 Proportion of companies characterized by ICT usage, by size of the company

	Small(<20)	*Medium (20–99)*	*Large (100 and over)*
Cert	0.094	0.244	0.502
Tech foreign	0.08	0.154	0.277
Web	0.313	0.546	0.769
Emailc	0.553	0.806	0.937
New prod	0.315	0.401	0.474
New prodmarket	0.651	0.673	0.693
Inn process	0.298	0.403	0.485
RD	0.118	0.221	0.35

Source: Own compilation based on data from ES World Bank (February 2021 release).

banks, supplier, credit, equity or stock sales, and other financing sources. On average, investments and working capital are financed mainly from internal funds. Table 3.3 presents the average shares of investments and working capital financed from different sources.

3.4 Empirical analysis

The empirical analysis is divided into three parts. First, the correlation between different forms of ICT usage and financial aspects and firms' performance (productivity) is analysed. Next, the determinants of enterprise involvement in internationalisation are examined. The characteristics of firms involved in the internationalisation process are compared to those

Table 3.3 Proportion of investments and working capital financed by different sources

Proportion of investments financed by	
internal funds	68.5
banks	17.9
supplier credit	5.0
equity or stock sales	4.2
other sources	4.4

Proportion of working capital financed by	
internal funds	72.2
banks	12.6
supplier credit	11.1
other sources	4.2

Note: Mean values over the whole sample of surveyed companies.

Source: Own compilation based on data from ES World Bank (February 2021 release).

which do not take part in the international process, e.g., exporters to non-exporters, importers to non-importers, etc. A logit function is estimated for an extensive margin of trade. Finally, the firms' adjustment to the shock caused by the COVID-19 pandemic is studied.

3.4.1 ICT, financial markets and firm productivity

As presented in the literature review, ICT usage and financial aspects can impact the firms' performance. Figure 3.1 presents the kernels showing the distribution of labour productivity (calculated as total sales per employee) among enterprises with a particular ICT usage and those without ICT usage. It can be clearly seen that for all different aspects of ICT, the labour productivity of companies with ICT usage is shifted to the right. In other words, the labour productivity of companies that use ICT is higher than those not using ICT, if other assumptions remain unchanged.

Since many other aspects influence the firm's performance and its productivity, we will check it more systematically. Following, the correlation between the firm's productivity and its characteristics, among them,

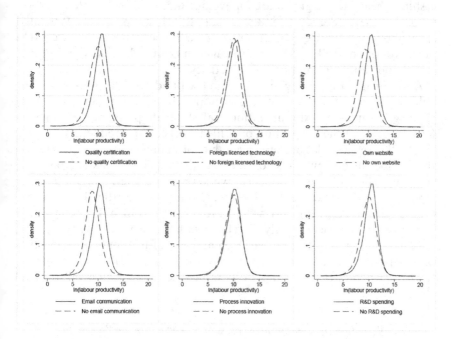

Figure 3.1 Productivity differences: firms using different forms of ICT vs. non-ICT companies.

Notes: Kernel density estimates, all countries and years pooled together.

Source: Own compilation based on data from ES World Bank (February 2021 release).

ICT usage and financial aspects will be verified using the estimation of the regression (1):

$$y_{it} = \beta_0 + \beta_1 ICT_{it} + \beta_2 Fin_{it} + \beta X_{it} + D_S + D_C + D_t + \varepsilon_{it}, \tag{3.1}$$

where y_{it} is the labour productivity[7] expressed in logs. Among the independent variables, there are different proxies of a firm's ICT usage (*ICT*), different measures of financial aspects (*Fin*), while X_i stands for other firm characteristics, such as size, age, qualification of employees, and ownership. Additionally, individual effects related to country (D_c), sector (D_s), and time (D_t) are taken into consideration to limit the possibility of errors connected with the omitted variables related, e.g., to institutional country aspects, sector characteristics or specific time events, such as business cycles. The results are presented in Table 3.4. Since different types of ICT usage can be correlated with each other, they are added in separate regressions (columns 1–8 in Table 3.4). It can be seen that smaller firms have lower labour productivity as well as younger enterprises (*Age* – based on the year in which the firm began operations). Companies with foreign ownership structure (*FDI* – firm is classified to have foreign ownership if at least 10% of ownership is held by foreigners) are on average more productive than domestic ones. Finally, the results indicate that all ICTs are positively correlated with labour productivity, which confirms our conclusion from Figure 3.1. In other words, controlling for firm size, age, and ownership, the usage of ICT is an important factor of firms' productivity.

Additionally, the analogous regression with additional right-hand variables is estimated: by describing the proportion of non-production workers (e.g., managers, administration, sales) in all permanent employees (*Non_prod*) and the proportion of skilled workers[8] in production workers (*Skill*). These variables are only available for manufacturing industries, so the number of observations considerably drops. The results indicate that the proportion of non-production workers is positively correlated with labour productivity while the *Skill* coefficient is not statistically significant (Table 3.1A in Appendix). However, the results for all ICT measures are confirmed – they are positively correlated with labour productivity. Finally, the interaction term between the given measure of ICT and the proportion of non-production (Eq. 3.2) or skilled workers (Eq. 3.3) are introduced – to check whether the impact of ICT on productivity depends on workers' characteristics.

$$y_{it} = \beta_0 + \beta_1 ICT_{it} + \beta_2 Non\_prod_{it} + \beta_3 ICT_{it} \times Non\_prod_{it} + \beta X_{it} + D_S$$
$$+ D_C + D_t + \varepsilon_{it}, \tag{3.2}$$

$$y_{it} = \beta_0 + \beta_1 ICT_{it} + \beta_2 Skill_{it} + \beta_3 ICT_{it} \times Skill_{it} + \beta X_{it} + D_S + D_C + D_t + \varepsilon_{it}, \tag{3.3}$$

Table 3.4 Labour productivity and ICT – estimates of Eq. (3.1)

	Cert	Tech foreign	Web	Email	Inn process	RD	New prod	New prodmarket
	(1)	(2)	(3)	(4)	(5)	(6)	(7)	(8)
Small	-0.215***	-0.426***	-0.157***	-0.130***	-0.293***	-0.280***	-0.296***	-0.266***
	[0.031]	[0.031]	[0.029]	[0.032]	[0.035]	[0.035]	[0.035]	[0.051]
Medium	-0.033	-0.182***	-0.019	-0.031	-0.099***	-0.089***	-0.103***	-0.105**
	[0.029]	[0.029]	[0.028]	[0.031]	[0.034]	[0.034]	[0.034]	[0.048]
Age	0.003***	0.001*	0.003***	0.004***	0.004***	0.004***	0.004***	0.006***
	[0.001]	[0.001]	[0.001]	[0.001]	[0.001]	[0.001]	[0.001]	[0.001]
FDI	0.458***	0.374***	0.442***	0.432***	0.536***	0.532***	0.523***	0.566***
	[0.031]	[0.038]	[0.031]	[0.034]	[0.039]	[0.039]	[0.039]	[0.061]
ICT	0.319***	0.255***	0.414***	0.604***	0.217***	0.245***	0.208***	0.078**
	[0.024]	[0.028]	[0.019]	[0.026]	[0.021]	[0.027]	[0.021]	[0.033]
N	114,712	65,981	117,399	97,173	86,036	86,330	87,439	28,212
R^2	0.4	0.48	0.41	0.41	0.41	0.41	0.41	0.43

Notes: * $p < 0.10$, ** $p < 0.05$, *** $p < 0.01$, Country, sector, and time dummies included. Ordinary least squares (OLS) regressions with weights based on the rescaled ES survey weights and robust standard errors

Source: Own compilation based on data from ES World Bank (February 2021 release).

Now, the marginal effect of ICT on labour productivity equals to $\frac{\delta y}{\delta ICT} = \beta_1 + \beta_3 Non\_prod$ (Eq. 3.2) and $\frac{\delta y}{\delta ICT} = \beta_1 + \beta_3 Skill$ (Eq. 3.3). For illustration purposes, the predicted labour productivity is presented over the proportion of non-production/skilled workers for ICT and non-ICT companies (Figure 3.1A in Appendix). The share of non-production workers is presented on the x-axis of panel A and the proportion of skilled workers is shown on the x-axis of panel B. On average, ICT companies are characterised by higher labour productivity than non-ICT ones, which confirms the results obtained from the basic model (Table 3.4). Additionally, for some types of ICT, the relationship between labour productivity and ICT depends on the characteristics of workers. A steeper line of ICT=1 indicates the positive coefficient for interaction terms.

Finally, the estimations were repeated, taking into account the financial constraints of the company. Table 3.5 presents the results.

Three different characteristics of firm financial conditions are focused on. *Fin1* indicates whether a firm identifies the access/cost of finance as a "major" or "very severe" obstacle. We can see that firms identifying access to finance as a major constraint are less productive on average (columns 1 and 2 of Table 3.5). The second variable, *Fin2*, describes the situation in which the company did not apply for a loan in the last fiscal year because the loan was not needed. On average, firms that do not need a loan are more

Table 3.5 Labour productivity and financial constraints – estimates of Eq. (3.1)

	Fin1	Fin1	Fin2	Fin2	Fin3	Fin3
	(1)	(2)	(3)	(4)	(5)	(6)
Small	−0.294***	−0.509***	−0.306***	−0.532***	−0.297***	−0.422***
	[0.029]	[0.031]	[0.030]	[0.032]	[0.050]	[0.059]
Medium	−0.084***	−0.235***	−0.091***	−0.250***	−0.156***	−0.239***
	[0.028]	[0.029]	[0.029]	[0.029]	[0.049]	[0.055]
Age	0.004***	0.001	0.003***	0.001	0.004***	0
	[0.001]	[0.001]	[0.001]	[0.001]	[0.001]	[0.001]
FDI	0.482***	0.360***	0.482***	0.368***	0.431***	0.484***
	[0.030]	[0.040]	[0.031]	[0.040]	[0.070]	[0.076]
FIN	−0.101***	−0.104***	0.046***	−0.006	−0.469***	−0.386***
	[0.019]	[0.022]	[0.017]	[0.021]	[0.065]	[0.071]
Non_prod		0.728***		0.736***		0.724***
		[0.060]		[0.061]		[0.129]
Skill		0.03		0.031		0.028
		[0.034]		[0.035]		[0.071]
N	115,966	60,490	112,507	58,983	15,032	7362
R^2	0.4	0.49	0.4	0.49	0.43	0.53

Notes: *p <0.10, **p <0.05, ***p <0.01, Country, sector, and time dummies included. OLS regressions with weights based on ES survey weights and robust standard errors.

Source: Own elaboration with data from ES.

productive (Column 3). When the workers' characteristics are added, the coefficient of *Fin2* loses its statistical significance. Finally – the results from columns 5 and 6 indicate that companies whose recent loan application was rejected (*Fin3*) are on average less productive. The above estimations show that financial constraints may determine the firms' productivity.

A similar analysis was conducted for companies from different regions, where no differences were found, and separately for manufacturing and services sectors. There, again, the results are very similar to the basic ones – all variables describing different types of ICT usage are positively correlated with enterprises' labour productivity as well as financial ones.[9] In the next subchapter, it is going to be checked whether the indicators of ICT usage and different aspects of a firm's financial condition are among the characteristics of the firm's presence in foreign markets.

3.4.2 ICT, financial markets and firm internationalisation

According to Melitz (2003) model, only the most productive firms should be engaged in international relations. Additionally to the variables that are usually taken into account as the determinants of exporters/non-exporters, the variables describing ICT usage and financial aspects of the company are added. Furthermore, the presented study is not limited to exporting[10] but also takes account of importing,[11] indirect involvement in trade activities: indirect exporting[12] and indirect importing,[13] as well as simultaneous importing and exporting.[14] It should be underlined that information about import is restricted to manufacturing companies only. Additionally, the classification of firms into "indirect importers" refers to companies whose import is solely indirect, while in the case of "indirect exporters," at least 1% of a firm's annual sales is derived from indirect exports (at the same time, a firm can also export part of its sales directly).

To identify the difference between the firms engaged in internationalisation and those which are not, the regression is estimated (4):

$$y_{it} = \begin{cases} 1, \beta_0 + \beta_1 ICT_{it} + \beta_2 Fin_{it} + \beta_3 Labour\_Prod_{it} + \beta X_{it} + D_S + D_C + D_t + \varepsilon_{it} \\ 0, else \end{cases}, \quad (3.4)$$

where y_{it} is a binary dependent variable that takes the value of one if a firm is involved in the internationalisation process and zero otherwise. *ICT, FIN, X_i, D_s, D_c, D_t* are defined as in the previous regression. Additionally, this time the regression is augmented with labour productivity (*Labour_Prod*). Equation (3.4) is estimated based on the logit model which is due to the fact of binary (1 or 0) type of the dependent variable. The regression (3.4) is estimated separately for all different types of internationalisation: export, import, indirect export, indirect import, and simultaneous export and import. Table 3.6 presents the results when ICT is proxied by the possession of a foreign certificate.

58   *Joanna Wolszczak-Derlacz*

Table 3.6 Results of estimations for participation in different forms of internationalisations (Eq. 3.4), ICT measured by foreign certificate

	Exporters	Indirect exporters	Importers	Indirect importers	Exporters & Importers
Small	−1.477***	−0.611***	−1.131***	−1.002***	−1.985***
	[0.024]	[0.033]	[0.031]	[0.219]	[0.036]
Medium	−0.769***	−0.142***	−0.632***	−0.429**	−0.986***
	[0.021]	[0.029]	[0.029]	[0.202]	[0.029]
Age	0.005***	0.003***	0.003***	0.004	0.004***
	[0.001]	[0.001]	[0.001]	[0.006]	[0.001]
FDI	0.960***	0.440***	0.870***	0.137	1.129***
	[0.027]	[0.032]	[0.040]	[0.256]	[0.036]
Labour_Prod	0.124***	−0.003	0.172***	0.035	0.158***
	[0.007]	[0.009]	[0.008]	[0.055]	[0.010]
Cert	0.828***	0.482***	0.439***	0.202	0.810***
	[0.020]	[0.028]	[0.027]	[0.189]	[0.028]
ll	−45964	−30903.2	−32432.5	−1042.99	−23528.4
Pseudo R2	0.254	0.11	0.267	0.747	0.306
N	113,311	114,080	63,832	6863	63,228

Notes: *p <0.10, **p <0.05, ***p <0.01, weighted logit regression with robust standard errors
Source: Own compilation based on data from ES World Bank (February 2021 release).

The results indicate that small and medium firms, compared to large firms, are less likely to be involved in international activities. Older firms and those with foreign capital are more likely to take part in international transactions (except for indirect import, when the coefficients of *Age* and *Foreign* are not statistically significant). Additionally, exporters, importers and two-way traders are more productive (the statistically significant coefficient of *Labour_Prod*). Finally, the variable being the main focus of the study – ICT usage – is positively correlated with internationalisation decisions, except for indirect importing for which the coefficient of *Cert* is not statistically significant. The probability of export, import, export indirectly as well as simultaneously export and import is higher for companies that are characterised by ICT usage. For firms that are engaged in international markets through indirect importing, the results are different. The only statistically significant coefficient is the firm's size – small and medium-sized firms, compared to large firms, are less likely to take part in indirect importing. However, none of the other coefficients is statistically significant. It is important to note that indirect import is restricted to manufacturing firms whose import is solely indirect. Therefore their internationalisation is rather limited.

The analogous estimates are repeated for all different proxies of ICT and very similar results are obtained (see Tables 3.2A–3.8A in Appendix). Company website, communication with clients and suppliers by email, introducing process innovation, spending on R&D, introducing a new product/service, and firms whose new product/service is also new to the main

market – are all positively related to the firm's decisions about internationalisation. Additionally, the exercise is repeated for the regression without
labour productivity among independent variables (to take into account
the possible endogeneity issues) and it is confirmed that the probability to
engage in any internationalisation process is higher for ICT companies.

Finally, the extensive margin of trade – the probability to participate
in trade against financial constraints – is analysed. Table 3.7 presents the
results when the regression is augmented with *FIN1* indicating that the
firm identifies access to finance as a major constraint. Here, some interesting results are obtained. Neither for export nor indirect exporters, the
coefficient of financial constraint is statistically significant. However, both
for import and indirect import, the coefficient is statistically significant
and positive, which means that firms with financial constraints are more
likely to take part in such a form of internationalisation. It may mean that
enterprises with financial constraints are importing directly or indirectly
(cheaper) inputs because their financial situation is not satisfactory. In
Tables 3.9A and 3.10A of the Appendix, the analogous results are shown,
when the financial aspects are measured either by a variable indicating
that a firm does not need a loan or that its recent loan application was
rejected. It can be observed that companies that do not need a loan are
less likely to take part in the internationalisation process (statistically significant and negative coefficients of FIN2 in Table 3.9A) and if their recent

Table 3.7 Results of estimations for participation in different forms of
internationalization – Eq. (3.4), FIN measured as indicating financial
constraints

	Exporters	*Indirect exporters*	*Importers*	*Indirect importers*	*Exporters & importers*
Small	−1.716***	−0.762***	−1.283***	−1.111***	−2.230***
	[0.023]	[0.031]	[0.029]	[0.212]	[0.034]
Medium	−0.921***	−0.240***	−0.737***	−0.509***	−1.148***
	[0.020]	[0.027]	[0.028]	[0.197]	[0.028]
Age	0.006***	0.004***	0.003***	0.004	0.005***
	[0.001]	[0.001]	[0.001]	[0.006]	[0.001]
FDI	1.036***	0.505***	0.920***	0.14	1.197***
	[0.026]	[0.032]	[0.040]	[0.249]	[0.036]
Lab_prod	0.151***	0.013	0.187***	0.043	0.189***
	[0.007]	[0.009]	[0.008]	[0.053]	[0.010]
FIN1	−0.013	0.053	0.110***	0.252*	0.015
	[0.020]	[0.047]	[0.023]	[0.136]	[0.028]
ll	−47704.2	−31691.4	−32951.5	−1041.68	−24530.1
Pseudo R2	0.239	0.105	0.264	0.749	0.29
N	114,468	115,253	64,603	6887	63,984

Notes: *p <0.10, **p <0.05, ***p <0.01, weighted logit regression with robust standard errors.
Source: Own compilation based on data from ES World Bank (February 2021 release).

loan application was rejected, they are less likely to be exporters or indirect importers (Table 3.10A). Contrary to the previous analysis, which considered the probability of taking part in internationalisation processes from the perspective of ICT, now, when the financial aspects are taken into account, no clear picture can be obtained. Generally, it may indicate that the nexus between financial constraints and being present in a foreign market is more complicated. Some enterprises can start their engagement in internationalisation processes as a result of financial constraints, e.g., they may be looking for cheaper materials and inputs from foreign markets or selling abroad to overcome their own financial constraints. Those results are partly matching those of Berman and Héricourt (2010), who studied 50,000 firms from nine developing countries. Even though their research shows the importance of the impact of firms' access to finance on their decision to enter the export market, at the same time, they highlight that better financial health increases neither the probability of remaining an exporter, nor the size of export.

3.4.3 Adjustment of firms to COVID-19

The COVID-19 pandemic, spreading since March 2020, caused an unprecedented and unforeseen shock impacting different aspects of the economy. Firms are hit by different and numerous factors, which are also the result of a country's policies, e.g., how quickly the lockdown was introduced, what kind of tools the countries employ to fight the short-run negative implications of the closure of the economy, etc. There are some recent studies in which the first effects of COVID-19 on firms' performance are analysed. For example, Beck et al. (2020), based on the data of nearly 500 firms from ten emerging markets, we find that the vast majority of firms have been negatively affected by COVID-19 and reacted by reducing investment rather than payroll.

In this part of the analysis, the data from ES World Bank follow-up surveys are used. The first round was carried out in May-June and the other one in September-October 2020. The analysis is limited to the countries for which the results of two rounds of the survey are already available. As a result, there are 8,477 enterprises from 15 countries[15] included in the study. The data contain information on small (47% of observations), medium (33%), and large (20%) enterprises from the manufacturing (52%) and services (48%) sectors. The majority of enterprises (70%) are located in ECA, while 20% in LAC and 10% in MNA. The survey includes questions regarding the firm's situation since the beginning of COVID-19, taking into account the changes in sales, employment, and financial aspects.

Figure 3.2 shows that 2.4% of small firms, 1.3% of medium ones, and 0.6% of large firms reported closure since the onset of COVID-19. These ratios significantly increase when a wider definition of firm termination is used:

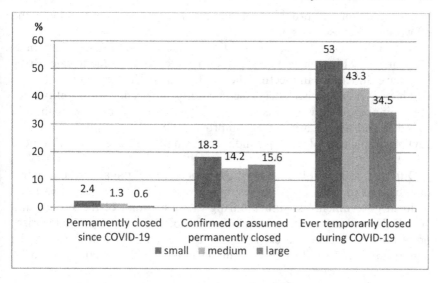

Figure 3.2 Shares of closed or temporarily closed enterprises during COVID-19.

Source: Own elaboration based on ES World Bank Follow-up.

not only firms with confirmed closure but also those that could not be contacted during fieldwork and therefore are assumed to have terminated their activity. Additionally, more than 50%, 40%, and 34% of small, medium, and large firms, respectively, indicate that they were temporarily closed at any time during COVID-19.

In Table 3.11A of the Appendix, some additional indicators describing the firms' performance during COVID-19 are presented, disaggregated by firm size. During the first round of the survey, around 72% of enterprises reported that their monthly sales decreased in comparison to the analogous period in the previous year. The ratio is the greatest for small companies. The average reduction in sales was between 13%, for large companies during the second round, to 39%, for small companies reported during the first round of the survey. In terms of the workforce, a considerable percentage of firms decided to decrease the total number of hours worked per week compared to the previous year. The results of the first round of the survey indicate that between May/June 2020 and May/June 2019, 55%, 53%, and 49% of small, medium, and large companies, respectively, reported a drop in total hours worked. When September/October 2020 is compared to September/October 2019, the differences are still significant but lower than in the previous round. Additionally, around 14% of firms reduced their workers' salaries or benefits due to COVID-19. According to Apedo-Amah et al. (2020), who used firm-level data from the World Bank across 51 countries, the main channel of employment adjustment to the pandemic shock was working hours reduction and providing employees with granted leave while laying off workers was used less often.

Due to the COVID-19 shock, the financial situation of many companies has worsened. Firms have to cover their fixed costs and, due to sales drop, they have difficulties in meeting their obligations. The percentage of firms that have ever experienced decreased liquidity or cash flow availability since the beginning of COVID-19 is not minor (e.g., 72.5% of small companies in round 1) and the situation is not improving (78.6% in round 2 of the survey). As in the case of previous indicators, small firms are usually hit more severely.

Different policy tools have been introduced to fight against the negative implications of COVID-19. On average, 36% of the firms received national or local government assistance during the first round of the survey, and 46% in the second round. Among different tools, the majority of enterprises point out fiscal relief and cash transfer as the most needed measure. The digital support was indicated by a small percentage of companies, up to 3% among medium enterprises.

As an adjustment to COVID-19, firms started or rose online business activity (35% of large companies surveyed during the second round) and increased remote work (60% of large enterprises). One-fifth of the firms introduced a new product or service in response to COVID-19 outbreak. According to the broader World Bank's data concerning 100,000 firms, 34% of enterprises increased usage of digital platforms and 17% invested in digital solutions (Apedo-Amah et al., 2020) as a response to the shock.

3.5 Conclusion

Although there is a consensus that the productivity paradox, namely, the proposition that ICT investments are not accompanied by growth, is not valid, the ICT-finance-growth nexuses are still largely debatable issues.

We actively take part in this debate by conducting a comprehensive empirical study to investigate the association between ICT, finance and firm-level productivity, covering almost 170,000 enterprises from 139 countries (2006–2019). We take into account different proxies of ICT capabilities and measures of financial constraints and relate them to (a) productivity, (b) firms' internationalisation decisions. We find that controlling for firm size, age, and ownership, enterprises using ICT are on average more productive. Additionally, we confirm that the ICT-productivity relationship is further contingent upon the labour force characteristics. Enterprises characterised by a higher proportion of non-production and skilled workers are obtaining higher productivity gains from ICT. Additionally, an important determinant of firms' productivity is also their financial situation: firms with healthier finance are more productive. At this point, we should also acknowledge some limitations of our study. We want to underline that based on our estimations, we should not draw strong conclusions about causality. There is a possible two-way relationship. The usage of ICT determines labour productivity and more productive firms are in turn more anxious or capable to employ ICT tools. The causal effect between productivity and ICT usage could be measured solely based on panel data analysis when one firm is reported over a given period, and its productivity is measured at the point before the ICT introduction and after. Such analysis should also take into account the changes in the productivity of enterprises that have not introduced ICT at all – not treated (difference-in-difference approach). However, such a study was not feasible with the data we worked with. Nevertheless, based on our simple analysis, we can obtain a general picture of the correlation between different firms' characteristics and their productivity, and provide some stylised facts rather than drawing strong causal conclusions.

The next part of our empirical analysis was dedicated to the estimation of logit regression with a binary dependent variable describing whether a given enterprise takes part in internationalisation. Different kinds of internationalisation processes are distinguished: exporting, importing, indirect exporting, indirect importing, and simultaneous importing and exporting. It is observed that on average, enterprises engaged in international processes are bigger, younger, with foreign capital, and ICT advanced. However, in terms of financial indicators, we could not confirm the robust correlation between financial constraints and a firm's decision to take part in internationalisation processes. Here, we should also consider the possible two-way relationship. More productive firms enter the foreign markets more easily, but because of learning through exporting and/or learning through importing, they can decide to make further ICT investments.

Finally, the first firm's adjustment to the COVID-19 pandemic is explored. Due to the sales drop, firms have been forced to decrease the total hours worked, and their financial situation considerably worsened. Generally, at this initial stage of the pandemic, small firms face more challenges.

We can assume with certainty that the topic of our analysis will be still present in future research agendas due to the expansion of smart technologies such as fintech, AI and 5G. There will be a need for studies analysing the effects of these new technological developments on firms' performance and/or firms' internationalisation. Additionally, albeit the great uncertainty about the future due to the COVID-19 pandemic, there is still hope that new technology and digitalisation will reduce the negative effects of this shock. At the moment, there is great uncertainty about how quickly the productivity of firms, as well as their engagement in international processes, can be recovered.

Appendix

Table 3.1A Determinants of labour productivity, additional variables describing workers qualifications

	Cert	Tech foreign	Web	Email	Inn process	RD	New prod	New prodmarket
Small	-0.413***	-0.493***	-0.390***	-0.359***	-0.499***	-0.476***	-0.511***	-0.524***
	[0.033]	[0.031]	[0.032]	[0.034]	[0.036]	[0.037]	[0.036]	[0.049]
Medium	-0.173***	-0.230***	-0.174***	-0.168***	-0.260***	-0.243***	-0.265***	-0.296***
	[0.029]	[0.029]	[0.029]	[0.031]	[0.033]	[0.033]	[0.033]	[0.045]
Age	0.000	0.001	0.000	0.000	0.001	0.001	0.001	0.001
	[0.001]	[0.001]	[0.001]	[0.001]	[0.001]	[0.001]	[0.001]	[0.001]
FDI	0.346***	0.339***	0.342***	0.341***	0.401***	0.394***	0.391***	0.373***
	[0.040]	[0.040]	[0.039]	[0.042]	[0.054]	[0.053]	[0.054]	[0.056]
Non_prod	0.703***	0.710***	0.666***	0.607***	0.696***	0.692***	0.689***	0.720***
	[0.060]	[0.060]	[0.060]	[0.065]	[0.071]	[0.071]	[0.071]	[0.097]
Skill	0.011	0.021	0.017	0.046	0.041	0.033	0.041	-0.001
	[0.034]	[0.034]	[0.034]	[0.037]	[0.043]	[0.042]	[0.043]	[0.058]
ICT	0.318***	0.258***	0.371***	0.559***	0.183***	0.215***	0.128***	0.007
	[0.026]	[0.029]	[0.023]	[0.030]	[0.026]	[0.030]	[0.025]	[0.034]
N	59,840	60,802	61,113	51,962	47,615	47,749	47,832	15,967
R²	0.5	0.49	0.5	0.5	0.48	0.48	0.48	0.52

Notes: *p <0.10, **p <0.05, ***p <0.01, Country, sector, and time dummies included. OLS regressions with weights based on ES survey weights and robust standard errors. Non_prod: proportion of non-production workers out of all permanent employees; Skill: proportion of skilled workers out of all production workers.

Source: Own elaboration with data from ES World Bank (February 2021 release).

Table 3.2A Results of estimations for participation in different forms of internationalisations and ICT, ICT measured by technology licensed from foreign companies

	Exporters	Indirect exporters	Importers	Indirect importers	Exporters & Importers
Small	−2.129***	−0.814***	−1.179***	−1.037***	−2.165***
	[0.030]	[0.039]	[0.030]	[0.214]	[0.034]
Medium	−1.101***	−0.223***	−0.676***	−0.449**	−1.109***
	[0.025]	[0.032]	[0.028]	[0.198]	[0.028]
Age	0.007***	0.004***	0.004***	0.003	0.005***
	[0.001]	[0.001]	[0.001]	[0.006]	[0.001]
FDI	1.080***	0.296***	0.833***	0.101	1.126***
	[0.035]	[0.039]	[0.040]	[0.250]	[0.036]
Labour_Prod	0.190***	0.020*	0.178***	0.039	0.180***
	[0.009]	[0.011]	[0.008]	[0.053]	[0.010]
Techn_foreign	0.444***	0.394***	0.638***	0.461**	0.543***
	[0.028]	[0.033]	[0.030]	[0.200]	[0.031]
ll	−29984.1	−21009.9	−32812.6	−1040.88	−24306
Pseudo R^2	0.259	0.099	0.268	0.749	0.296
N	65,255	65,680	64,727	6880	64,116

Notes: *p <0.10, **p <0.05, ***p <0.01, weighted logit regression with robust standard errors
Source: Own elaboration with data from ES World Bank (February 2021 release).

Table 3.3A Results of estimations for participation in different forms of internationalisations and ICT, ICT measured by having its own website

	Exporters	Indirect exporters	Importers	Indirect importers	Exporters & importers
Small	−1.470***	−0.602***	−1.053***	−0.927***	−1.990***
	[0.024]	[0.032]	[0.030]	[0.227]	[0.035]
Medium	−0.802***	−0.168***	−0.611***	−0.384*	−1.028***
	[0.021]	[0.028]	[0.028]	[0.202]	[0.028]
Age	0.005***	0.003***	0.002***	0.003	0.004***
	[0.001]	[0.001]	[0.001]	[0.006]	[0.001]
FDI	0.997***	0.482***	0.886***	0.114	1.186***
	[0.026]	[0.031]	[0.039]	[0.245]	[0.035]
Labour_Prod	0.116***	−0.006	0.159***	0.031	0.153***
	[0.007]	[0.009]	[0.008]	[0.054]	[0.010]
Web	0.790***	0.465***	0.610***	0.391**	0.807***
	[0.019]	[0.026]	[0.023]	[0.179]	[0.027]
ll	−47339.8	−31877.1	−32959	−1054.13	−24279.8
Pseudo R2	0.252	0.109	0.271	0.748	0.303
N	115,873	116,664	65,276	6935	64,651

Notes: *p <0.10, **p <0.05, ***p <0.01, weighted logit regression with robust standard errors.
Source: Own elaboration with data from ES World Bank (February 2021 release).

Table 3.4A Results of estimations for participation in different forms of
internationalisations and ICT, ICT measured by communicate with
clients and suppliers by e-mail

	Exporters	Indirect exporters	Importers	Indirect importers	Exporters & importers
Small	−1.554***	−0.596***	−1.128***	−0.805***	−2.053***
	[0.026]	[0.036]	[0.034]	[0.213]	[0.039]
Medium	−0.889***	−0.180***	−0.711***	−0.423**	−1.128***
	[0.022]	[0.031]	[0.031]	[0.197]	[0.031]
Age	0.006***	0.004***	0.004***	0.002	0.005***
	[0.001]	[0.001]	[0.001]	[0.006]	[0.001]
FDI	1.009***	0.506***	0.861***	0.09	1.172***
	[0.029]	[0.035]	[0.043]	[0.251]	[0.039]
Labour_Prod	0.122***	−0.009	0.155***	0.023	0.161***
	[0.008]	[0.010]	[0.009]	[0.054]	[0.012]
Email	0.937***	0.607***	0.753***	0.886***	1.104***
	[0.031]	[0.040]	[0.030]	[0.173]	[0.047]
ll	−38575.6	−25071.8	−27076	−1043.95	−19907.5
Pseudo R^2	0.244	0.11	0.292	0.751	0.302
N	95,930	96,548	55,181	6940	54,655

Notes: *p <0.10, **p <0.05, ***p <0.01, weighted logit regression with robust standard errors.
Source: Own elaboration with data from ES World Bank (February 2021 release).

Table 3.5A Results of estimations for participation in different forms of
internationalisations and ICT, ICT measured by introduction a
process innovation

	Exporters	Indirect exporters	Importers	Indirect importers	Exporters & importers
Small	−1.709***	−0.682***	−1.197***	−0.894***	−2.166***
	[0.027]	[0.036]	[0.034]	[0.345]	[0.038]
Medium	−0.937***	−0.224***	−0.714***	−0.331	−1.128***
	[0.024]	[0.032]	[0.032]	[0.247]	[0.031]
Age	0.006***	0.004***	0.004***	0.01	0.005***
	[0.001]	[0.001]	[0.001]	[0.008]	[0.001]
FDI	1.085***	0.525***	0.980***	1.509**	1.236***
	[0.032]	[0.037]	[0.049]	[0.689]	[0.042]
Labour_Prod	0.156***	0.006	0.188***	0.173*	0.186***
	[0.008]	[0.010]	[0.010]	[0.092]	[0.012]
Inn process	0.478***	0.450***	0.522***	0.669**	0.521***
	[0.021]	[0.028]	[0.026]	[0.274]	[0.030]
ll	−35977.5	−23993.6	−24671.8	−422.321	−19208.1
Pseudo R^2	0.241	0.113	0.297	0.835	0.295
N	84,913	85,492	50,663	5266	50,167

Notes: *p <0.10, **p <0.05, ***p <0.01, weighted logit regression with robust standard errors.
Source: Own elaboration with data from ES World Bank (February 2021 release).

Table 3.6A Results of estimations for participation in different forms of internationalisations and ICT, ICT measured by R&D spending

	Exporters	Indirect exporters	Importers	Indirect importers	Exporters & Importers
Small	−1.654***	−0.634***	−1.156***	−0.900***	−2.099***
	[0.027]	[0.036]	[0.034]	[0.346]	[0.039]
Medium	−0.902***	−0.189***	−0.689***	−0.342	−1.086***
	[0.024]	[0.032]	[0.032]	[0.245]	[0.031]
Age	0.006***	0.004***	0.003***	0.01	0.005***
	[0.001]	[0.001]	[0.001]	[0.008]	[0.001]
FDI	1.090***	0.525***	0.970***	1.436**	1.240***
	[0.032]	[0.037]	[0.049]	[0.706]	[0.042]
Labour_Prod	0.150***	0.003	0.185***	0.155*	0.180***
	[0.008]	[0.010]	[0.010]	[0.090]	[0.012]
R&D	0.706***	0.572***	0.654***	0.550**	0.740***
	[0.023]	[0.030]	[0.030]	[0.228]	[0.031]
ll	−35949.4	−24078.4	−24717	−422.871	−19145.5
Pseudo R^2	0.245	0.115	0.298	0.836	0.3
N	85,199	85,782	50,823	5266	50,327

Notes: *p <0.10, **p <0.05, ***p <0.01, weighted logit regression with robust standard errors
Source: Own elaboration with data from ES World Bank (February 2021 release).

Table 3.7A Results of estimations for participation in different forms of internationalisations and ICT, ICT measured by introduction a new product/service

	Exporters	Indirect exporters	Importers	Indirect importers	Exporters & importers
Small	−1.699***	−0.694***	−1.191***	−0.889**	−2.168***
	[0.026]	[0.035]	[0.033]	[0.346]	[0.038]
Medium	−0.930***	−0.227***	−0.712***	−0.325	−1.128***
	[0.023]	[0.031]	[0.032]	[0.247]	[0.031]
Age	0.006***	0.004***	0.003***	0.009	0.005***
	[0.001]	[0.001]	[0.001]	[0.008]	[0.001]
FDI	1.087***	0.532***	0.981***	1.553**	1.236***
	[0.032]	[0.036]	[0.049]	[0.719]	[0.042]
Labour_Prod	0.156***	0.007	0.187***	0.162*	0.185***
	[0.008]	[0.010]	[0.010]	[0.093]	[0.012]
New prod	0.444***	0.319***	0.648***	0.787***	0.574***
	[0.020]	[0.027]	[0.024]	[0.241]	[0.028]
ll	−36536.6	−24445	−24672.1	−419.903	−19293.2
Pseudo R^2	0.24	0.11	0.301	0.837	0.296
N	86,295	86,877	50,911	5279	50,416

Notes: *p <0.10, **p <0.05, ***p <0.01, weighted logit regression with robust standard errors.
Source: Own elaboration with data from ES World Bank (February 2021 release).

Table 3.8A Results of estimations for participation in different forms of
internationalisations and ICT, ICT measured by introduction new
product/service that is also new to the main market

	Exporters	Indirect exporters	Importers	Indirect importers	Exporters & importers
Small	−1.550***	−0.485***	−1.251***	−0.962*	−2.050***
	[0.044]	[0.057]	[0.061]	[0.510]	[0.062]
Medium	−0.900***	−0.161***	−0.801***	−0.09	−1.148***
	[0.038]	[0.050]	[0.056]	[0.323]	[0.050]
Age	0.008***	0.006***	0.003**	0.006	0.005***
	[0.001]	[0.001]	[0.001]	[0.010]	[0.001]
FDI	0.918***	0.394***	0.875***	−0.208	1.096***
	[0.049]	[0.056]	[0.084]	[1.867]	[0.068]
Labour_Prod	0.159***	−0.017	0.232***	0.188	0.224***
	[0.013]	[0.016]	[0.018]	[0.123]	[0.020]
New prod markt	0.137***	0.152***	0.081*	0.24	0.191***
	[0.033]	[0.043]	[0.043]	[0.328]	[0.045]
ll	−13137.5	−9042.75	−7761.77	−230.703	−7332.86
Pseudo R²	0.237	0.098	0.322	0.589	0.299
N	27,676	27,955	17,096	1912	16,845

Notes: *p <0.10, **p <0.05, ***p <0.01, weighted logit regression with robust standard errors.
Source: Own elaboration with data from ES World Bank (February 2021 release).

Table 3.9A Results of estimations for participation in different forms of
internationalisations – Eq. (3.4), FIN2 measured by firm indication
that loan is not needed

	Exporters	Indirect exporters	Importers	Indirect importers	Exporters & importers
Small	−1.715***	−0.748***	−1.282***	−0.906***	−2.244***
	[0.023]	[0.032]	[0.030]	[0.221]	[0.034]
Medium	−0.924***	−0.235***	−0.735***	−0.558***	−1.166***
	[0.021]	[0.028]	[0.028]	[0.208]	[0.028]
Age	0.006***	0.004***	0.004***	0.004	0.005***
	[0.001]	[0.001]	[0.001]	[0.007]	[0.001]
FDI	1.022***	0.492***	0.918***	0.205	1.186***
	[0.027]	[0.032]	[0.041]	[0.266]	[0.036]
Lab_prod	0.165***	0.022**	0.203***	0.155**	0.204***
	[0.007]	[0.009]	[0.009]	[0.063]	[0.010]
FIN2	−0.126***	−0.158***	−0.153***	−0.246	−0.096***
	[0.017]	[0.023]	[0.021]	[0.162]	[0.025]
ll	−46336.8	−30819.1	−31518.4	−819.015	−23791.5
Pseudo R2	0.24	0.105	0.268	0.787	0.29
N	111,055	111,839	62,208	6370	61,606

Notes: *p <0.10, **p <0.05, ***p <0.01, weighted logit regression with robust standard errors.
Source: Own elaboration with data from ES World Bank (February 2021 release).

Table 3.10A Results of estimations for participation in different forms of internationalisations – Eq. (3.4), FIN measured by firm indication that the recent loan application was rejected

	Exporters	Indirect exporters	Importers	Indirect importers	Exporters & importers
Small	−1.442***	−0.552***	−1.264***	−1.689**	−2.206***
	[0.062]	[0.078]	[0.082]	[0.754]	[0.096]
Medium	−0.760***	−0.1	−0.752***	−0.267	−1.162***
	[0.051]	[0.064]	[0.073]	[0.628]	[0.071]
Age	0.008***	0.005***	0.002	−0.057	0.005**
	[0.002]	[0.002]	[0.002]	[0.035]	[0.002]
FDI	1.040***	0.405***	1.034***	−1.348	1.121***
	[0.078]	[0.085]	[0.128]	[1.033]	[0.105]
Lab_prod	0.153***	−0.001	0.201***	−0.034	0.165***
	[0.019]	[0.023]	[0.025]	[0.195]	[0.027]
FIN3	−0.154*	−0.117	−0.14	−0.877**	−0.053
	[0.087]	[0.111]	[0.101]	[0.433]	[0.122]
ll	−6907.07	−4922.87	−3911.68	−84.785	−3504.67
Pseudo R2	0.259	0.115	0.251	0.496	0.281
N	14,778	14,911	7754	311	7679

Notes: *p <0.10, **p <0.05, ***p <0.01, weighted logit regression with standard errors.
Source: Own elaboration with data from ES World Bank (February 2021 release).

Table 3.11A Firm's characteristics under COVID-19

	Round1			Round 2		
	Small	Medium	Large	Small	Medium	Large
	Sales					
Share of firms experiencing decreased monthly sales compared to one year ago	75.7	71.2	65.4	67.5	61.7	53.0
Average change in monthly sales compared to one year ago	−38.7	−31.9	−25.1	−25.5	−19.5	−13.5
	Workforce and salaries					
Share of firms that decreased total hours worked per week compared to one year ago	55.0	52.8	49.0	40.5	35.2	29.3
Share of firms that reduced workers' salaries or benefits due to the COVID-19				14.5	13.5	13.8

(*Conttinued*)

Table 3.11A Firm's characteristics under COVID-19 (Continued)

	Round1			Round 2		
	Small	*Medium*	*Large*	*Small*	*Medium*	*Large*
Finance						
Share of firms ever experienced decreased liquidity or cash flow availability since COVID-19 began	72.5	66.9	57.2	78.6	73.2	61.9
Share of firms ever delay payments to suppliers, landlords, tax authorities since COVID-19 began	40.7	38.6	36.8	51.5	48.2	45.2
Share of firms that applied for a loan since COVID-19 began				20.7	23.7	26.3
Policy tools						
Share of firms that received national or local government assistance	34.6	37.9	38.7	47.4	50.5	47.9
Share of firms that expect to receive national or local government assistance	8.8	6.6	8.1	7.1	6.1	7.3
Needed measures: % of firms						
Cash transfers				31.5	22.2	23.1
Deferral of payments				11.4	14.1	14.2
Access to new credit				10.0	8.2	7.6
Fiscal relief				27.6	30.9	31.2
Wage subsidies				11.7	16.6	16.4
Digital support				2.3	3.1	2.9
Other assistance				5.5	4.8	4.7
Adjustment						
Share of firms adjusting or converting their production or services	24.5	28.5	30.6	43.6	46.7	48.3
Share of firms that started or increased online business activity	19.9	26.0	26.4	29.1	36.4	35.4
Share of firms that started or increased remote work	21.5	37.0	54.3	26.4	42.8	60.1

Notes: Data refers to enterprises from 15 countries: BGR, CYP, GEO, GRC, GTM, HND, ITA, JOR, MDA, MLT, NIC, POL, ROU, SLV, SVN, surveyed: May/June 2020 (round 1) and October/December 2020 (round 2).

Source: Own elaboration based on ES World Bank Follow-up.

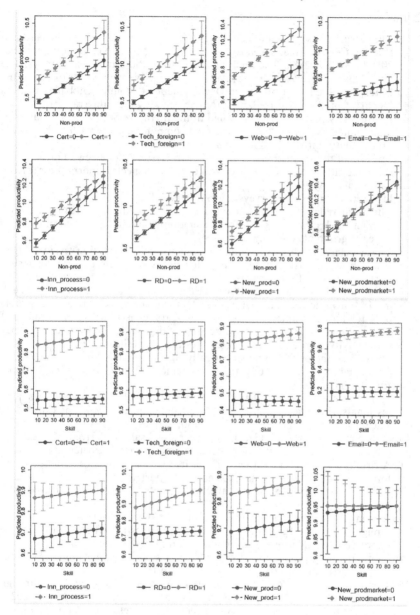

Figure 3.1A Determinants of productivity: the results of regression with interaction terms between ICT and proportion of non-production workers (Eq. 3.2).

Panel A. The interaction between ICT and non-production workers.
Panel B. The interaction between ICT and skilled workers.

Source: Own elaboration with data from ES World Bank (February 2021 release).

Notes

1. The research has been conducted within the project financed by the National Science Centre, Poland (Narodowe Centrum Nauki NCN) grant number 2015/19/B/HS4/02884. The analysis is based on the Enterprise Surveys, The World Bank, http://www.enterprisesurveys.org. We would like to thank the Enterprise Analysis Unit of the Development Economics Global Indicators Department of the World Bank Group for making the data available.
2. Productivity paradox is often called in the literature Solow paradox as originally noted by Solow, "you can see the computer age everywhere but in the productivity statistics" (Solow, 1987).
3. The aim of this chapter is not to present the systematic review of growth theories but rather to concentrate on some specific aspects important for further empirical analysis.
4. https://www.enterprisesurveys.org/en/methodology
5. The original data covers 146 countries, however we do not take into account: Sweden, Belgium, Greece, Italy, Luxembourg, Malta, Portugal in order to have the group of emerging economies.
6. These include: methods of manufacturing products or offering services; logistics, delivery, or distribution methods for inputs, products, or services; or supporting activities for processes.
7. There are also data available on TFP derived either from output model: YKLM or value added model: VAKL. Unfortunately, these data are available only for limited number of sectors and years, consequently, the number of observations drops considerably. Because of that we decided to stick to labour productivity. However, the analogous estimates as those in Eq. (1) were conducted and the positive and statistically significant correlation between four out of eight measures of ICT and TFP (namely: *Cert, Tech_foreign, Web and Email*) was obtained.
8. Skilled workers are defined as workers in highly skilled production jobs, professionals whose tasks require extensive theoretical and technical knowledge.
9. The results are available from author upon request.
10. A firm is an exporter if at least 1% of its annual sales is derived from exports (direct or indirect exports), otherwise classified as non-exporter.
11. A firm is an importer if at least 1% of its material inputs or supplies are of foreign origin, otherwise classified as non-importer.
12. A firm is an indirect exporter if at least 1% of its annual sales is derived from indirect exports.
13. A firm is an importer if at least 1% of its material inputs or supplies is of foreign origin and the negative answer to the question whether any of these imported material inputs and supplies are imported directly.
14. Simultaneously proportion of exported total sales is greater than 1% and the proportion of imported inputs is greater than 1%.
15. The data from ES World Bank follow-up surveys is freely available through https://www.enterprisesurveys.org/en/data (downloaded on 1 March 2021). The original data refers to almost 30,000 enterprises from 36 countries, but only in the case of 15 countries (BGR, CYP, GEO, GRC, GTM, HND, ITA, JOR, MDA, MLT, NIC, POL, ROU, SLV, SVN), the information of the two rounds is provided.

References

Abbasi, T., & Weigand, H. (2017). The impact of digital financial services on firm's performance: A literature review. *arXiv preprint arXiv:1705.10294.*

Apedo-Amah, M. C., Avdiu, B., Cirera, X., Cruz, M., Davies, E., Grover, A., ... & Tran, T. T. (2020). *Unmasking the impact of covid-19 on businesses: Firm level evidence from across the world.* Policy Research Working Paper 9434, World Bank Group.

Aral, S., & Weill, P. (2007). IT assets, organizational capabilities, and firm performance: How resource allocations and organizational differences explain performance variation. *Organization Science, 18*(5), 763–780.

Attewell, P. (1994). Information technology and the productivity paradox. *Organizational Linkages: Understanding the Productivity Paradox,* 13–53.

Beck, T., Flynn, B., & Homanen, M. (2020). Covid-19 in emerging markets: Firm-survey evidence. Covid Economics, Vetted and Real-Time Papers 38, VoxEU.

Berman, N., & Héricourt, J. (2010). Financial factors and the margins of trade: Evidence from cross-country firm-level data. *Journal of Development Economics, 93*(2), 206–217. doi: https://doi.org/10.1016/j.jdeveco.2009.11.006.

Brynjolfsson, E. (1993). The productivity paradox of information technology. *Communications of the ACM, 36*(12), 66–77.

Brynjolfsson, E., & Hitt, L. M. (2003). Computing productivity: Firm-level evidence. *Review of Economics and Statistics, 85*(4), 793–808.

Brynjolfsson, E., & Yang, S. (1996). Information technology and productivity: A review of the literature. *Advances in Computers, 43,* 179–214.

Brynjolfsson, E., Rock, D., & Syverson, C. (2019). Chapter 1. Artificial intelligence and the modern productivity paradox: A clash of expectations and statistics. In Agrawal, Gans, and Goldfarb (Eds.), *The economics of artificial intelligence: An agenda* (pp. 23–60).

Cooley, T. F., & Quadrini, V. (2001). Financial markets and firm dynamics. *American Economic Review, 91*(5), 1286–1310.

Dedrick, J., Gurbaxani, V., & Kraemer, K. L. (2003). Information technology and economic performance: A critical review of the empirical evidence. *ACM Computing Surveys (CSUR), 35*(1), 1–28

Díaz-Chao, Á, Sainz-González, J., & Torrent-Sellens, J. (2015). ICT, innovation, and firm productivity: New evidence from small local firms. *Journal of Business Research, 68*(7), 1439–1444.

Hagsten, E., & Kotnik, P. (2017). ICT as a facilitator of internationalization in small-and medium-sized firms. *Small Business Economics, 48*(2), 431–446.

Head, K., & Mayer, T. (2013). What separates us? Sources of resistance to globalization. *Canadian Journal of Economics, 46*(4), 1196–1231.

Luo, Y., & Bu, J. (2016). How valuable is information and communication technology? A study of emerging economy enterprises. *Journal of world business, 51*(2), 200–211.

Meijers, H. (2014). Does the internet generate economic growth, international trade, or both? *International Economics and Economic Policy, 11*(1), 137–163.

Melitz, M. (2003). The impact of trade on intra-industry reallocations and aggregate industry productivity. *Econometrica, 71,* 1695–1725.

Nwankpa, J. K., & Roumani, Y. (2016). IT capability and digital transformation: A firm performance perspective.

Pilat, D. (2005). The ICT productivity paradox: Insights from micro data. *OECD Economic Studies, 2004*(1), 37–65.

Polák, P. (2017). The productivity paradox: A meta-analysis. *Information Economics and Policy, 38*, 38–54.

Sassi, S., & Goaied, M. (2013). Financial development, ICT diffusion and economic growth: Lessons from MENA region. *Telecommunications Policy, 37*(4–5), 252–261.

Schweikl, S., & Obermaier, R. (2020). Lessons from three decades of IT productivity research: towards a better understanding of IT-induced productivity effects. *Management Review Quarterly, 70*, 461–507.

Singh, S., Sahni, M. M., & Kovid, R. K. (2021). Exploring trust and responsiveness as antecedents for intention to use FinTech services. *International Journal of Economics and Business Research, 21*(2), 254–268.

Stoel, M. D., & Muhanna, W. A. (2009). IT capabilities and firm performance: A contingency analysis of the role of industry and IT capability type. *Information & Management, 46*(3), 181–189.

Stanley, T. D., Doucouliagos, H., & Steel, P. (2018). Does ICT generate economic growth? A meta-regression analysis. *Journal of Economic Surveys, 32*(3), 705–726.

Solow, R. (1987), New York Book Review. July 12, 1987.

Wagner, J. (2007). Exports and productivity: A survey of the evidence from firm-level data. *The World Economy, 30*(1), 60–82.

Vu, K., Hanafizadeh, P., & Bohlin, E. (2020). ICT as a driver of economic growth: A survey of the literature and directions for future research. *Telecommunications Policy, 44*(2), 101922.

4 Determinants of the sustainability of microfinance institutions

Delineating the role of digitization of micro finance services

Amar Nath Das and Arindam Laha

4.1 Introduction

Private lending institutions may fail to allocate credit efficiently, because of information asymmetry problems in the market for small business loans (Stiglitz & Weiss, 1981). In such situation of imperfect information of the borrowers' characteristics, lenders design their credit contracts so as to alleviate the problems of adverse selection and moral hazards. Consequently, it leads to the problem of credit rationing in the institutional credit market (Craig et al., 2007). To address the problem of credit market failure of the formal financial services, microfinance is seen as an innovative solution since 1970 in outreaching its doorstep financial services to the poor and low-income households. In fact, microfinance approach addresses the problems of credit market imperfections (moral hazard, adverse selection, contract enforcement) through innovations in contract design, that make use both of local knowledge and social networks and of adaptive organizational structures (Duflo et al., 2007).

However, microcredit is perceived as a business serving high-risk borrowers with low returns on investment due to high transaction and information costs (Pollinger et al., 2007). A significant number of microfinance programmes depend on donors' fund from government or investors to meet this high cost of transactions. At present, MFIs are experiencing increasing competitions in securing scarce donor funds and outreaching underserved market due to the presence of small banking institutions in the domain of microfinance business (Hermes et al., 2011). In this scenario, MFIs require to achieve borrower's loyalty resulting from spill over effect of efficient management system. Borrowers' loyalty could address the problem of scarcity of loanable funds, and ensure survival in cutting edge competition. This can be expected to have a far-reaching implication on the sustainability of MFIs. Sustainability indicates the ability of MFIs to recover operating cost, to serve more poor people efficiently without reliance on government subsidies or donor funds. It leads to operational self-sufficiency, financial self-sufficiency, and substantial outreach performance (Barres et al., 2005; CGAP, 2009; Morduch, 2000; Rosenberg et al., 2009).

DOI: 10.4324/9781003199076-4

For the purpose of achieving sustainability, microfinance industry across the globe has been exploiting the potential of Information and Communication Technology (ICT). It is well documented that use of ICT in the operation of MFIs could reduce their operating costs, enhance staff productivity, decrease uncertainty as well as improve their revenue generation which make them less reliant of donors' funds (Augsburg et al., 2011; Banda, 2012; Diniz et al., 2008; Hengst & Sol, 2001; Jiménez-Zarco et al., 2006; Krishnaveni & Meenakumari, 2010). For instance, Jawadi et al. (2010) found the positive impact of ICT adoption on expansion and performance of microfinance services in Europe. Kipesha (2013) studied the effect of ICT in Microfinance operations, cost management in Tanzania. Some other studies also identified ICT adoption can improve information accessibility and provides effective ways to deliver customer services (Hengst & Sol, 2001; Melville et al., 2004). On the other hand, some researchers focussed solely on sustainability perspective of MFIs. Bhanot and Bapat (2015) developed sustainability index to measure the progress of Indian MFIs on financial performance and outreach dimensions. They also investigated some contributory factors affecting the sustainability of MFIs. In addition, Tehulu (2013) empirically investigated the determinants of financial sustainability of microfinance institutions in East Africa. However, these studies did not include ICT adoption as one of the factor in explaining sustainability.

While several researchers suggested that ICT adoption improves the efficiency of MFIs, however, there is still paucity of comprehensive empirical works in investigating the role of ICT on sustainability of MFIs across countries of the world. This study, therefore, objectively tries to address this research gap in the existing literature by developing a multidimensional sustainability index and to explore how ICT together with other contributory factors can influence sustainability of MFIs.

For convenience, this chapter is divided into five sections. The next section analysed the conceptual framework on sustainability of MFIs and its determinants. Section 4.3 considers the data sources and methodological aspects relating to measure of sustainability and its determinants. In Section 4.4, empirical evidences on sustainability scores of MFIs and ICT adoption across five world regions are presented. Also, the effects of various factors in determining sustainability are identified. The concluding remarks are presented in Section 4.5.

4.2 Sustainability and its determinants: A conceptual framework

The microfinance sector came into limelight in the policy circles after the success of Grameen Bank in Bangladesh, where almost collateral free financing led to a significant change in the financial and social scenario for the targeted poor population. In 2018, MFIs served 139.9 million borrowers across the world, compared to just 98 million in 2009. Although, the operating expense ratio decreased by 2.7 points but average cost per borrower increased by 56% over the period. Since, 2012 the average annual growth rate of borrower is 7% (MIX Market, 2018).

In the context of MFI, sustainability conceptualized in different ways in the existing literature. In some studies, sustainability has been considered as the long-term financial viability of MFIs (Chavan & Ramakumar, 2002; Pati, 2009), others regarded managerial efficiency coupled with satisfactory financial performance (Shetty, 2009; Srinivasan, 2008). From dependency perspective, sustainability was perceived as the ability to survive without donors' subsidy (Parida & Sinha, 2010). In fact, sustainability is a never-ending process. It needs to be maintained till the last mile of the institution. MFIs can sustain if they achieve acceptable financial and outreach performance (Bhanot & Bapat, 2015). As per generic understanding, it implies the ability to recover the cost of operation as well as reaching to poor clients in substantial numbers without government grant or donors' subsidy. Eventually the entire process of ensuring sustainability in operation is expected to enable the poor to get out of poverty.

The Sustainable Development Goals (SDGs) were adopted by United Nations Member States (170 countries and territories) in 2015 as a universal call to alleviate poverty, and ensure that all people enjoy peace and prosperity by 2030 (UNDP, 2016). It recognizes the contribution of microfinance in scaling down poverty and overall socio-economic development. For the purpose of achieving this global mission, MFIs need to reduce operating cost in the process of outreaching its operation. Rendering satisfactory service at minimum cost to the customer is perceived as a confidence building measure from the perspective to both client and service providers.

At the juncture of present technological advancement, digitizing financial services is no longer an option to the MFIs. It becomes an essential tool to remain competitive in the financial market through outreaching its services to the excluded sections of the population. Digital financial services deliver facilities like basic money transfer, bill payments, savings, insurance, merchant payments, crowd funding, bulk disbursement, and other value-added services. Digital solution reduces data management cost, deepen customer engagement, and offers a range of financial services to customer. MFI agents can deliver financial services to the door steps of the customers through digital financial devices. It increases liquidity, loan recovery and enlarge loan portfolios. Digitization of services replaces the concept of physical presence of a branch by virtual or mobile branches. In such way, MFIs render better customer experience in minimum time, increase staff productivity and reduce operating cost (Riggins & Weber, 2016). This trend helps traditional MFIs to overcome high operating cost coupled with high credit risk, and eventually reach out to the unbanked sections of the population (Musa et al., 2012).

Most of researches in the field of sustainability of MFIs identified the determinants of sustainability. Nawaz (2010) observed that delivering of credit to poor borrower in small size increase transaction cost and, therefore, induces to charge higher interest rate. Eventually, design of an innovative interest rate leads to improve financial performance by lowering dependency on donors' fund and enhance sustainability. However, existing literature establishes a positive significant relationship among asset size and sustainability (Bogan, 2012; Cull et al., 2007; Mersland and Strøm, 2007), large number of borrowers and sustainability (Logotri, 2006), breadth of outreach and sustainability (Nyamsogoro, 2010). On the other hand, a negative and significant relationship between ratio of gross outstanding loan portfolio to total assets and sustainability also empirically supported (Okumu, 2007). In the context of Indian MFIs, Bhanot and Bapat (2015) observed a positive and significant relationship between large loan portfolio, staff productivity and return on assets (ROA) with sustainability of MFIs. Portfolio at risk (PAR) is also inversely related to the sustainability. From the insights of the existing empirical evidences, a conceptual framework is presented to document a list of positive contributions to sustainability of MFIs with the help of upright pyramid. On the other hand, negative contributions to sustainability are shown by an inverted pyramid (Figure 4.1).

Researches in the field of adoption of ICT in microfinance operation revealed almost identical outcome in majority of the studies. ICT facilitates in achieving operational efficiency, improvement in decision making, enhance greater outreach of customer service delivery, credit monitoring services (Kamau, 2014; Melville et al., 2004; Musa et al., 2012;

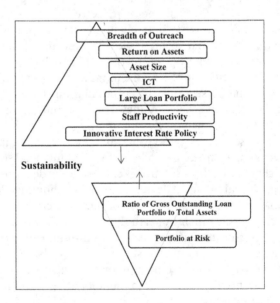

Figure 4.1 Determinants and their relationship with sustainability.

Source: Authors' own presentation.

Ssewanyama, 2009). However, ICT adoption is observed to be costly and less beneficial in areas with low population density and poor communication infrastructure. Sometimes lower education level in client base is emerged as a challenge in the usage of digitized micro finance services (Hishigsuren, 2006).

4.3 Materials and methods

In this study, three individual indicators are compiled to construct a multidimensional index of sustainability. These three indicators are operational self-sufficiency ratio, average loan balance per borrower (ALPB), and number of active borrowers (NAB) (following Bhanot & Bapat, 2015). After estimating sustainability score of our sample MFIs, a panel regression analysis is performed to identify the factors affecting the sustainability of such MFIs.

4.3.1 Sample profile

This study is exclusively based on secondary sources of data. Relevant indicators of a sample of 106 MFIs for the purpose of the study is obtained from the Microfinance Information Exchange (MIX) database. In fact, a panel dataset on 106 MFIs across the world is compiled from MIX database for the years 2017 and 2018. For these years, data were available for 3114 MFIs. However, after removing the entries of missing values the sample is narrowed down to a sample of 106 MFIs. This yields a balanced panel dataset of 212 observations (i.e., a dataset of 106 MFIs for two respective years). The selection of the time period of the analysis is mainly driven by the availability of data on digitization of microfinance services. A descriptive statistics for the explanatory variables as used in our study is listed in Table 4.1A (see in Appendix).

4.3.2 Model specification

Composite sustainability score is derived from three individual indicators. First, operational self-sufficiency ratio (OSS), a financial performance indicator, is measured by using the following formula: OSS = [Financial Revenue/(Financial Expense + Net Impairment Loss + Operating Expense)]. Second, ALPB is considered as an indicator of depth of outreach and third, NAB represents a measure of breadth of outreach indicator. We have transformed ALPB and NAB into natural logarithm as they are collected in absolute terms.

Technique for Order Preference by Similarity to the Ideal Solution (TOPSIS) method is used to compile the scores of MFIs on individual indicators and thereby obtain their relative ranking on the basis of overall measure of sustainability. This technique was developed by Hwang and Yoon (1981) and extensively applied in different studies (Bhanot & Bapat, 2015;

Cheng *et al.*, 2003; Deng *et al.*, 2000; Montanari, 2004; Opricovic and Tzeng, 2004; Tzeng *et al.*, 2005; Zavadskas et al., 2002). TOPSIS is used for solving Multiple Criteria Decision-Making (MCDM) problems (Roszkowska, 2011). This technique provides best alternative that should have the shortest Euclidian distance from the positive ideal solution (most preferable alternative) and the farthest from the negative ideal solution (least preferable alternative) (Benitez et al., 2007). The positive ideal solution maximizes the benefit criteria (Beneficial attribute) and minimizes the cost criteria (Non-beneficial attribute). In this way, TOPSIS technique considers the distances to both the ideal and the negative-ideal solutions simultaneously to ranks a number of possible alternatives according to their relative closeness to the ideal solution. (Hwang & Yoon, 1981; Yonghong, 2002). This method is consists of following steps:

The first step of TOPSIS involves the construction of a decision matrix. TOPSIS is used to rank P alternatives associated with N criteria, when the score of each alternative with respect to each criterion is available. In our model, P = 106 (total number of sample MFIs) and N=3 (three criteria, i.e., OSS, ALPB, NAB). In the second step, we normalized the dataset of each indicator by using the following normalization formula:

$$ r_{ij} = \frac{x_{ij}}{\sqrt{\sum_{i=1}^{P} (x_{ij})^2}} $$

where individual element in $P \times N$ matrix is represented by x_{ij}, $i \in P$, $j \in N$.

In the third step, we multiply each element of the normalized decision matrix (r_{ij}) by their respective weights (w_j) to quantify the relative importance of the different selection criteria, i.e., $v_{ij} = w_j r_{ij}$. The objective weights[1] associated with the respective indicators are estimated by following Principal Component Analysis (OECD, 2008). Following the Organisation for Economic Co-operation and Development(OECD) guidelines, the weights are constructed from the matrix of factor loadings after rotation, given that the square of factor loadings represents the proportion of the total unit variance of the indicator which is explained by the factor. In this approach, individual indicators are grouped with the highest factors loadings into *intermediate* composite indicators. In this study, two intermediate composites are aggregated by assigning a weight to each one of them equal to the proportion of the explained variance in the data set.

In the fourth step, the positive and negative ideal solutions are determined. In fact, TOPSIS ranks different alternatives based on their positive ideal and negative ideal solution. Depending on whether a criterion is to be maximized or minimized, ideal nature of solution is chosen. In this study, operational self-sufficiency and NAB are considered as positive ideal criteria which need to be maximised. On the other hand, average loan per borrower is taken as negative ideal criteria, which is required to be minimised.

The positive ideal (A⁺) and the negative ideal (A⁻) solutions are defined according to the weighted decision matrix.

$$A^+ = \left\{ v_1^+, v_2^+, v_3^+ \right\}, \text{ where}: v_j^+ = \left\{ \left(\max\left(v_{ij}\right) if \ j \in J \right); \left(min \ v_{ij} \ if \ j \in J' \right) \right\}$$

$$A^- = \left\{ v_1^-, v_2^-, v_3^- \right\}, \text{ where}: v_j^- = \left\{ \left(\min\left(v_{ij}\right) if \ j \in J \right); \left(max \ v_{ij} \ if \ j \in J' \right) \right\}$$

where, J indicates beneficial attributes (OSS, NAB) and J' stands for non-beneficial attribute (ALPB). In the step five, we measure Euclidian distance for each MFI from the positive ideal, (S_{i+}) and that of from negative ideal solutions (S_{i-}) as follows

$$S_{i+} = \sqrt{\sum_{j=1}^{3}\left(v_{ij} - v_{j+}\right)^2} \ for \ i = 1,2,3\ldots\ldots\ldots106$$

$$S_{i-} = \sqrt{\sum_{j=1}^{3}\left(v_{ij} - v_{j-}\right)^2} \ for \ i = 1,2,3\ldots\ldots\ldots106$$

Finally, relative closeness of each MFI to the ideal solution[2] is calculated as

$$C_{i+} = \frac{S_{i-}}{S_{i+} + S_{i-}}, \ 0 < C_{i+} < 1, \ for \ i = 1,2,3\ldots\ldots\ldots106$$

The relative closeness of each MFI is calculated in such a way that, best alternative (which is nearest to the positive ideal and farthest from negative ideal solution) can be traced out. The values of C_{i+} (*i.e.*,C_1 to C_{106}) indicate the sustainability score of each sample MFIs in our study In other words, sustainability score is calculated for each of our sample MFIs. A higher value of C_{i+}, indicates higher relative closeness to the ideal solution (i.e., C_{i+}approaches to 1), higher-ranking order and better performance than other alternatives. If we rank the score in descending order, then MFI closest to the positive ideal will comes at the top position and the MFI farthest to the positive ideal, is placed at the lowest position of the ranking. Therefore, TOPSIS helps us to get a relative sustainability score of sample MFIs across the world regions on the basis of distance from positive ideal and negative ideal solutions.

After calculating sustainability score of the respective MFIs by using TOPSIS method, we have tried to identify the factors that can explain the variation in sustainability score. For this purpose, we have chosen a set of independent variables, which are relevant for their impact on the sustainability score of MFIs. We have compiled the following determining variables of the MFIs, for the same time frame 2017 and 2018, from MIX database: gross loan portfolio (GLP), PAR, borrower per staff member (BSM), ROA, debt equity ratio (DE), deposits (DP), and ICT adaptation. As such there is no direct measure of ICT in MIX database. Alternatively, we have considered six variables which are attributed as digital delivery channel in MIX database. All these variables execute financial transactions of MFIs through digital channel (Keivin et al., 2011), and, therefore, affected by the ICT. These six digital delivery channels are percentage of total transactions at merchant POS, percentage of total transactions at ATMs, percentage of total transactions by internet, percentage of total transactions by mobile banking, percentage of total transactions at roving staff and percentage of total transactions by alternative delivery channels (ADCs). In fact, highest observed percentage value among these six variables is considered as a proxy of ICT adaptation. In this way, we have tried to capture the contribution of ICT in explaining sustainability of MFIs. All these variables in our analysis are either expressed as ratios (e.g., ICT) or were transformed using natural logarithm function.

The empirical models can be specified as:

$$Sustainability\ Score_{it} = \alpha + \beta_1 GlP_{it} + \beta_2 PR_{it} + \beta_3 BSM_{it} + \beta_4 ROA$$
$$+ \beta_5 DE + \beta_6 DP_{it} + \beta_7 ICT_{it} + u_{it} \dots\dots\dots \tag{4.1}$$

where $t = 1, 2, 3, \dots\dots\dots T$ and $i = 1, 2, 3, \dots\dots n$

In model (1), sustainability score is the dependent variable, α is the intercept term, β are the $k \times 1$ vectors of parameters to be estimated, and u_{it} represents the error term. The description of explanatory variables along with their expected sign of hypothesised relationship with sustainability score are presented in Table 4.1.

In the panel data regression framework, three empirical models are available: Constant Coefficient Model (CCM), Random Effects Model (REM), and Fixed Effect Model (FEM). Although prior to the application of FEM or REM, it is imperative to know underlying regression framework: panel data regression or the pooled regression (i.e., CCM). Therefore, at first, Breusch-Pagan (BP) test is applied to ensure the application of FEM or REM instead of CCM A significant χ^2 value (5.04) at 1% level of significance suggests that Panel regression framework is appropriate. Second, in a balanced panel dataset, Hausman test guides us in selecting an appropriate model (fixed effect panel regression, or random effect panel regression). In this study, Fixed effect panel regression is ultimate selected by following Hausman test results (see Appendix Table 4.2A).

4.4 Results and discussion

4.4.1 *Sustainability score of MFIs: TOPSIS results*

For our convenience, five regions (i.e., Africa, East Asia and the Pacific, Eastern Europe and Central Asia, Latin America and The Caribbean, South Asia) are considered across countries of the world depending on their

Table 4.1 List of independent variables along with their hypothesised relationship with sustainability score

Variables	Description	Category	Hypothesised relation
Gross loan portfolio	Gross outstanding principals due for all outstanding client loans	Size of MFI	+
Deposits	The total value of funds placed in an account with a financial institution that are payable to a depositor	Deposits	+
Debt to equity ratio	Total liabilities/Total equity	Financing structure	–
Return on assets	(Net operating income – Taxes)/Average total assets	Financial performance	+
Borrowers per staff member	Number of active borrowers/Number of personnel	Productivity and efficiency	–
Portfolio at risk >30 days	Outstanding balance overdue >30 Days + renegotiated portfolio/ Gross loan portfolio	Risk and liquidity	–
ICT	Percentage of total transactions at merchant POS, at ATMs, by internet, by mobile banking, at roving staff and alternative delivery channels	Infrastructure	+

Source: Authors' own estimation.

presence of MFIs. World region wise mean and standard deviation of sustainability score of MFIs and their components are listed in Table 4.2.

It is evident from Table 4.2 that South Asian region is emerged as the harbour of most sustainable MFIs in the world, and it is followed by MFIs in other regions, viz. East Asia and the Pacific, Eastern Europe and Central Asia, Latin America and Caribbean continent and Africa. Eventually, out of top five most sustainable micro finance institutions in the world, three are from South Asian region. As regard to the component of sustainability score, an increase in operational self-sufficiency results in higher sustainability score (Anduanbesssa, 2009). In respect of outstanding balance per borrower and NAB a mixed outcome are observed.

ICT adaptation of MFIs

In assessing the impact of ICT on sustainability of MFIs, six ICT adoption related indicators are considered, namely, percentage of total transactions

Table 4.2 World region wise calculation of sustainability score and its components

Region	Sustainability score	Number of active borrowers	Average loan balance per borrower	Operational self sufficiency
	Mean ± SD	*Mean ± SD*	*Mean ± SD*	*Mean ± SD*
Africa	0.549 ± 0.101	66196 ± 151902	2063.02 ± 2574.08	1.004 ± 0.164
East Asia and the Pacific	0.611 ± 0.103	88075 ± 115471	2631.4 ± 2237.74	1.196 ± 0.148
Eastern Europe and Central Asia	0.600 ± 0.096	46060 ± 31566	1469.1 ± 925.30	1.153 ± 0.297
Latin America and the Caribbean	0.562 ± 0.090	90396 ± 142671	6022.87 ± 6710.04	1.117 ± 0.107
South Asia	0.670 ± 0.134	325338 ± 361199	506.43 ± 146.03	1.176 ± 0.229

Source: Authors' own calculation.

at merchant POS, at ATMs, by internet, by mobile banking, at roving staff and ADCs. World region wise components of digital delivery channels of MFIs are listed in Table 4.3. Mobile banking services provides greater convenience and instant facility to customer. Higher transaction rate through this channel is observed in African and European regions. ADCs, ATMs, and roving staff are appeared as three major digital delivery channels used in South Asian regions. A considerable portion of transactions are taken place through these channels followed by mobile banking, merchant POS and internet banking. Each region has its own popular digital transaction channels. As per our study, we can safely argue that choice of ICT channels is depend on generic features of individual regions.

4.4.2 Panel regression

The regression result in Table 4.4 explains the determinants of sustainability scores obtained by using TOPSIS. It is evident that GLP, PAR, ROA, and ICT are crucial in explaining variation in sustainability score of MFIs.

GLP has positively influence (significant at 1% level) on sustainability of MFIs. Higher GLP implies a sizable volume of outstanding principal, which resulting in incremental interest income. Larger credit portfolio is an outcome of a considerable scale of operation, which helps to achieve economies of scale resulting in greater outreach services, eventually improving sustainability. This finding is consistent with Bogan (2012), Cull et al. (2007),

Table 4.3 World region wise components of digital delivery channels

Region	Percentage of total transactions at merchant POS Mean ± SD	Percentage of total transactions at ATMs Mean ± SD	Percentage of total transactions by internet Mean ± SD	Percentage of total transactions by mobile banking Mean ± SD	Percentage of total transactions at roving staff Mean ± SD	Percentage of total transactions at ADCs Mean ± SD
Africa	0.0286 ± 0.144	0.110 ± 0.243	0.023 ± 0.105	0.394 ± 0.432	0.126 ± 0.310	0.633 ± 0.478
East Asia and the Pacific	0.0218 ± 0.049	0.551 ± 0.426	0.071 ± 0.257	0.102 ± 0.243	0.052 ± 0.200	0.464 ± 0.505
Eastern Europe and Central Asia	0.135 ± 0.322	0.260 ± 0.393	0.096 ± 0.238	0.197 ± 0.368	0	0.501 ± 0.492
Latin America and The Caribbean	0.033 ± 0.101	0.557 ± 0.406	0.059 ± 0.126	0.101 ± 0.248	0.001 ± 0.007	0.356 ± 0.472
South Asia	0.024 ± 0.066	0.266 ± 0.363	0.012 ± 0.0271	0.137 ± 0.288	0.125 ± 0.341	0.312 ± 0.478

Source: Authors' own calculation.

Table 4.4 The results of the determinants of sustainability of MFIs

Dependent variable	Independent variable	Coefficient (β)	t-stat
Sustainability score	Gross loan portfolio	0.556	0.001***
	Portfolio at risk	−0.484	0.041**
	Borrower per staff member	0.000	0.654
	Return on assets	0.665	0.024**
	Debt equity ratio	0.000	0.744
	Deposit	−0.140	0.265
	ICT	0.091	0.004***
	Constant	5.941	0.000***

Note: *** and ** indicate that the coefficient is significant at the 0.01 and 0.05 level of significance, respectively.

Source: Author's own calculation.

and Bhanot and Bapat (2015). The coefficient of PAR is found negative and significant at 5% level. Higher value of PAR implies, a sizable percentage of loan portfolio is bearing default risk. Non-remittance of credit leads to loss of principal amount along with interest income and restrict outreach venture which eventually appear as a threat to sustainability of MFI. Higher PAR involves inefficient loan recovery policy, improper timing for loan disbursement (e.g., agrarian credit) and lack of understanding of borrowers' livelihood (Godquin, 2004). MFIs, those who primarily focus on extending credit for income generating activity, do have adequate understanding over clients' credit absorption capacity. It helps them to minimise default cases and ensuring sustainability.

The coefficient of ROA is observed to be positive in explaining sustainability of MFIs and statistically significant (at 1% level).It suggests that the practice of earning profit over assets helps MFIs to improve sustainability level. ROA is a profitability indicator. It measures how efficiently an MFI uses its assets to make surplus and continue to grow in future. When an MFI has surplus, it can be reinvested in scaling up its business operation which improve its outreach capability and reduce dependency on donor's fund. However, expansion of business does not always ensure sustainability (Bhanot & Bapat, 2015). Sustainability also requires ploughing back of profit into the business to increase portfolio size and reducing equity funding or external borrowing. For the purpose of maintaining better ROA, an MFI requires to achieve high staff productivity, higher loan portfolio, extended outreach facility and above all good collection capability. A number of studies provide empirical evidence in supporting this relationship (Berger et al. 2006; Godquin, 2004).

In this study ICT represents as an indicator of digital delivery channel with enormous potential in microfinance industry. Transaction through merchant POS, ATMs, internet, mobile banking, and roving staff provide a multichannel digital platform to serve the clients. The paradigm shifts from brick-and-mortar system to digital delivery channel accelerate intensity of the competition among the players of microfinance industry. In this backdrop, ICT is seen to have a significant effect on sustainability of MFIs with a positive coefficient at 1% level. It is due to the fact that ICT usage removes time and distance constraint on accessing information, and processing transaction in real time basis. It leads to augment the scale of operational efficiency by reducing operating cost, staff fraud and error, risk of handling cash, increasing staff productivity and exploiting economies of scale by achieving greater geographical outreach of MFIs. From clients' end, digital delivery channels offer more convenience, as it opens up a wide range of financial services at the doorstep, even in remote areas. Roving staff visit customer and collect savings, repayment of credit, insurance payments, assist in credit formalities using digital devices. Customer can perform similar type of transactions through internet, mobile banking, or visiting merchant POS. It enables faster transaction, getting transaction history instantly. Eventually, ICT has made an ease in banking experience of MFI customer. They no longer need to cover a long distance with cash to visit branches. Therefore, it reduces risk of theft, distance travel, time and transaction cost. Through these linkage effects, ICT eventually helps in enhancing sustainability of the MFIs. The findings of our study are similar with other country based empirical studies (Banda, 2012; Hishigsuren, 2006; Jawadi et al., 2010; Rai, 2012; Ssewanyama, 2009; Washington, 2006). The rest of the variables like, GLP, deposit mobilisation, debt-equity ratio, borrowers per staff member and PAR are found statistically insignificant as per model output.

4.5 Conclusions

This study made an attempt to measure sustainability of MFIs in the parlance of self-sufficiency and outreach of microfinance services. It also tried to identify determinants of overall sustainability, specifically, the impact of digitization of financial services on the sustainability of MFIs. A quantitative approach (TOPSIS) is followed in measuring sustainability of MFIs across the regions of the world. A comprehensive sample of 106 MFIs across countries of the world is compiled from MIX database. Our observation reveals that MFIs in South Asia secure higher sustainability score in the world regions, and it is followed by other regions, viz. East Asia and the Pacific, Eastern Europe and Central Asia, Latin America and The Caribbean and Africa. This study provides an insight of the importance of ICT adaptation for future survival of MFIs. ICT adaptation is believed to be helpful for the microfinance industry to render the increasing demand on micro-financial services efficiently with lower transaction cost. The study also identifies GLP, PAR, ROA and ICT as significant determinants in explaining the sustainability of MFIs across the regions of the world. GLP is a measure of credit capacity of an MFI, and therefore reflects economies of scale in operation. Our results show that higher loan portfolio size helps MFIs to secure higher level of sustainability. PAR is found negatively affect sustainability of MFIs. Higher portfolio risk increases the chance of credit default by the client. As a result, it dampens interest income, recovery rate of principal amount and adversely affecting sustainability of MFIs. Better understanding on clients' risk profile can significantly reduces such type of risk. ROA is a measure how efficiently an MFI uses its assets to make surplus. When an MFI has surplus, the same can be ploughing back into the business to increase portfolio size, to reduce dependency on donor's fund. The result supports the claim of positive impact of ROA on sustainability of MFIs.

Another interesting finding is that, ICT adaptation in credit digital delivery channels bears a strong linkage effect on the sustainability of MFIs. In fact, digital delivery channels could improve operational performance of MFIs and offer more convenience to customers. Particularly, it helps MFIs to reach unbanked population at a lowest cost, offer more accessibility, faster transaction, reducing risk, instant transaction history, above all deliver better customer experience to secure greater customer loyalty, eventually sustainability.

Although, we have tried to generalise the results but this study is not exhaustive in nature. In addition to the limitation of sample MFIs, the MIX Market data does not allow us to consider other socio-economic factors from different countries and territories. There is further scope of study by considering social performance data set of MFIs to account for their effect on sustainability of MFIs.

Appendix

Table 4.1A Descriptive statistics of variables

Variables	Observations	Mean	SD	Minimum	Maximum
Dependent variables					
Number of active borrowers	212	97908.92	173709.30	662	1181037
Average loan balance per borrower	212	3763.09	5202.96	19	41297
Operational self-sufficiency	212	1.10	0.19	0.00	1.78
Independent variables					
Gross loan portfolio	212	227,000,000	451,000,000	715,008	3,540,000,000
Deposits	212	204,000,000	438,000,000	157,361	3,570,000,000

Table 4.1A (Continued)

Variables	Observations	Mean	SD	Minimum	Maximum
Debt to equity ratio	212	11.48	85.19	0.25	1245.33
Return on assets	212	0.01	0.03	−0.10	0.21
Borrowers per staff member	212	86.54	58.84	15.00	349.00
Portfolio at risk > 30 days	212	0.07	0.07	0.00	0.54
ICT	212	0.86	0.27	0.00	1.00

Source: Author's own calculation.

Table 4.2A Diagnostic tests in panel regression framework

Breusch-Pagan /Cook-Weisberg Test for Heteroskedasticity:
H0: Constant variance
Variables: fitted Values of Sustainability Score
Chi2(1) = 20.59
Prob>chi2 = 0.00
Hausman fixed random test

	(b) Fixed	(B) Random	(b-B) Difference	S.E.
Gross Loan	0.55	0.10	0.66	0.16
Deposits	−0.14	−0.07	−0.06	0.12
Debt_to equity	0.00	0.00	−0.00	0.00
Return_on_assets	0.66	1.31	−0.64	0.23
Borrowers per SM	0.00	0.00	−0.00	0.00
Portfolio Risk	−0.48	−0.16	−0.32	0.21
ICT	0.09	0.02	0.06	0.02

Note: chi2(7) = 74.36. Prob>chi2 = 0.00.
Source: Author's own calculation.

Notes

1. The subjective choice to assign equal weights to the indicators is the simplest solution, but not "neutral" or without critics (OECD, 2008). So, unlike in other studies (Bhanot and Bapat, 2015), this study utilizes objective approach in determining weights. In the statistical measurement, weights are calculated from the observed values of the variables, and therefore data driven in nature.
2. Ideal solution refers to nearest to the positive ideal and farthest from the negative ideal solution.

References

Anduanbessa, T. (2009). Statistical analysis of the performance of microfinance institutions: The Ethiopian case. *Savings and Development, 33*(2), 183–198.

Augsburg, B., Schmidt, J. P., & Krishnaswamy, K. (2011). Free & open source software for microfinance: Increasing efficiency. *Advanced Technologies for Microfinance*, 18.

Banda, J. (2012). ICT for business services: The case of Ugandan microfinance institutions. *International Journal of Research Reviews in Applied Sciences, 11*(1), 140–152.

Barres, I., Curran, L., Nelson, E., Bruett, T., Escalona, A., & Norell, D. (2005). *Measuring performance of microfinance Institutions: A framework for reporting, analysis and monitoring*. The Seep Network and Alternative Credit Technologies, LLC.

Benitez, J., Martin, J., & Roman, C. (2007). Using fuzzy number for measuring quality of service in the hotel industry. *Tourism Manage, 28*(2), 544–555.

Berger, M., Otero, M., & Schore, G. (2006). *Pioneers in the commercialization of microfinance: The significance and future of upgraded microfinance institutions, inside view of Latin American microfinance* (pp. 37–77). Inter-American Development Bank.

Bhanot, D., & Bapat, V. (2015). Sustainability index of micro finance institutions (MFIs) and contributory factors. *International Journal of Social Economics, 42*(4), 387–403.

Bogan, V. L. (2012). Capital structure and sustainability: An empirical study of microfinance Institutions. *Review of Economics and Statistics, 94*(4), 1045–1058.

Chavan, P., & Ramakumar, R. (2002). Micro-credit and rural poverty: An analysis of empirical evidence. *Economic and Political Weekly, 37*(10), 955–965.

Cheng, S., Chan, C. W., & Huang, G. H. (2003). An integrated multi-criteria decision analysis and inexact mixed integer linear programming approach for solid waste management. *Engineering Applications of Artificial Intelligence, 16*(5–6), 543–554.

Craig, B. R., Jackson, W. E., & Thomson, J. B. (2007). Credit market failure intervention: Do government sponsored small business credit programs enrich poorer areas? *Small Business Economics, Small Bus Econ, 30*(4), 345–360.

Cull, R., Demirgüç-Kunt, A., & Morduch, J. (2007). Financial performance and outreach: A global analysis of leading microbanks. *The Economic Journal, 117*(517), F107–F133.

CGAP (2009). *Financial analysis for microfinance institutions*. Retrieved from www. cgap.org/sites/default/files/CGAP-Training-Financial-Analysis-Course-2009.pdf.

Deng, H., Yeh, C. H., & Willis, R. J. (2000). Inter-company comparison using modified TOPSIS with objective weights. *Computers and Operations Research, 27*(10), 963–973.

Diniz, E. H., Pozzebon, M., & Jayo, M. (2008). Banking technology to scale microfinance: The case of correspondent banking in Brazil, ICIS 2008 Proceedings, 144.

Duflo, A., Tripathi, R., & Walton, M. (2007). Credit market failures and microfinance: From promise to practice – A case study of the Andhra Pradesh crisis. Retrieved from http://www.michaelwalton.info/wp-content/uploads/2011/08/Microfinance-the-crisis-in-Andhra-Pradesh.pdf.

Godquin, M. (2004). *Microfinance repayment performance in Bangladesh: How to improve the allocation of loans by MFIs. World Development, 32*(11), 1909–1926.

Hengst, M., & Sol, H. (2001). The impact of information and communication technology on inter-organizational coordination: Guidelines from theory. *Journal of Informing Science: Special Series on Information Exchange in Electronic Markets*, *4*(3), 130–138.

Hermes, N., Lensink, R., & Meesters, A. (2011). *Outreach and efficiency of microfinance institutions*. World Development, *39*, 939–948.

Hishigsuren, G. (2006). Information and Communication Technology and Microfinance: Options for Mongolia. ADB Institute Discussion Paper No. 42.

Hwang, C. L., & Yoon, K. (1981). *Multiple attribute decision making methods and applications*. Springer.

Jawadi, F., Jawadi, N., & Dechamps, D. (2010). European Microfinance institutions and information and communication technologies: An empirical qualitative investigation in the French context. *Journal of Electronic Commerce in Organizations*, *8*(3), 38–48.

Jiménez-Zarco, A., Martínez-Ruiz, M., & Llamas-Alonso, M. (2006). Analysis of ICTs opportunities on firm's success: An innovation process. *Problems and Perspectives in Management*, *4*(4), 84–94.

Kamau, S. K. (2014). *The effect of ICT adoption on the financial performance of micro-finance institutions in Kenya*. University of Nairobi. Unpublished MBA Project.

Keivin, P., & Pierre, P. (2011). *Mobile money:An overview for global telecommunications operators* (6th ed.). Ernst &Young Press.

Kipesha (2013). Impact of ICT utilization on efficiency and financial sustainability of microfinance institutions in Tanzania. *Interdisciplinary Studies on Information Technology and Business*, *1*(1), 67–82.

Krishnaveni, R., & Meenakumari, J. (2010). Usage of ICT for information administration in higher education Institutions: A study. *International Journal of Environmental Science and Development*, *1*(3), 282–286.

Logotri (2006). *Building sustainable microfinance system: A growth of catalyst for the poor*. Local government training and research institute, society for development studies, Retrieve from: http://www.logotri.net.

Melville, N., Kraemer, K., & Gurbaxani, V. (2004). Information technology and organizational performance: An integrative model of IT business value. *MIS Quarterly*, *28*(22), 283–322.

Mersland, R., & Strøm, R. O. (2007). *Performance and corporate governance in microfinance institutions*. Agder University.

Mix Market. (2018). *Global Outreach & Financial Performance Benchmark Report*. https://www.themix.org/sites/default/files/publications/mix_global_regional_benchmark_report.pdf

Montanari, R. (2004). Environmental efficiency analysis for enel thermo-power plants. *Journal of Cleaner Production*, *12*(4), 403–414.

Morduch, J. (2000). The microfinance schism. *World Development*, *28*(4), 617–629.

Musa, M., Akodo, M., Mukooza, R., Kaliba, M., & Mbarika, R. (2012). Impact of investment in information and communication technology on performance and growth of microfinance institutions in Uganda. *Applied econometrics and international development Journal*, *12*(2), 151–164.

Nawaz, A. (2010). Issues in subsidies and sustainability of microfinance: An empirical investigation. *CEB Working paper No. 10/010*. Pakistan Institute of Development Economics.

Nyamsogoro, G. D. (2010). *Financial sustainability of rural microfinance institutions in Tanzania*, Published Doctoral Thesis, University of Greenwich, London.

OECD (2008). *Handbook on constructing composite indicators: Methodology and user guide*. Joint Research Centre-European Commission. OECD publishing.

Okumu, L. J. (2007). *The Microfinance Industry in Uganda: Sustainability, Outreach and Regulation*. Unpublished PhD Dissertation, University of Stellenbosch.

Opricovic, S., & Tzeng, G. H. (2004). Compromise solution by MCDM methods: A comparative analysis of VIKOR and TOPSIS. *European Journal of Operational Research, 156*(2), 445–455.

Parida, P., & Sinha, A. (2010). Performance and sustainability of self-help groups in India: A gender perspective. *Asian Development Review, 27*(1), 80–103.

Pati, A. (2009). Subsidy impact on sustainability of SHGs: An empirical analysis of micro lending through SGSY scheme. *Indian Journal of Agricultural Economics, 64*(2), 1–13.

Pollinger, J. J., Outhwaite, J., & Guzmán, H. C. (2007). The question of sustainability for microfinance institutions. *Journal of Small Business Management, 45*(1), 23–41.

Rai, A. (2012). The role and impact of information and communication technologies in microfinance institutions. *International Journal of Management and Strategy, 3*(4), 1–11.

Riggins, F. J., & Weber, D. M. (2016). Impact of ICT on market structure in the microfinance industry. *The African Journal of Information Systems, 8*(3), 1–19.

Rosenberg, R., Gonzales, R., & Narain, S. (2009). *The new moneylenders: Are the poor being exploited by high microcredit interest rates?* CGAP.

Roszkowska, E. (2011). Multi-criteria decision making models by applying the topsis method to crisp and interval data. *Multiple Criteria Decision Making, 6*(Mcdm), 200–230.

Shetty, N. (2009). Index of microfinance group sustainability: Concepts, issues and empirical evidence from rural India. *The Microfinance Review, 1*(1), 131–152.

Ssewanyama, J. (2009). ICT usage in microfinance Institutions in Uganda. *The African Journal of Information Systems, 1*(3), 5–28.

Srinivasan, N. (2008). Sustainability of SHGs. In *Microfinance in India*. Sage Publication.

Stiglitz, J. E., & Weiss, A. (1981). Credit rationing in markets with imperfect information. *American Economic Review, 71*, 393–410.

Tehulu, T. (2013). Determinants of financial sustainability of microfinance Institutions in East Africa. *European Journal of Business and Management, 5*(17).

Tzeng, G. H., Lin, C. W., & Opricovic, S. (2005). Multi-criteria analysis of alternative fuel buses for public transportation. *Energy Policy, 33*(11), 1373–1383.

UNDP (2016). *The Sustainable Development Goal Report*. https://unstats.un.org/sdgs/report/2016/ The Sustainable Development Goals Report 2016.pdf

Washington, D. (2006). *Client focused technology usage in microfinance Institutions*. USAID.

Yonghong, H. (2002). The improvement of the application of TOPSIS method to comprehensive evaluation. *Mathematics in Practice and Theory, 32*(4), 572–575.

Zavadskas, E. K., Ustinovichius, L., Turskis, Z., Peldschus, F., & Messing, D. (2002). LEVI 3.0 – Multiple criteria evaluation program for construction solutions. *Journal of Civil Engineering and Management, 8*(3), 184–191.

5 Impact of digital technologies on reliability of risk forecasting models – case study of enterprises in three global financial market regions

Tomasz Korol

5.1 Introduction

Advancements in digital technologies have led to the adaption of decision support systems for risk forecasting (Tsai, 2020). The globalization process has led to a complex network of relationships in the business environment. Correct processing of information aims at skillful use and analysis of information available to the enterprise. Nowadays, the complexity of the phenomena occurring around and in business increases. Their uncertainty and volatility increase too. This causes the increased reliance on the quality of human-made decisions on the quality of the information they possess. This quality can be improved if appropriate original information processing methods at the company's disposal are applied. Digital technologies represent such a powerful tool for enhancing effectiveness and easiness in conducting financial risk analyses (Lin et al., 2012; Luo et al., 2017; Veganzones & Severin, 2018; Zelenkov et al., 2017).

Risk forecasting models are vital for economists who must forecast the financial situation of enterprises. Such models often provide early warning signs of potential corporate bankruptcy risk. Although bankruptcy forecasting is a well-researched area in finance, a retrospective analysis of the financial crisis during the 2007–2012 period shows that even the best enterprises must constantly monitor their financial situation. Moreover, the current global coronavirus pandemic has dramatically increased the risk of insolvencies throughout the world. Many financial institutions, such as Goldman Sachs or the Fitch rating agency forecast a decline in global Gross Domestic Product (GDP) by 1.9%, with the EU and US economy expected to be hit hardest (with projected decreases by 7–8%). Any enterprise can experience a bankruptcy threat because today's business environment is increasingly undergoing uncertainty and facing competition. The consequences of financial failure are enormous for financial creditors, managers, shareholders, investors, employees, and even a country's economy. That is why financial institutions require effective prediction models in order to make appropriate lending decisions. Accurate financial risk prediction usually leads to many benefits, such as cost reduction in credit analysis, better

DOI: 10.4324/9781003199076-5

monitoring, and an increased debt-collection rate. Thus, risk forecasting at financial markets has become of major interest and is gaining much more importance currently. Today, the question is not if one should use risk forecasting models, but which forecasting methods are the most effective for enterprises in different parts of world.

While a vast amount of literature focuses on developing a single or a few bankruptcy prediction models using various individual statistical or artificial intelligence techniques for firms in specific regions of world, no attempts have been made to verify the effectiveness of a broad number of forecasting techniques (both traditional statistical and artificial intelligence) on the basis of different populations of enterprises to determine the most effective methods according to a specific global region. The verification of the effectiveness of a broad variety of techniques of financial distress prediction and the development of models adapted to the particular financial market region characteristics is an important quest for a reliable tool that can predict company failure.

The objective of this chapter is to evaluate the impact of ICT on reliability of risk forecasting models. To conduct this goal, the author estimated five traditional statistical and five soft computing models separately for the enterprises from three different financial markets (Latin American, European, and Far-East Asian), which amounts to 30 different forecasting models. Such research approach allows to identify the best predictive model among created statistical models and among soft computing techniques and to select the most effective model from ten different techniques used together. A further goal is to evaluate which method is characterized by the smallest decrease of effectiveness in increasing the forecast horizon for each group of enterprises separately. It allows to compare the behavior of traditional techniques and the latest IT techniques in short- and long-term use.

This chapter adds to the literature in several important ways. First, it verifies the effectiveness of models developed with the use of ten different forecasting techniques – five traditional (multivariate discriminant analysis, logit analysis, probit analysis, decision tree – C&RT and Random Forests [RF] model) and five artificial intelligence methods (feedforward multilayer neural network, support vector machines, self-organizing maps [SOM], fuzzy sets, and genetic algorithms). It identifies the most effective technique among a large array of methods thus it shows also the impact of ICT on reliability of models used at financial markets. Second, the above-mentioned models are estimated separately for enterprises from three different financial markets. The author developed three populations of enterprises: one from Latin America (from such countries as Mexico, Argentina, Chile, Peru, Brazil, and Colombia), from Europe (from such countries as Germany, France, Spain, Finland, Italy, Poland, and Sweden), and from Far-East Asia (from such countries as Taiwan, Japan, China, South Korea, and Malaysia). Such a research approach allows us to identify the most appropriate technique for companies in each specific region. Third, it allows us to analyze which method has the smallest decrease in effectiveness in extending the forecast horizon from one to two and to three years. Very few studies in the literature focus on this crucial aspect. By evaluating and identifying the predictive properties of models in longer forecasting periods, we can build a decision-support system that gives managers more time in the decision-making process. Fourth, it distinguishes the differences in forecasting processes, namely, the type of financial ratios used in three different populations of business entities and it identifies the most significant ones with the highest predicting properties. Fifth, based on ten different forecasting techniques tested on enterprises from three different regions of the world, this study discusses the advantages and disadvantages of each technique in different environments from the point of view of both short- and long-term forecasting horizons.

This work consists of five sections. In the Introduction, the author justifies the topic, the study objectives and the contributions and innovations to the literature. Section 5.2 presents an overview of the literature on development of ICT in financial risk prediction studies. Section 5.3 introduces this study's assumptions. In Section 5.4, the author presents thirty different financial risk prediction models and discusses the results of their effectiveness tests based on 1800 enterprises. Section 5.5 concludes the chapter.

5.2 Literature review

In the XX century, financial ratio analyses have become popular managerial tools, as well as tools for determining the financial risk of firms (Sayari & Mugan, 2017). A large number of empirical studies highlight the importance and the ability of financial ratios in detecting early warnings of corporate financial distress (e.g., Alaka et al., 2018; Altman, 2018; Delen et al., 2013; Dong et al., 2018; Jardin, 2009; Jardin, 2017; Jayasekera, 2018; Laitinen et al., 2014; Liang & Shih, 2016; Ooghe & Balcaen, 2006; Sun et al., 2014; Tian & Yu, 2017; Tian et al., 2015).

Although the basis of financial ratio analyses can be traced back to 300 BCE, in the fifth book of the Elements of Euclid, who systematized the mathematical knowledge of that time (Horrigan, 1968), the first use of financial ratios to assess the economic situation of enterprises dates back to the second half of the nineteenth century in the USA, where rapid industrial development created the need to analyze the financial statements of enterprises. These analyses were primarily aimed at assessing loan repayment ability. The first ratio in history was the current liquidity ratio. During the years 1900–1919, the range of financial ratios used to assess the financial situation of the companies analyzed was significantly expanded. In 1919, A. Wall published an article listing ratio analyses of 981 enterprises (Wall, 1919). Its publication has become a catalyst for the development of new ratios and areas of their use. In the years 1920–1929, the need to categorize financial ratios according to their research area (liquidity, debt, profitability, etc.) was apparent. The 1930s are characterized by two achievements in the development of the ratio analyses:

- The search for the most effective measures within each group of financial ratios began (Foulke, 1933, 1934),
- The first attempts to forecast the financial situation of companies were carried out. The first published research on the use of ratio analyses in forecasting the economic condition of enterprises is the article by Winakor and Smith (1930), who analyzed a ten-year trend for the average values of 21 financial ratios of 29 enterprises with financial problems in the USA. Next, P. Fitzpatrick was the first to study the predictive power of 13 financial ratios of 20 companies that went bankrupt in the USA in the years 1920–1929 (Fitzpatrick, 1932).

During the next stage of the development of financial analyses methods (1940–1967), important research by Merwin (1942) and Beaver (1966) focused on the use of ratio analyses in one-dimensional models. Merwin used a profile analysis to compare solvent and insolvent companies using financial ratios. A profile analysis consists in presenting in time (years prior to the occurrence of insolvency), using a line chart, the arithmetic averages of a given financial ratio calculated for a group of solvent and insolvent companies. On the other hand, Beaver's significant contribution to forecasting the financial standing of firms is the introduction of a dichotomous classification test. He defined the critical value for each ratio, used to separate enterprises into two groups – bankrupt and nonbankrupt.

It is worth noting that economists quickly modernized the approaches to conducting the economic analysis of enterprises along with the development of new statistical models. In the short period after the publication of the probit function in 1934 (Bliss, 1934), the discriminatory function in 1936 (Fischer, 1936) and the logit function in 1944 (Berkson, 1944), these models were adapted to the needs of financial analyses of enterprises.

A milestone in the development of methods for assessing the financial standing of enterprises was the use by E. Altman (1968) of multidimensional discriminant analysis to forecast the risk of bankruptcy of companies. In 1968, he published the first model of such an analysis, based on the use of five financial ratios, in the Journal of Finance (Altman, 1968), after which there was a dynamic development of this type of model. In the years 1970–2000, statistical models (logit, probit models [PROB], and multidimensional discriminant analysis) were already widely used in financial analyses. The development of the C&RT algorithm of decision trees in 1984 (Breiman et al., 1984) and RF by T.K. Ho in 1995 (Ho, 1995) are further examples of the successful implementation of statistical methods in economics. Examples of the latest studies using statistical models (multivariate discriminant analysis, logit models, PROB, decision trees – C&RT and RF) in forecasting corporate bankruptcy risk include the following:

Barboza et al., 2017; Ho et al., 2013; Hosmer et al., 2013; Jackson & Wood, 2013; Kieschnick et al., 2013; Kim & Gu, 2006; Lyandres & Zhdanov, 2013; Mihalovic, 2016; Singhal & Zhu, 2013; Sun, 2007; Wanke et al., 2015; and Xu & Zhang, 2009.

There is no doubt that changes in computing technology have drastically altered both the real and potential ways enterprises conduct business analysis. An example of technological progress is the use of models of artificial neural networks and models of genetic algorithms in forecasting economic phenomena. The theoretical assumptions of neural networks were presented in 1943 by Pitts (Warren & Pitts, 1943) and genetic algorithms in the 1960s by Holland (1975). The first practical application in finance of these models occurred in the 1980s and 1990s. Another example of the development of soft computing methods with practical implementations in financial analysis is the Support Vector Machine model developed by Cortes and Vapnik in 1995 (Cortes & Vapnik, 1995). The latest examples of studies on predicting corporate bankruptcy with the use of artificial intelligence (genetic algorithms, artificial neural networks, fuzzy sets, support vector machine) are the following: Acosta- González and Fernández-Rodríguez, 2014; Chauhan et al., 2009; Chen et al., 2009; Hua et al., 2007; Kim & Kang, 2010; Lee, 2007; Lee & Choi, 2013; Lensberg et al., 2006; Min & Lee, 2005; Min et al., 2006; Tsai, 2008; Wu et al., 2007; and Zanganeh et al., 2011.

All the above methods of forecasting a firm's financial situation are based on the use of ratio analysis, in which the basic assumption is the use of financial ratios developed on the basis of classical logic – zero-one (true/ false). The concept of the fuzzy set was introduced in 1965 by Zadeh (1965). The classic set theory assumes that any element belongs or does not belong to a given set. In contrast, in the theory of fuzzy sets, an element may partly belong to a certain set, and this affiliation can be expressed by means of a real number from the interval [0,1]. The theory of fuzzy logic arose as a result of difficulties that arose during the evaluation of phenomena using bivalent logic. Classical logic makes it impossible to describe mathematical phenomena of an inaccurate and ambiguous nature, for example, "high profit" and "greater economic risk." Interestingly, even though the fuzzy set theory was introduced back in 1965, it is still not as widely used in financial analysis as in engineering and medical applications.

5.3 Data, samples, and variables

The objective of this research was to assess the impact of ICT on effectiveness of risk forecasting models. To conduct this goal, the author estimated five traditional statistical and five soft computing models separately for the enterprises from three different financial market regions (Latin America, Europe, and Far-East Asia), which amounts to 30 different forecasting models. The second main goal was to identify the best predictive model among created statistical models and among soft computing techniques and to select the most effective model from ten different techniques used together. A further goal was to evaluate which method is characterized by the smallest decrease of effectiveness in increasing the forecast horizon for each group of enterprises separately. To distinguish the differences in forecasting processes, namely, the type of financial ratios used in three different populations of business entities, identifying the most significant one with the highest predictable properties was another objective of the research conducted.

Firms' financial accounts were used to calculate 20 ratios, and these ratios were used to estimate the forecasting models. The list of variables used is presented in Table 5.1. The research relies on six samples of firms. Three samples are learning samples, and three are testing samples. The learning and testing samples comprise enterprises from three different regions of world: Latin America (Mexico, Argentina, Chile, Peru, Brazil, Colombia), Europe (Germany, France, Spain, Finland, Italy, Poland, Sweden), and Asia (Taiwan, Japan, China, South Korea, Malaysia). Each testing sample includes 300 bankrupt and 300 nonbankrupt enterprises, while each learning sample includes 100 bankrupt and 100 nonbankrupt firms. The fact that the company is in a good financial situation was assumed based on the overall analysis of financial statements. In the assessment, profitability, liquidity and debt ratios were mainly considered. The companies were selected for

Table 5.1 The financial ratios used in the study

Symbol of input variable	Computing formula
X1	Profit on sales / total assets
X2	(current assets – current liabilities) / total assets
X3	(net income + depreciation) / total liabilities
X4	Operational costs / current liabilities
X5	Stockholders' equity / total liabilities
X6	(stockholders' equity + noncurrent liabilities) / fixed assets
X7	Total revenues / total assets
X8	Current assets / current liabilities
X9	Current liabilities / total assets
X10	Income before tax / current liabilities
X11	Total assets / total liabilities
X12	(Current assets – inventories) / current liabilities
X13	Income before tax / total revenues
X14	Inventories / total revenues
X15	Net income / total assets
X16	EBIT / total assets
X17	Current liabilities / stockholders' equity
X18	Cash / total assets
X19	EBIT / interest paid
X20	Current assets / total liabilities

Source: Own studies.

which there was no doubt that they are not at risk of falling. The enterprises at risk of bankruptcy were chosen based on the following three criteria:

- information from the firm's authorities about the threat of collapse,
- court judgments declaring bankruptcy, and
- liquidation of the company.

The forecasting horizon for all enterprises and all models comprises three periods: one year, two years, and three years prior to bankruptcy. Depending on the enterprise, the three-year financial statements taken for analysis covered the period from 2013 to 2018.

To examine the quality of the 30 created models, three evaluation metrics are calculated for each testing sample, which are overall effectiveness and Type I and Type II errors (due to space limitations, the metrics for the learning samples are not presented). Overall effectiveness is calculated based on how many enterprises are correctly classified by the forecasting model in a given testing sample. Type I error is a measure of the number of companies in which the model incorrectly classifies a bankrupt firm into a nonbankrupt class, while Type II error is a measure that accounts for the number of firms classified as bankrupt when they actually belong to a nonbankrupt class.

5.4 Results

The first estimated model from a group of traditional statistical methods was the multivariate discriminant analysis (MDA) model. This model differs from most models of discriminant analysis found in the literature, not only in consisting of two functions in the model but also in how it classifies companies into those at risk and those not at risk of bankruptcy. Depending on the higher value Z_{BAN} or Z_{NON} a company is classified into one of the populations (nonbankrupt, bankrupt) of companies. Thus, if $Z_{BAN} > Z_{NON}$, the company is considered to be at risk of bankruptcy; when $Z_{BAN} < Z_{NON}$, the risk does not exist and the company's financial situation is assessed positively.

Using a forward stepwise regression method, the following forms of MDA models were estimated:
- for European enterprises:

$$Z_{ban} = -2.98 - 2.71 * X_1 - 6.65 * X_2 - 0.67 * X_3 + 1.9 * X_6 + 0.89 * X_7$$

$$Z_{non} = -2.99 + 7.12 * X_1 + 1.15 * X_2 + 2.21 * X_3 + 0.51 * X_6 + 2.0 * X_7$$

- for Asian enterprises:

$$Z_{ban} = -10.23 + 2.59 * X_6 - 3.15 * X_8 - 9.16 * X_{10} + 0.19 * X_{14} - 0.021 * X_{18}$$

$$Z_{non} = -10.72 + 1.32 * X_6 + 4.89 * X_8 + 6.45 * X_{10} + 1.73 * X_{14} + 0.192 * X_{18}$$

- for Latin American enterprises:

$$Z_{ban} = -4.15 - 1.25*X_1 - 2.19*X_3 - 3.95*X_4 + 1.9*X_6 + 1.29*X_{16}$$

$$Z_{non} = -4.59 + 9.37*X_1 + 4.17*X_3 + 0.55*X_4 + 0.51*X_6 + 3.32*X_{16}$$

It is worth noting that all three models comprise five financial ratios, but for Asian enterprises, the model contains very different ratios than is the case for European and Latin American firms. The models for European and Latin American companies share the three same ratios (with different coefficients): X_1, X_3, and X_6.

In the second step, the logit model (LOG) was estimated. This model was also developed using forward stepwise regression. For individual samples of enterprises, the following forms of this model have been estimated:
- for European firms:

$$Z = 2.0 - 10.19*X_1 - 4.58*X_3 - 0.57*X_4$$

- for Asian firms:

$$Z = -1.12 - 0.29*X_2 - 7.21*X_{15} - 1.83*X_{18}$$

- for Latin American firms:

$$Z = 1.25 - 12.05*X_1 - 0.87*X_4 - 2.78*X_{12}$$

The third type of model of a group of statistical methods developed to predict the bankruptcy of companies was a PROB. Like the first two models, it was also estimated using forward stepwise regression. This model has the following functions for each group of firms:
- for European entities:

$$Z = 1.13 - 5.61*X_1 - 2.08*X_3 - 0.34*X_4$$

- for Asian entities:

$$Z = 0.61 - 1.28*X_2 - 4.73*X_{15} - 0.98*X_{18}$$

- for Latin American entities:

$$Z = 1.44 - 7.02*X_1 - 0.48*X_3 - 1.18*X_4$$

Once again, it is interesting to observe that in case of the PROB for European and Latin American firms, the models share as many as three common financial ratios (X_1, X_3, X_4), and in case of logit models two ratios are the

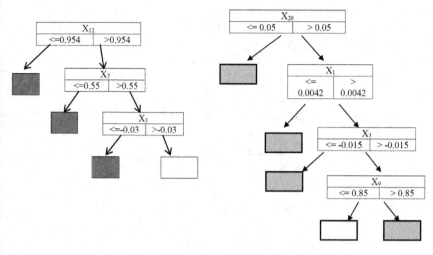

Figure 5.1 The structure of the C&RT decision tree for European (left side) and Latin American (right side) enterprises. Note: Gray box indicates companies at risk of bankruptcy; white box, nonbankrupt firms.

Source: Own studies.

same (X_1 and X_4), the models for Asian companies comprise distinct ratios in both cases (logit and probit).

Other models developed from a group of statistical methods are the decision tree model (C&RT) and the RF model. Figure 5.1 shows the structure of the decision tree model for European and Latin American samples of firms. Figure 5.2 shows the structure of such decision trees for the analysis of Asian companies. As can be seen, all three models are very different and all share only one common financial ratio: X_3.

The RF model is based on the action of many decision trees. The author assumed the use of 100 decision trees and four predictors (financial ratios) in the RF method. The following four explanatory variables demonstrated the greatest importance in predicting the bankruptcy of companies:

- for European firms: X_2, X_3, X_5, X_8
- for Asian entities: X_1, X_2, X_7, X_{18}
- for Latin American enterprises: X_9, X_{11}, X_{13}, X_{19}

As in case of C&RT models, the RF models share no similarities among the three samples of enterprises.

The next five models created are models of soft computing techniques. The purpose of these models is the classification of enterprises into one of two groups of companies: endangered or not at risk of bankruptcy. The output of these models in the learning process takes the value of zero or one. It should be noted, however, that the output values generated by the tested

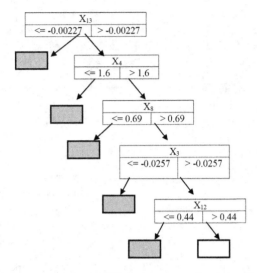

Figure 5.2 The structure of the C&RT decision tree for Asian firms. Note: Gray box indicates companies at risk of bankruptcy; white box, nonbankrupt firms.

Source: Own studies.

model with the use of testing samples are not equal to the values specified in the learning sample but take values from the interval (0,1). The author has adopted a threshold boundary of 0.5, which means that firms for which the model output adopts values below 0.5 are classified as being at risk of bankruptcy. In contrast, model output values above 0.5 indicate that these companies are nonbankrupt ones.

Inputs to the artificial neural network models and genetic algorithms models are based on the correlation matrix by choosing only those features that are poorly correlated with each other and strongly correlated with the grouping variable, representing information about the threat of bankruptcy or lack of risk of bankruptcy. This approach ensured the selection of such features, which do not duplicate information provided by other financial ratios, while being good representatives of the ratios not selected as diagnostic. On this basis, the following financial ratios were set:

- for European companies: X_1, X_6, X_7, X_{12}
- for Asian firms: X_1, X_{12}, X_{14}, X_{18}
- for Latin American enterprises: X_1, X_4, X_6, X_7, X_{12}, X_{16}

Due to the large number of models at this stage in our research, we presented graphically the architecture of selected models only, while all models will be characterized using the description n – h – o, where:

- n – number of neurons in the input layer,
- h – number of neurons in the hidden layer,
- o – number of neurons in the output layer.

Using the above assumptions for our study, the following models were developed:

- Artificial feedforward multilayer neural network (MLP ANN):

  for European firms 4 – 9 – 2 (Figure 5.3),
  for Asian entities 4 – 9 – 2 (Figure 5.3),
  for Latin American enterprises 6 – 12 – 6 – 2 (This model comprises two hidden layers);

- Artificial neural network based on genetic algorithms (GA ANN): This model is based on the multilayer perceptron structure in which all the learning samples used a genetic algorithm with the following

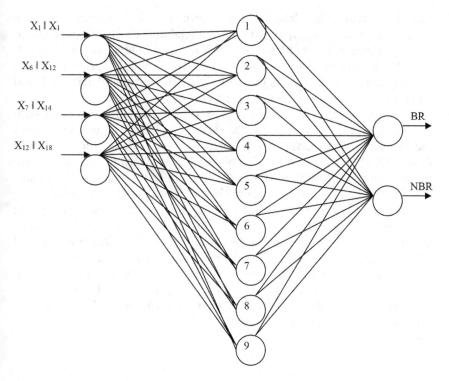

Figure 5.3 Architecture of artificial feedforward multilayer neural network for analysis of companies from Europe (left side of entry variables) and Asia (right side of entry variables).

Source: Own studies.

parameters: the number of generations 100 and the size of the population 50. This model has the following architecture:

for European entities $4 - 4 - 1$,
for Asian firms $4 - 4 - 1$,
for Latin American companies $6 - 6 - 1$.

- Support vector machines (SVM): in all analyzed samples of firms, the support vector machine was estimated using support vectors with a radial basis function (RBF). This model differed in the number of predictor variables and vectors in the various samples of companies:

  for European firms: 20 predictors (financial ratios from X_1 to X_{20}); number of support vectors – 47,
  for Asian entities: 20 predictors (financial ratios from X_1 to X_{20}); number of support vectors – 39,
  for Latin American firms: 20 predictors (financial ratios from X_1 to X_{20}); number of support vectors – 59.

In all three types of models, the architecture of models for Latin American enterprises is the most expanded. The artificial neural network model comprises as much as two hidden layers with 12 and 6 hidden neurons (the network for European and Asian firms comprise only one hidden layer with nine neurons – Figure 5.3). In the case of the artificial neural network based on genetic algorithms, the model for Latin American firms comprises two more hidden neurons than is the case for the models of the two other samples of enterprises. In addition, the support vector machines model uses the highest number of support vectors, 59, while the model for European firms uses 47 and for Asian firms only 39. It is evidence that the process of forecasting the risk of bankruptcy for firms in Latin America is the most complicated due to dynamic changes in the environment of enterprises.

The next model developed in the group of methods of soft computing techniques was the fuzzy logic model. This model requires no assumptions about the learning process and is developed based on expert knowledge and experience. It should be noted that this is one of the first attempts to use fuzzy logic to predict the bankruptcy of enterprises in all three regions in this study. Knowledge is a key element of the expert model. To better distinguish this type of model from previous bankruptcy prediction models, several unique features of the expert model based on the operation of fuzzy logic are presented:

- explicit knowledge;
- the ability to explain how to solve the problem (as opposed to the artificial neural network model that operates on a "black box" principle);
- the ability to solve problems not based on an algorithm written explicitly but using different methods of inference (reasoning); and

• the ability to use mainly the processing of symbols and, to a lesser degree, of numerical calculations.

The decision-making center of the fuzzy logic model is the basis of rules taking the form of IF – THEN, written by the author, in which expert knowledge is stored and required for an effective, factually correct interpretation of the financial ratios at the model input. The output of the model is a variable representing the forecast of the financial situation of the audited company.

For each input – that is, the financial ratio – the author defined two fuzzy sets: BAD and GOOD and their membership functions. Fuzzy sets and the shape of membership functions have been arbitrarily set by the author. The assessment ratio (as "good" or "bad") is based on statistical analysis. The author counted the value of the first and third quartile for each financial ratio, separately for companies in good financial condition and separately for companies threatened with bankruptcy for one, two and three years back. The third quartile value for bankrupt companies has served as a critical value (the index has been recognized as "bad" below the critical value). These values are shown in Table 5.2.

For each sample of enterprises, the author has developed 25 decision-making "IF–THEN" rules (the rules are given in Appendix).

The last type of created bankruptcy forecasting model in the group of methods of soft computing techniques is the SOM model. Using a learning

Table 5.2 Critical values of financial ratios used in the fuzzy logic model

Indicator symbol	Critical value in fuzzy logic model
For European companies	
X_1	0.015
X_2	0.11
X_5	0.75
X_8	1.05
X_{13}	0.01
For Asian firms	
X_1	0.023
X_3	0.153
X_{10}	0.214
X_{12}	0.65
X_{17}	0.8
For Latin American enterprises	
X_1	0.028
X_6	0.87
X_7	0.475
X_8	1.12
X_{13}	0.035

Source: Own studies.

C	C	C	C	D	D	E	F	F	F
C	C	C	C	D	D	E	F	F	F
B	B	B	B	C	D	E	F	F	F
B	B	B	B	C	D	E	E	E	E
B	B	B	B	B	C	C	D	D	D
A	A	A	A	A	B	B	C	D	D
A	A	A	A	A	B	B	C	D	D
A	A	A	A	A	B	B	C	C	C
A	A	A	A	A	B	B	C	C	C
A	A	A	A	A	B	B	C	C	C

Figure 5.4 Map of the self-organizing network with designated classes of risk of bankruptcy for European firms.

Source: Own studies.

sample comprising 200 companies described by 20 financial ratios (from X_1 to X_{20} in Table 5.1), a model of size 10 neurons (rows) × 10 neurons (columns) was developed for European firms (Figure 5.4), Asian entities (Figure 5.5), and Latin American enterprises (Figure 5.6). On the map of all three models, the author distinguished the following six risk classes:

- A – the highest level of credibility (a company with outstanding credit reliability);
- B – very good solvency of the enterprise;

C	C	C	C	D	D	E	F	F	F
C	C	C	C	D	D	E	F	F	F
B	B	B	C	D	D	E	F	F	F
B	B	B	C	D	D	E	E	E	E
B	B	B	C	D	D	D	D	D	D
B	B	B	B	C	C	C	D	D	D
A	A	A	A	B	B	C	D	D	D
A	A	A	A	B	B	C	C	C	C
A	A	A	A	B	B	C	C	C	C
A	A	A	A	B	B	C	C	C	C

Figure 5.5 Map of the self-organizing network with designated classes of risk of bankruptcy for Asian companies.

Source: Own studies.

C	C	C	D	E	E	F	F	F	F
C	C	C	D	E	E	F	F	F	F
B	B	C	D	E	E	F	F	F	F
B	B	C	D	D	E	F	F	F	F
B	B	C	C	D	E	E	E	E	E
B	B	B	B	D	D	D	D	E	E
B	B	B	B	C	D	D	D	D	D
A	A	A	B	C	D	D	D	D	D
A	A	A	B	C	C	C	C	D	D
A	A	A	B	C	B	B	C	C	C

Figure 5.6 Map of the self-organizing network with designated classes of risk of bankruptcy for Latin American firms.

Source: Own studies.

- C – average solvency capabilities with visible risk;
- D – the possible repayment of liabilities, increased uncertainty, and problematic credit exposure;
- E – liabilities are at high risk, and the company is vulnerable to bankruptcy; and
- F – a bankrupt company with unacceptable risk.

As a result, the manager can use this map not only to evaluate the risk of bankruptcy of the analyzed company but also to assess the good financial situation of the company and to visualize the trajectory of the risk class migrations during the "life" of the enterprises. In addition, the black bold line is the distinguishing area in which the company is at risk of bankruptcy and the zone of good economic situation of enterprises.

Although the structure of the SOM is the same for all three samples of firms (10 × 10 neurons), it is interesting to note that the number of specific risk classes differ in all three models. As can be seen, the highest number of high-risk bankruptcies (classes D, E, and F) occurs in the SOM model for Latin American firms. Once again this is evidence that the enterprises in Latin America are much more at the risk of financial failure due to dynamic changes in the markets of Latin American countries than the companies in the other two analyzed regions.

Tables 5.3, 5.4, and 5.5 present the results of all created models for European, Asian, and Latin American enterprises obtained by testing the samples separately for three forecasting periods: one year, two years, and three years prior to bankruptcy.

Analyzing the results for European firms (Table 5.3), it can be seen that the highest effectiveness was achieved using the fuzzy logic model, with

Table 5.3 The results of the effectiveness of models for European firms (testing sample)

European firms	One year before			Two years before			Three years before		
	S	E1	E2	S	E1	E2	S	E1	E2
MDA	95.33%	5.33% (16)	4.00% (12)	93.00%	8.00% (24)	6.00% (18)	87.33%	12.00% (36)	13.33% (40)
LOG	92.00%	10.00% (30)	6.00% (18)	90.00%	12.00% (36)	8.00% (24)	83.00%	18.67% (56)	15.33% (46)
PROB	89.67%	11.33% (34)	9.33% (28)	87.67%	13.33% (40)	11.33% (34)	81.33%	19.33% (58)	18.00% (54)
C&RT	91.33%	9.33% (28)	8.00% (24)	88.67%	12.67% (38)	10.00% (30)	80.00%	18.67% (56)	21.33% (64)
RF	90.67%	10.67% (32)	8.00% (24)	88.00%	13.33% (40)	10.67% (32)	81.67%	20.00% (60)	16.67% (50)
SVM	91.67%	5.33% (16)	11.33% (34)	89.67%	6.67% (20)	14.00% (42)	79.67%	18.67% (56)	22.00% (66)
MLP ANN	94.67%	4.67% (14)	6.00% (18)	92.00%	7.33% (22)	8.67% (26)	85.33%	14.00% (42)	15.33% (46)
FL	97.33%	2.00% (6)	3.33% (10)	93.67%	6.00% (18)	6.67% (20)	90.00%	9.33% (28)	10.67% (32)
GA ANN	91.00%	6.00% (18)	12.00% (36)	88.00%	9.33% (28)	14.67% (44)	82.67%	14.00% (42)	20.67% (62)
SOM	95.67%	4.00% (12)	4.67% (14)	93.00%	6.00% (18)	8.00% (24)	89.00%	9.33% (28)	12.67% (38)

Legend: MDA – multivariate discriminant analysis; LOG – logit model; PROB – probit model; C&RT – Classification and Regression Trees; RF – Random forests; SVM – support vector machines; MLP ANN – multilayer perceptron of artificial neural networks; FL – fuzzy logic; GA ANN – genetic algorithms in artificial neural networks; SOM – self-organizing map. Numbers in brackets mean number of enterprises wrongly classified.

Source: Own studies and calculations.

97.33% correct classifications one year before bankruptcy, 93.67% correct forecasting in analysis two years prior to financial failure and 90.00% in a forecasting horizon of three years. What it is more important to note is that the fuzzy logic and SOM models have the fewest Type I errors. Such errors indicate how many bankrupt companies are classified as nonbankrupt firms. Type I errors, for obvious financial reasons, are far more dangerous than Type II errors. Based on overall effectiveness and Type I errors among all ten models, the fuzzy logic and SOM models are shown to be the best bankruptcy predictive techniques for European companies in all three years prior to bankruptcy. It is also interesting to note that most soft computing models generated many fewer Type I errors than did traditional statistical models (aside from the multivariate discriminant analysis model). Among statistical models, the multivariate discriminant model has the best predictive properties. It is the third best model (after the SOM and FL models), if we take into account overall effectiveness and Type I errors. Another important aspect to explore is how the models performed in a long forecasting horizon. It is worth noting that the fuzzy logic and SOM models show the smallest decrease in overall effectiveness with the increase in the forecasting period from one to three years prior to bankruptcy, with a decrease of 7.33 and 6.67 percentage points, respectively.

Looking at the results obtained by five statistical and five soft computing models in the testing sample of Asian enterprises (Table 5.4), very similar tendencies to European firms can be observed. Although the overall effectiveness is slightly worse than in the case of models for European companies, results are still very good. The fuzzy logic model is again characterized by the highest effectiveness (96.33% one year, 94.67% two years, and 91.00% three years before bankruptcy). Among statistical models, the multivariate discriminant model has best predictive power, with 94.00% effectiveness one year prior bankruptcy, 91.67% correct classifications two years before the financial failure of enterprises, and 86.67% effectiveness in the longest forecasting horizon of three years. The same as in the case of European firms, the soft computing models generated many fewer Type I errors than the statistical models. The fuzzy logic model and SOM models show the smallest decrease in effectiveness, while increasing the forecasting horizon from one year to three years prior to bankruptcy (5.33 percentage points for the FL model and 5.66 for the SOM model).

Evaluating the results obtained with the use of models developed for Latin American firms (Table 5.5), the following observations can be noted: (a) once again, the fuzzy logic and SOM models outperform the other eight forecasting models; (b) among statistical models, the multivariate discriminant model shows the best results; (c) the overall effectiveness of all ten models is slightly worse one year prior to bankruptcy compared to the effectiveness received in testing Asian and European enterprises (e.g., for the fuzzy logic model, it is 1 percentage point worse than the Asian sample and 2 percentage points worse than the European sample) and much worse in the forecasting horizon

Table 5.4 The results of the effectiveness of models for Asian firms (testing sample)

Asian firms	One year before			Two years before			Three years before		
	S	E1	E2	S	E1	E2	S	E1	E2
MDA	94.00%	6.67% (20)	5.33% (16)	91.67%	8.67% (26)	8.00% (24)	86.67%	14.00% (42)	12.67% (38)
LOG	91.33%	11.33% (34)	6.00% (18)	88.33%	13.33% (40)	10.00% (30)	82.33%	18.67% (56)	16.67% (50)
PROB	89.33%	12.00% (36)	9.33% (28)	87.00%	14.00% (42)	12.00% (36)	81.67%	19.33% (58)	17.33% (52)
C&RT	90.33%	10.67% (32)	8.67% (26)	87.33%	13.33% (40)	12.00% (36)	80.00%	20.67% (62)	19.33% (58)
RF	90.33%	10.00% (30)	9.33% (28)	89.00%	11.33% (34)	10.67% (32)	80.33%	20.00% (60)	19.33% (58)
SVM	91.00%	7.33% (22)	10.67% (32)	88.00%	9.33% (28)	14.67% (44)	79.00%	21.33% (64)	20.67% (62)
MLP ANN	94.00%	4.00% (12)	8.00% (24)	92.33%	6.67% (20)	8.67% (26)	83.00%	16.00% (48)	18.00% (54)
FL	96.33%	2.67% (8)	4.67% (14)	94.67%	4.67% (14)	6.00% (18)	91.00%	8.00% (24)	10.00% (30)
GA ANN	90.67%	6.00% (18)	12.67% (38)	87.00%	10.00% (30)	16.00% (48)	83.33%	15.33% (46)	18.00% (54)
SOM	94.33%	4.67% (14)	6.67% (20)	92.33%	6.00% (18)	9.33% (28)	88.67%	8.67% (26)	14.00% (42)

Legend: MDA – multivariate discriminant analysis; LOG – logit model; PROB – probit model; C&RT – Classification and Regression Trees; RF – Random forests; SVM – support vector machines; MLP ANN – multilayer perceptron of artificial neural networks; FL – fuzzy logic; GA ANN – genetic algorithms in artificial neural networks; SOM – self-organizing map. Numbers in brackets mean number of enterprises wrongly classified.

Source: Own studies and calculations.

Table 5.5 The results of the effectiveness of models for Latin American firms (testing sample)

Latin American firms	One year before			Two years before			Three years before		
	S	E1	E2	S	E1	E2	S	E1	E2
MDA	93.33%	7.33% (22)	6.00% (18)	90.33%	10.00% (30)	9.33% (28)	81.67%	16.67% (50)	20.00% (60)
LOG	89.67%	11.33% (34)	9.33% (28)	86.00%	15.33% (46)	12.67% (38)	78.67%	23.33% (70)	19.33% (58)
PROB	88.67%	12.67% (38)	10.00% (30)	84.33%	17.33% (52)	14.00% (42)	75.67%	24.67% (74)	24.00% (72)
C&RT	88.00%	12.00% (36)	12.00% (36)	85.00%	15.33% (46)	14.67% (44)	75.00%	24.00% (72)	26.00% (78)
RF	86.33%	14.00% (42)	13.33% (40)	82.67%	17.33% (52)	17.33% (52)	73.33%	27.33% (82)	26.00% (78)
SVM	89.67%	8.00% (24)	12.67% (38)	86.67%	10.67% (32)	16.00% (48)	74.33%	24.00% (72)	27.33% (82)
MLP ANN	93.00%	6.00% (18)	8.00% (24)	90.00%	8.67% (26)	11.33% (34)	82.33%	16.00% (48)	19.33% (58)
FL	95.33%	4.00% (12)	5.33% (16)	93.00%	6.00% (18)	8.00% (24)	86.67%	12.67% (38)	14.00% (42)
GA ANN	88.33%	9.33% (28)	14.00% (42)	85.67%	11.33% (34)	17.33% (52)	78.33%	19.33% (58)	24.00% (72)
SOM	94.33%	5.33% (16)	6.00% (18)	91.33%	8.00% (24)	9.33% (28)	84.00%	13.33% (40)	18.67% (56)

Legend: MDA – multivariate discriminant analysis; LOG – logit model; PROB – probit model; C&RT – Classification and Regression Trees; RF – Random forests; SVM – support vector machines; MLP ANN – multilayer perceptron of artificial neural networks; FL – fuzzy logic; GA ANN – genetic algorithms in artificial neural networks; SOM – self-organizing map. Numbers in brackets mean number of enterprises wrongly classified.

Source: Own studies and calculations.

of three years prior to bankruptcy (none of the models gained higher than 87.00% effectiveness in this forecast period, while in the Asian sample two models and in the European sample, as much as three models received such high results); and (d) as a result of our previous conclusion, it can be said that models for Latin American firms show a relatively higher decrease in forecasting performance, which could be caused by the higher complexity of markets and the complexity of the forecasting process itself.

5.5 Conclusions

Digital technologies effectively deal with imprecisely defined problems, incomplete data, imprecision and uncertainty. The issue of predicting financial risk has all of the above characteristics. In addition, digital technologies are suitable for use in systems which are designed to fit certain internal parameters to changing environmental conditions in a dynamic way (so-called learning systems). Presented study shows how the development of ICT can improve the reliability of such financial risk forecasting models. The financial situation of enterprises is affected by many internal and external factors, which cannot be defined precisely and unambiguously. The traditional zero-one (good/bad) evaluation criteria for ratios have lost their relevance. In addition, a finding that a company is in a "good" or "bad" financial situation is imprecise because in the current economic reality, analysts rarely have to deal with 100% "good" or 100% "bad" enterprises. Majority of the models are based on the classical set theory that makes it difficult to determine the precise degree of risk. It is evident that fuzzy sets models are superior to traditional forecasting models in terms of overall effectiveness but also due to its "open form" structure. The programmed fuzzy models are presented in the form of "open" applications with unlimited possibilities of adaptations to its own needs by entities at different financial markets.

Although many studies have aimed to propose new models for financial risk prediction, very few have focused on creating and testing models with such a wide variety of forecasting techniques (traditional versus artificial intelligence ones) and, more importantly, by estimating these models separately for three different regions worldwide. The proposed models can be widely used in Latin America, Europe, and Asia by scientists, economists, financial analysts, and decision-makers. Presented empirical study reveals that in all three samples of enterprises, the most effective models are the fuzzy logic and SOM models in both the short-term (one year prior to financial failure) and long-term forecasting horizon (two and three years prior to bankruptcy). Additionally, soft computing models showed fewer Type I errors than Type II errors, as opposed to the traditional models, which generate more Type I errors than Type II errors. In other words, traditional models generate a higher cost of the misclassification of enterprises than do artificial intelligence models.

Another important conclusion is that the forecasting models for European and Latin American enterprises very often use the same type of financial ratios, which means that similar financial information is necessary to evaluate the process of forecasting the risk of financial failure. On the other hand, the models for European firms are much more stable with the increase of the forecasting horizon than the models for Latin American companies. This can be a sign that Latin American enterprises operate in more dynamic and unpredictable environments and markets. In case of the models for Asian firms, they use different types of financial ratios than the models for the other two regions studied, but they show a similar stability over the forecast periods as the models for European enterprises.

This chapter's conclusions show the enormous role of digital technologies in forecasting the company's financial situation to help efficiently process the information held by the enterprise.

Acknowledgment

This work has been prepared within the grant project No. 2015/19/B/HS4/00377, "Trajectories of life and the collapse of companies in Poland and in the world – identification, evaluation and forecast." Research funded by the National Science Centre in Poland (Narodowe Centrum Nauki).

Appendix

The set of 25 decision-making "IF–THEN" rules for each sample of enterprises:

• for European firms:

(1) If $X_1 <= 0.015$ and $X_2 <= 0.11$ and $X_5 <= 0.75$ and $X_8 <= 1.05$ and $X_{13} <= 0.01$ then 0

(2) If $X_1 <= 0.015$ and $X_2 <= 0.11$ and $X_5 <= 0.75$ and $X_8 <= 1.05$ and $X_{13} > 0.01$ then 0

(3) If $X_1 <= 0.015$ and $X_2 <= 0.11$ and $X_5 <= 0.75$ and $X_8 > 1.05$ and $X_{13} > 0.01$ then 0

(4) If $X_1 <= 0.015$ and $X_2 <= 0.11$ and $X_5 > 0.75$ and $X_8 > 1.05$ and $X_{13} > 0.01$ then 1

(5) If $X_1 <= 0.015$ and $X_2 > 0.11$ and $X_5 > 0.75$ and $X_8 > 1.05$ and $X_{13} > 0.01$ then 1

(6) If $X_1 > 0.015$ and $X_2 > 0.11$ and $X_5 > 0.75$ and $X_8 > 1.05$ and $X_{13} > 0.01$ then 1

(7) If $X_1 <= 0.015$ and $X_2 <= 0.11$ and $X_5 > 0.75$ and $X_8 <= 1.05$ and $X_{13} > 0.01$ then 0

(8) If $X_1 <= 0.015$ and $X_2 > 0.11$ and $X_5 <= 0.75$ and $X_8 <= 1.05$ and $X_{13} > 0.01$ then 0

(9) If $X_1 > 0.015$ and $X_2 <= 0.11$ and $X_5 <= 0.75$ and $X_8 <= 1.05$ and $X_{13} > 0.01$ then 0

(10) If $X_1 <= 0.015$ and $X_2 <= 0.11$ and $X_5 <= 0.75$ and $X_8 > 1.05$ and X_{13} $<= 0.01$ then 0

(11) If $X_1 <= 0.015$ and $X_2 <= 0.11$ and $X_5 > 0.75$ and $X_8 <= 1.05$ and X_{13} $<= 0.01$ then 0

(12) If $X_1 <= 0.015$ and $X_2 > 0.11$ and $X_5 <= 0.75$ and $X_8 <= 1.05$ and X_{13} $<= 0.01$ then 0

(13) If $X_1 > 0.015$ and $X_2 <= 0.11$ and $X_5 <= 0.75$ and $X_8 <= 1.05$ and X_{13} $<= 0.01$ then 0

(14) If $X_1 <= 0.015$ and $X_2 > 0.11$ and $X_5 > 0.75$ and $X_8 > 1.05$ and $X_{13} <= 0.01$ then 1

(15) If $X_1 <= 0.015$ and $X_2 <= 0.11$ and $X_5 > 0.75$ and $X_8 > 1.05$ and $X_{13} <= 0.01$ then 0

(16) If $X_1 <= 0.015$ and $X_2 > 0.11$ and $X_5 <= 0.75$ and $X_8 > 1.05$ and $X_{13} <= 0.01$ then 0

(17) If $X_1 <= 0.015$ and $X_2 > 0.11$ and $X_5 > 0.75$ and $X_8 <= 1.05$ and $X_{13} <= 0.01$ then 0

(18) If $X_1 > 0.015$ and $X_2 <= 0.11$ and $X_5 > 0.75$ and $X_8 <= 1.05$ and $X_{13} <= 0.01$ then 0

(19) If $X_1 > 0.015$ and $X_2 <= 0.11$ and $X_5 <= 0.75$ and $X_8 > 1.05$ and $X_{13} <= 0.01$ then 0

(20) If $X_1 > 0.015$ and $X_2 <= 0.11$ and $X_5 <= 0.75$ and $X_8 > 1.05$ and $X_{13} > 0.01$ then 1

(21) If $X_1 > 0.015$ and $X_2 > 0.11$ and $X_5 <= 0.75$ and $X_8 > 1.05$ and $X_{13} > 0.01$ then 1

(22) If $X_1 > 0.015$ and $X_2 > 0.11$ and $X_5 <= 0.75$ and $X_8 <= 1.05$ and $X_{13} > 0.01$ then 1

(23) If $X_1 > 0.015$ and $X_2 > 0.11$ and $X_5 > 0.75$ and $X_8 <= 1.05$ and $X_{13} <= 0.01$ then 1

(24) If $X_1 > 0.015$ and $X_2 > 0.11$ and $X_5 <= 0.75$ and $X_8 > 1.05$ and $X_{13} <= 0.01$ then 1

(25) If $X_1 > 0.015$ and $X_2 <= 0.11$ and $X_5 > 0.75$ and $X_8 > 1.05$ and $X_{13} > 0.01$ then 1

- For Far-East Asian firms:

  (1) If $X_1 <= 0.023$ and $X_3 <= 0.153$ and $X_{10} <= 0.214$ and $X_{12} <= 0.65$ and $X_{17} <= 0.8$ then 0

  (2) If $X_1 <= 0.023$ and $X_3 <= 0.153$ and $X_{10} <= 0.214$ and $X_{12} <= 0.65$ and $X_{17} > 0.8$ then 0

  (3) If $X_1 <= 0.023$ and $X_3 <= 0.153$ and $X_{10} <= 0.214$ and $X_{12} > 0.65$ and $X_{17} > 0.8$ then 0

  (4) If $X_1 <= 0.023$ and $X_3 <= 0.153$ and $X_{10} > 0.214$ and $X_{12} > 0.65$ and $X_{17} > 0.8$ then 1

  (5) If $X_1 <= 0.023$ and $X_3 > 0.153$ and $X_{10} > 0.214$ and $X_{12} > 0.65$ and $X_{17} > 0.8$ then 1

(6) If $X_1 > 0.023$ and $X_3 > 0.153$ and $X_{10} > 0.214$ and $X_{12} > 0.65$ and $X_{17} > 0.8$ then 1

(7) If $X_1 <= 0.023$ and $X_3 <= 0.153$ and $X_{10} > 0.214$ and $X_{12} <= 0.65$ and $X_{17} > 0.8$ then 0

(8) If $X_1 <= 0.023$ and $X_3 > 0.153$ and $X_{10} <= 0.214$ and $X_{12} <= 0.65$ and $X_{17} > 0.8$ then 0

(9) If $X_1 > 0.023$ and $X_3 <= 0.153$ and $X_{10} <= 0.214$ and $X_{12} <= 0.65$ and $X_{17} > 0.8$ then 0

(10) If $X_1 <= 0.023$ and $X_3 <= 0.153$ and $X_{10} <= 0.214$ and $X_{12} > 0.65$ and $X_{17} <= 0.8$ then 0

(11) If $X_1 <= 0.023$ and $X_3 <= 0.153$ and $X_{10} > 0.214$ and $X_{12} <= 0.65$ and $X_{17} <= 0.8$ then 0

(12) If $X_1 <= 0.023$ and $X_3 > 0.153$ and $X_{10} <= 0.214$ and $X_{12} <= 0.65$ and $X_{17} <= 0.8$ then 0

(13) If $X_1 > 0.023$ and $X_3 <= 0.153$ and $X_{10} <= 0.214$ and $X_{12} <= 0.65$ and $X_{17} <= 0.8$ then 0

(14) If $X_1 <= 0.023$ and $X_3 > 0.153$ and $X_{10} > 0.214$ and $X_{12} > 0.65$ and $X_{17} <= 0.8$ then 1

(15) If $X_1 <= 0.023$ and $X_3 <= 0.153$ and $X_{10} > 0.214$ and $X_{12} > 0.65$ and $X_{17} <= 0.8$ then 0

(16) If $X_1 <= 0.023$ and $X_3 > 0.153$ and $X_{10} <= 0.214$ and $X_{12} > 0.65$ and $X_{17} <= 0.8$ then 0

(17) If $X_1 <= 0.023$ and $X_3 > 0.153$ and $X_{10} > 0.214$ and $X_{12} <= 0.65$ and $X_{17} <= 0.8$ then 0

(18) If $X_1 > 0.023$ and $X_3 <= 0.153$ and $X_{10} > 0.214$ and $X_{12} <= 0.65$ and $X_{17} <= 0.8$ then 0

(19) If $X_1 > 0.023$ and $X_3 <= 0.153$ and $X_{10} <= 0.214$ and $X_{12} > 0.65$ and $X_{17} <= 0.8$ then 0

(20) If $X_1 > 0.023$ and $X_3 <= 0.153$ and $X_{10} <= 0.214$ and $X_{12} > 0.65$ and $X_{17} > 0.8$ then 1

(21) If $X_1 > 0.023$ and $X_3 > 0.153$ and $X_{10} <= 0.214$ and $X_{12} > 0.65$ and $X_{17} > 0.8$ then 1

(22) If $X_1 > 0.023$ and $X_3 > 0.153$ and $X_{10} <= 0.214$ and $X_{12} <= 0.65$ and $X_{17} > 0.8$ then 1

(23) If $X_1 > 0.023$ and $X_3 > 0.153$ and $X_{10} > 0.214$ and $X_{12} <= 0.65$ and $X_{17} <= 0.8$ then 1

(24) If $X_1 > 0.023$ and $X_3 > 0.153$ and $X_{10} <= 0.214$ and $X_{12} > 0.65$ and $X_{17} <= 0.8$ then 1

(25) If $X_1 > 0.023$ and $X_3 <= 0.153$ and $X_{10} > 0.214$ and $X_{12} > 0.65$ and $X_{17} > 0.8$ then 1

- for Latin American companies:

(1) If $X_1 <= 0.028$ and $X_6 <= 0.87$ and $X_7 <= 0.475$ and $X_8 <= 1.12$ and $X_{13} <= 0.035$ then 0

(2) If $X_1 <= 0.028$ and $X_6 <= 0.87$ and $X_7 <= 0.475$ and $X_8 <= 1.12$ and $X_{13} > 0.035$ then 0

(3) If $X_1 <= 0.028$ and $X_6 <= 0.87$ and $X_7 <= 0.475$ and $X_8 > 1.12$ and $X_{13} > 0.035$ then 0

(4) If $X_1 <= 0.028$ and $X_6 <= 0.87$ and $X_7 > 0.475$ and $X_8 > 1.12$ and $X_{13} > 0.035$ then 1

(5) If $X_1 <= 0.028$ and $X_6 > 0.87$ and $X_7 > 0.475$ and $X_8 > 1.12$ and $X_{13} > 0.035$ then 1

(6) If $X_1 > 0.028$ and $X_6 > 0.87$ and $X_7 > 0.475$ and $X_8 > 1.12$ and $X_{13} > 0.035$ then 1

(7) If $X_1 <= 0.028$ and $X_6 <= 0.87$ and $X_7 > 0.475$ and $X_8 <= 1.12$ and $X_{13} > 0.035$ then 0

(8) If $X_1 <= 0.028$ and $X_6 > 0.87$ and $X_7 <= 0.475$ and $X_8 <= 1.12$ and $X_{13} > 0.035$ then 0

(9) If $X_1 > 0.028$ and $X_6 <= 0.87$ and $X_7 <= 0.475$ and $X_8 <= 1.12$ and $X_{13} > 0.035$ then 0

(10) If $X_1 <= 0.028$ and $X_6 <= 0.87$ and $X_7 <= 0.475$ and $X_8 > 1.12$ and $X_{13} <= 0.035$ then 0

(11) If $X_1 <= 0.028$ and $X_6 <= 0.87$ and $X_7 > 0.475$ and $X_8 <= 1.12$ and $X_{13} <= 0.035$ then 0

(12) If $X_1 <= 0.028$ and $X_6 > 0.87$ and $X_7 <= 0.475$ and $X_8 <= 1.12$ and $X_{13} <= 0.035$ then 0

(13) If $X_1 > 0.028$ and $X_6 <= 0.87$ and $X_7 <= 0.475$ and $X_8 <= 1.12$ and $X_{13} <= 0.035$ then 0

(14) If $X_1 <= 0.028$ and $X_6 > 0.87$ and $X_7 > 0.475$ and $X_8 > 1.12$ and $X_{13} <= 0.035$ then 1

(15) If $X_1 <= 0.028$ and $X_6 <= 0.87$ and $X_7 > 0.475$ and $X_8 > 1.12$ and $X_{13} <= 0.035$ then 0

(16) If $X_1 <= 0.028$ and $X_6 > 0.87$ and $X_7 <= 0.475$ and $X_8 > 1.12$ and $X_{13} <= 0.035$ then 0

(17) If $X_1 <= 0.028$ and $X_6 > 0.87$ and $X_7 > 0.475$ and $X_8 <= 1.12$ and $X_{13} <= 0.035$ then 0

(18) If $X_1 > 0.028$ and $X_6 <= 0.87$ and $X_7 > 0.475$ and $X_8 <= 1.12$ and $X_{13} <= 0.035$ then 0

(19) If $X_1 > 0.028$ and $X_6 <= 0.87$ and $X_7 <= 0.475$ and $X_8 > 1.12$ and $X_{13} <= 0.035$ then 0

(20) If $X_1 > 0.028$ and $X_6 <= 0.87$ and $X_7 <= 0.475$ and $X_8 > 1.12$ and $X_{13} > 0.035$ then 1

(21) If $X_1 > 0.028$ and $X_6 > 0.87$ and $X_7 <= 0.475$ and $X_8 > 1.12$ and $X_{13} > 0.035$ then 1

(22) If $X_1 > 0.028$ and $X_6 > 0.87$ and $X_7 <= 0.475$ and $X_8 <= 1.12$ and $X_{13} > 0.035$ then 1

(23) If $X_1 > 0.028$ and $X_6 > 0.87$ and $X_7 > 0.475$ and $X_8 <= 1.12$ and $X_{13} <= 0.035$ then 1

(24) If $X_1 > 0.028$ and $X_6 > 0.87$ and $X_7 <= 0.475$ and $X_8 > 1.12$ and $X_{13} <= 0.035$ then 1

(25) If $X_1 > 0.028$ and $X_6 <= 0.87$ and $X_7 > 0.475$ and $X_8 > 1.12$ and $X_{13} > 0.035$ then 1

References

Acosta-González, E., & Fernández-Rodríguez, F. (2014). Forecasting financial failure of firms via genetic algorithms. *Computational Economics, 43*, 133–157.

Alaka, H. A., Oyedele, L. O., Owolabi, H. A., Kumar, V., Ajayi, S. O., Akinade, O. O., & Bilal, M. (2018). Systematic review of bankruptcy prediction models: Towards a framework for tool selection. *Expert Systems With Applications. No, 94*, 164–184.

Altman, E. I. (1968). Financial ratios, discriminant analysis and the prediction of corporate bankruptcy. *Journal of Finance, 4*, 589–609.

Altman, E. I. (2018). Applications of distress prediction models: What have we learned after 50 years from the z-score models? *International Journal of Financial Studies, 70*(6), 1–15.

Barboza, F., Kimura, H., & Altman, E. I. (2017). Machine learning models and bankruptcy prediction. *Expert Systems with Applications, 83*, 405–417.

Beaver, W. H. (1966). Financial ratios as predictors of failure. *Journal of Accounting Research, 4*, 71–111.

Berkson, J. (1944). Application of the logistic function to bio-assay. *Journal of the American Statistical Association, 9*, 357–365.

Bliss, C. (1934). The method of probits. *Science, 79*, 409–410.

Breiman, L., Friedman, J., Olshen, R., & Stone, C. (1984). *Classification and regression trees*. Wadsworth International Group.

Chauhan, N., Ravi, V., & Chandra, D. K. (2009). Differential evolution trained wavelet neural networks: Application to bankruptcy prediction in banks. *Expert Systems with Applications, 36*(4), 7659–7665.

Chen, H. J., Huang, S. Y., & Lin, C. S. (2009). Alternative diagnosis of corporate bankruptcy: A neuro fuzzy approach. *Expert Systems with Applications, 36*(4), 7710–7720.

Cortes, C., & Vapnik, V. (1995). Support-vector network. *Machine Learning, 20*, 1–25.

Delen, D., Kuzey, C., & Uyar, A. (2013). Measuring firm performance using financial ratios: A decision tree approach. *Expert Systems with Applications, 40*, 3970–3983.

Dong, M. C., Tian, S., & Chen, C. W. S. (2018). Predicting failure risk using financial ratios: Quantile hazard model approach. *North American Journal of Economics and Finance, 44*, 204–220.

Fischer, R. (1936). The use of multiple measurements in taxonomic problems. *Annals of Eugenics, 7*, 179–188.

Fitzpatrick, P. (1932). *A comparison of the ratios of successful industrial enterprises with those of failed companies*. The Accountants Publishing Company.

Foulke, R. (1933). Three important balance sheet ratios. *Dun & Bradstreet Monthly Review,8*.

Foulke, R. (1934). Three important sales ratios. *Dun & Bradstreet Monthly Review, 5*.

Ho, C. Y., McCarthy, P., Yang, Y., & Ye, X. (2013). Bankruptcy in the pulp and paper industry: market's reaction and prediction. *Empirical Economics*, 45, 1205–1232.

Ho, T. K. (1995). Random decision forests. Proceedings of the 3rd international conference on document analysis and recognition, Montreal, QC, 278–282.

Holland, J. (1975). *Adaptation in natural and artificial systems*. University of Michigan Press.

Horrigan, J. (1968). A short history of financial ratio analysis. *The Accounting Review*, 4, 284–294.

Hosmer, J. R., Lemeshow, S., & Sturdivant, R. X. (2013). *Applied logistic regression*. John Wiley & Sons.

Hua, Z., Wang, Y., Xu, X., Zhang, B., & Liang, L. (2007). Predicting corporate financial distress based on integration of support vector machine and logistic regression. *Expert Systems with Applications*, 33(2), 4434–4440.

Jackson, R. H. G., & Wood, A. (2013). The performance of insolvency prediction and credit risk models in the UK: A comparative study. *The British Accounting Review*, 45, 183–202.

Jardin, P. (2009). Bankruptcy prediction models: How to choose the most relevant variables? *Bankers, Markets & Investors*, 98, 39–46.

Jardin, P. (2017). Dynamics of firm financial evolution and bankruptcy prediction. *Expert Systems With Applications*, 75, 25–43.

Jayasekera, R. (2018). Prediction of company failure: Past, present and promising directions for the future. *International Review of Financial Analysis*, 55, 196–208.

Kieschnick, R., La Plante, M., & Moussawi, R. (2013). Working capital management and shareholders' wealth. *Review of Finance*, 17, 1827–1852.

Kim, H., & Gu, Z. (2006). Predicting restaurant bankruptcy: A logit model in comparison with a discriminant model. *Journal of Hospitality and Tourism Research*, 30(4), 474–493.

Kim, M. J., & Kang, D. K. (2010). Ensemble with neural networks for bankruptcy prediction. *Expert Systems with Applications*, 37(4), 3373–3379.

Laitinen, E. K., Lukason, O., & Suvas, A. (2014). Behaviour of financial ratios in firm failure process: An international comparison. *International Journal of Finance and Accounting*, 3(2), 122–131.

Lee, Y. (2007). Application of support vector machine to corporate credit rating prediction. *Expert Systems with Applications*, 33(1), 67–74.

Lee, S., & Choi, W. S. (2013). A multi-industry bankruptcy prediction model using back-propagation neural network and multivariate discriminant analysis. *Expert Systems with Applications*, 40(8), 2941–2946.

Lensberg, T., Eilifsen, A., & McKee, T. E. (2006). Bankruptcy theory development and classification via genetic programming. *European Journal of Operational Research*, 169, 677–697.

Liang, D., & Shih, G. (2016). Financial ratios and corporate governance indicators in bankruptcy prediction: A comprehensive study. *European Journal of Operational Research*, 252, 561–572.

Lin, W. Y., Hu, Y. H., & Tsai, C. F. (2012). Machine learning in financial crisis prediction: A survey. *IEEE Transactions on Systems, Man, and Cybernetics*, 42(4), 421–436.

Luo, C., Wu, D., & Wu, D. (2017). A deep learning approach for credit scoring using credit default swaps. *Engineering Applications of Artificial Intelligence*, 65, 465–470.

Lyandres, E., & Zhdanov, A. (2013). Investment opportunities and bankruptcy prediction. *Journal of Financial Markets, 16,* 439–476.

Merwin, C.L. (1942). Financing Small Corporations: In Five Manufacturing Industries, 1926-1936. *New York, National Bureau of Economic Research,* 1–191.

Mihalovic, M. (2016). Performance comparison of multiple discriminant analysis and logit models in bankruptcy prediction. *Economics and Sociology, 9*(4), 101–118.

Min, J., & Lee, Y. (2005). Bankruptcy prediction using support vector machine with optimal choice of kernel-function parameters. *Expert Systems with Applications, 28*(4), 603–614.

Min, S., Lee, J., & Han, I. (2006). Hybrid genetic algorithms and support vector machines for bankruptcy prediction. *Expert Systems with Applications, 31*(3), 652–660.

Ooghe, H., & Balcaen, S. (2006). 35 years of studies on business failure – An overview of the classic statistical methodologies and their related problems. *The British Accounting Review, 38,* 63–93.

Sayari, N., & Mugan, C. (2017). Industry specific financial distress modeling. *Business Research Quarterly, 20,* 45–62.

Singhal, R., & Zhu, Y. (2013). Bankruptcy risk, costs and corporate diversification. *Journal of Banking and Finance, 37,* 1475–1489.

Sun, L. (2007). A re-evaluation of auditors' opinions versus statistical models in bankruptcy prediction. *Review of Quantitative Finance and Accounting, 28,* 55–78.

Sun, J., Li, H., Huang, Q., & He, K. (2014). Predicting financial distress and corporate failure – A review from the state-of-the-art definitions, modeling, sampling, and featuring approaches. *Knowledge-Based Systems, 57,* 41–56.

Tian, S., Yu, Y., & Guo, H. (2015). Variable selection and corporate bankruptcy forecasts. *Journal of Banking & Finance. No, 52,* 89–100.

Tian, S., & Yu, Y. (2017). Financial ratios and bankruptcy predictions: An international evidence. *International Review of Economics and Finance, 51,* 510–526.

Tsai, C. (2008). Financial decision support using neural networks and support vector machines. *Expert Systems, 25*(4), 380–393.

Tsai, C. F. (2020). Two-stage hybrid learning techniques for bankruptcy prediction. *Statistical Analysis and Data Minin, 13*(6), 565–572.

Wall, A. (1919). Study of credit barometrics. *Federal Reserve Bulletin,* March, 229–243.

Wanke, P., Barros, C. P., & Faria, J. R. (2015). Financial distress drivers in Brazilian banks: A dynamic slacks approach. *European Journal of Operational Research, 240*(1), 258–268.

Warren, M., & Pitts, W. (1943). A logical calculus of ideas immanent in nervous activity. *Bulletin of Mathematical Biophysics, 5*(4), 115–133.

Winakor, A., & Smith, R. (1930). A test analysis of unsuccessful industrial companies. Bulletin. No 31, University of Illinois.

Veganzones, D., & Severin, E. (2018). An investigation of bankruptcy prediction in imbalanced datasets. *Decision Support Systems, 112,* 111–124.

Wu, C., Tzeng, G., Goo, Y., & Fang, W. (2007). A real-valued genetic algorithm to optimize the parameters of support vector machine for predicting bankruptcy. *Expert Systems With Applications, 32*(2), 397–408.

Zadeh, L. (1965). Fuzzy sets. *Information and Control, 8*(3), 338–353.

Zanganeh, T., Rabiee, M., & Zarei, M. (2011). Applying adaptive neuro-fuzzy model for bankruptcy prediction. *International Journal of Computer Applications*, *20*(3), 15–21.

Zelenkov, Y., Fedorova, E., & Chekrizov, D. (2017). Two-step classification method based on genetic algorithm for bankruptcy forecasting. *Expert Systems With Applications*, *88*, 393–401.

Xu, M., & Zhang, C. (2009). Bankruptcy prediction: The case of Japanese listed companies. *Review of Accounting Studies*, *14*, 534–558.

6 Digital financial services, gendered digital divide, and financial inclusion

Evidence from South Asia

Rashmi Umesh Arora

6.1 Introduction

Financial access and an inclusive financial system have a range of benefits and can lead to reduction in poverty and inequality. An inclusive financial system provides opportunities for investment in new or existing businesses, allows households to build savings, increases consumption and improves overall wellbeing (Aghion & Bolton, 1997; Arora, 2014; Banerjee & Newman, 1993; Claessens & Perotti, 2007; Demirguc-Kunt & Levine, 2008; Demirguc-Kunt & Levine, 2009; Galor and Zeira, 1993; Gine & Townsend, 2004; Piketty, 1997).

Theoretically, the assumption is that financial services are accessible to all; therefore, there are no distributional implications. In the real world, however, various complexities such as, high transaction costs, asymmetric information and risk and uncertainty on project outcomes can limit people's access to financial services (Beck & de la Torre, 2006). Several groups of population and regions such as rural areas, elderly, disabled, homeless, and migrants can remain excluded from the financial system. There is also a sharp gender divide in access to financial services. Globally, the number of adults with account at a financial institution (including mobile money providers) was 51% in 2001 increasing to 69% in 2017, about 72% of men and 65% of women had account at a financial institution and globally about 980 million women are still unbanked.

Unequal access to women in education, wages, employment and finance not only impacts labour productivity, but also has implications on savings and investment made by women, consumption, exports, and overall economic growth (Seguino & Floro, 2003). Access to finance is also considered as an important tool for enhancing women empowerment (Arora, 2020). Furthermore, it can also help in reducing gender inequalities and increase participation of women in the paid workforce (Popov & Zaharia, 2016). Women investors as being more risk averse (Byder et al., 2019), also play a greater role in building resilience and financial stability (Sahay et al. 2018).[1]

This gender divide is even sharper when taking access to digital financial services into account and the gap is particularly pervasive in

DOI: 10.4324/9781003199076-6

developing countries.[2] In recent years, considerable focus is being placed on employing technology to increase financial inclusion of women (Van der Spuy & Souter, 2020). Various benefits of financial services through technology (digital finance) which have been documented in case of developing countries include increased empowerment of women within households as it improves their access to financial services; increased role of women in household decision making and improved occupational choices (Demirguc-Kunt, et al. 2018; Docquier et al., 2009; Haider, 2018; Kusimba, 2018).

In this study, we, therefore, examine the extent of digital divide in access to digital financial service to women and its role in financial inclusion. Our region of interest is South Asia as gender inequality is pervasive in the South Asian countries. Also, this region (primarily Bangladesh) considered as the birthplace of modern microfinance, has targeted women as its prime beneficiaries with the objectives of reducing poverty and improving household well-being.[3] Table 6.1 provides a brief snapshot of the major indicators in the region.

In this chapter, we aim to address three major research questions: What is the level of women's access to digital financial services in South Asia? What are the barriers they face in accessing digital financial services? Can increased regulation reduce cyber security and overcome trust issues and reduce the digital divide?

Our study is novel in a number of ways. There are very few studies available on digital financial services in general. Moreover, hardly any academic literature (although several government reports/philanthropic organisations such as Bill Gates Foundation – the so-called grey literature have emerged in recent years) exists on digital financial services to women and more so, in South Asia, although a good body of literature is available on mobile money in African context, especially Kenya. Poor access to digital services to women and low financial access in general deprives approximately half of the population devoid of opportunities for instance, starting a business, education, savings, and consequently impacting economic growth.

Our study employs cross-country data for selected South Asian countries from Global Findex database, a comprehensive demand side database on how adults save, borrow, make payments, and manage risk. This data on more than 100 indicators including digital financial services to both men and women is collected in partnership with Gallup, Inc., through nationally representative surveys of more than 150,000 adults in over 140 economies. We also employ data from other sources such as supply-side data from International Monetary Fund (IMF) Financial Access Survey (FAS) on financial institutions and also Financial Inclusion Insights Survey on financial literacy and access to digital financial services.

Rest of the chapter is organised as follows. Section 6.2 reviews the related literature in the area. Section 6.3 provides an overview of the state of financial access and digital financial services in particular to women in South

Table 6.1 Some indicators on South Asia

Country	Population (millions) (2019)	% of total	GDP per capita (average)	GDP growth rate (2001–2015 avg)	% of adults having accounts at financial institution (2014)	Ranking in Human Development Index 2018	Poverty headcount ratio (@1.90$ a day) % of population
Bangladesh	161.35	9.2	744.9	6.0	29.4	136	14.8 (2016)
Nepal	28.08	1.6	574.1	3.7	33.8	149	15 (2010)
Pakistan	212.21	10.9	1028.9	4.4	8.7	150	3.9 (2015)
India	1,352.62	75.0	1276.6	7.4	45.5	130	21.2 (2011)
Sri Lanka	21.67	1.2	2755.0	5.9	82.7	76	0.8 (2016)

Source: World Bank indicators, World Bank.

Asia. It also highlights the extent of digital divide existing in the region. Section 6.4 discusses the barriers facing women in South Asia in accessing digital financial services. Finally, the last section concludes.

6.2 Related literature

Despite women's strong role in economic growth and development, as has been well acknowledged in the literature (Dollar & Gatti, 1999; Stotsky, 2006), women often face various deprivations to education, finance and employment. Several studies have pointed out in this context that gender sensitive policies reduce gender inequality, allow women to participate in economic activities and contribute to economic growth. For instance, Dollar and Gatti (1999) noted that 1% increase in the share of women with secondary education leads to an increase in per capita income by 0.3%. Gender focused approach also has a positive impact on development as women tend to spend more on children's education, health, nutrition and lead to increased household welfare (Duflo, 2012; Quisumbing & Maluccio, 2003). A number of studies have shown that access to finance provides opportunities to women start their businesses, increase their savings, and empowers them (Dupas and Robinson, 2013; Popov & Zaharia, 2016). Yet women's access to finance has remained low and their access to digital financial services is even lower, particularly in South Asia. In the paragraphs below we look at the literature on digital financial services and its relationship to financial inclusion in general and for women in particular. Also, we briefly examine literature on digital financial services and its impact on various development indicators.

The theoretical literature on financial markets has pointed out to the problems of incomplete information, high transaction costs, difficulties in enforcing contracts in financial markets and incentives especially in the developing countries (Stiglitz, 1989). However, the issues related to gender in financial markets were not been explored. Johnson (2004) notes that while various theories and rules exist in financial markets on lending, enforcement and regulation, gender does not figure in this discussion. Further, she notes:

Nor have theories of saving been purposefully disaggregated by gender although there is the potential to do so, for example, Friedman's permanent income hypothesis in which consumption is based on the agents view of her long-term income and short term changes-or transitory income – are saved; or Modigliani's life-cycle theory in which age is the main factor influencing saving in anticipation of retirement needs

Ke (2018) hypothesised that households in countries with traditional gender norms are likely to invest less in the stock markets. The study provides evidence that gender norms play an important role in decisions of households to invest in stock markets and this varies from country to country.

6.2.1 Digital financial services and financial inclusion

Digital financial services have been defined as a medium of delivering all financial services using internet without the need to visit physical bank branch (Arora, 2020). Acknowledging that there is no standard definition of digital financial services, Ozili (2018) argues that "there is some consensus that digital finance encompasses all products, services, technology, and/ or infrastructure that enable individuals and companies to have access to payments, savings, and credit facilities via the internet (online) without the need to visit a bank branch or without dealing directly with financial service provider." Gomber et al. (2017) define it as "all electronic products and services of the financial sector, e.g., credit and chip cards, electronic exchange systems, home banking, and home trading services (Banks, 2001) as well as automated teller machines (ATMs). Furthermore, it involves all mobile and app services."

The adoption of technology eases financial sector functions of monitoring and corporate control (functions as identified by Levine (1997)) and also reduces information and transaction costs in the financial sector. It also reduces asymmetric information and price volatility, characteristics of the financial sector (Aminuzzaman et al. 2003; Sassi & Goaied, 2013). Moreover, rapid diffusion of ICT through the channel of technological innovation also contributes to growth. For instance, Andrianaivo and Kpodar (2012) confirmed that financial inclusion supported with ICT diffusion contributes positively to growth and the joint interaction between mobile penetration and financial inclusion contributes positively to growth.

Empirical studies have also confirmed that technology can assist in financial inclusion. For instance, Agarwal et al. (2020) using data on 417,578 loan applications from mobile fintech lending platform examine whether usage of mobile data can predict and using alternate credit scoring methods. They argue that mobile footprints of individuals are better predictors of their ability to obtain credit and repay their loans. This is a better alternative to traditional credit scoring systems. They found that loan applicants with higher credit score, education, and salary are more likely to be approved. Further, their results also show that applicants with higher mobile footprints for instance, number of contacts, number of installed apps, call made or received, also financial or mobile loan apps are more likely to get their loans approved. Similarly, other studies such as Chava et al. (2017), D'Acunto et al. (2019), Fuster et al. (2018, 2019), Rossi and Utkus (2019), and Yiming and Clark (n.d.) have also explored impact of financial technology on consumer welfare. Their study, however, does not distinguish on the basis of gender. Asongu et al. (2019) too examined the role of mobile phones in promoting good governance (three dimensions of governance-political, economic, and institutional) employing cross country data for 47 Sub-Saharan countries for the period 2000–2012. Findings of their study showed a positive impact of mobile phones on governance in general.

Also, the impact of mobile phones on governance is much higher compared to individual dimensions.

Several other studies have observed positive impact of digitisation on financial inclusion (Bharadwaj & Suri, 2020). For instance, Agyekum et al. (2016) in their study showed that a 1% increase in mobile subscription leads to 1.19% increase in credit to the private sector. Other benefits of digitisation of financial services especially for the poor include ease of conducting financial transactions without the need to visit physical bank branches, thus avoiding related travel costs. For instance, Bachas et al. (2018) by employing a natural experiment in the Mexican context on technological intervention such as debit card provide evidence that it reduces indirect transaction costs such as travel costs and cost of forgone wages. The authors found that beneficiaries of Mexican cash transfer program with the use of debit card reduced their road distance travel from 4.8 km earlier to 1.3. Also, the proportion of beneficiaries who had to forgo housework, child care or work for accessing money from bank dropped from 84% earlier to 25%. Also, debit card enabled increased frequency of other financial activities such as checking balances, etc.

6.2.2 Impact of digital financial services and access to women and development

Various studies have found that providing digital financial services to women leads to increased empowerment, household decision making and improved choices in terms of occupations (Demirguc-Kunt, 2017; Docquier et al., 2009; Haider, 2018; Hendriks, 2019; Kusimba, 2018). It also leads to increased privacy for women and allows them increased control over funds over rest of the household (Aker et al., 2013). Morawczynski and Pickens (2009) showed that mobile money transfers allowed women to access remittances from their husbands in Kenya. Some studies also observed that smartphone financial apps increase welfare of women as it enables increased financial information and enables informed financial choices (Carlin et al., 2017).

Acknowledging the lack of diversity of women in financial services sector, Oliver Wyman's report (2020) notes:

The lack of women in technology is becoming increasingly important to address as the industry digitizes. In the future, many of the roles with the most impact on the industry and on customers will be digital. If we do not recruit, train, and re-skill women accordingly, there will be a gap in the most influential positions. With automation, many of the front-line roles traditionally held by women in branches and call centers are likely to be endangered (Women in Financial Services 2020: A Panoramic Approach, Oliver Wyman 2020).

Technological interventions can also help women in reducing or overcoming the problem of asymmetric information by using innovative credit scoring models such as social media presence on various digital platforms, mobile data usage and can increase their financial inclusion. As Arora (2020) observed:

Digital applications such as mobile banking and electronic payment solutions can overcome some of the socio-cultural barriers such as the customary requirement for male relatives to permit access to credit to women or overcome barriers of restricted women's mobility in many communities as it allows them to carry out financial transactions in the privacy of their own home in their own time without needing to physically travel to visit a bank branch and constrained by bank branch's working hours.

6.3 State of digital financial services and gendered digital divide

Globally, the number of adults with account at financial institutions was 51% in 2001 increasing to 69% in 2017 (World Bank). This however, varies considerably across developed and developing countries with account ownership around 94% in developed countries, while in developing countries it was 63% (Figure 6.1). Account ownership also varies across different developing countries with some countries such as, Brazil having account ownership of 70%; China 80% and countries in Sub-Saharan Africa Congo 26%, Ethiopia 35% and Guinea 23% in 2017. It also varies by income and education. Thus, the probability of owning an account is higher for those with higher incomes and with education. Around 1.7 billion adults still remain unbanked without an account at any financial institution or even a

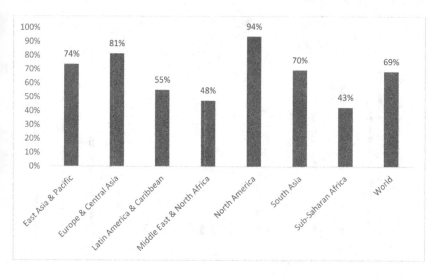

Figure 6.1 Account ownership in different regions, 2017.

Source: Global Findex Database, World Bank.

mobile money provider. Nearly half of the unbanked population is in just seven countries: Bangladesh, India, China, Indonesia, Mexico, Nigeria, and Pakistan.

Gender gap in account ownership is also substantial with globally nearly 56% of women still remaining unbanked. Gender gap is almost non-existent in the developed countries, while a gap of about 10% each persists in low income and lower middle-income countries. Across the regions, gender gap is highest at 19% in Middle East & North Africa followed by 11% each in South Asia and Sub-Saharan Africa (Figure 6.2).

However, reverse trends have also been observed in financial access gender gap in countries like Chile and Moldova where commercial bank deposit accounts held by women exceed that of men. In case of microfinance, gender disaggregated data shows that women continue to be the major borrowers from microfinance institutions. For example, women were the major borrowers in MFIs in Bangladesh (IMF 2020). Yet, the numbers given below may not provide an adequate picture for instance, in Pakistan the accounts may be in women's name, yet it may be controlled by men. As Zulfiqar (2017) observed, "even when the loans are in women's names, a good proportion of the women lack control or even knowledge of how the loans are used (Anne-Marie Goetz and Sen R. Gupta, 1994). In Pakistan, Aban Haq and Mehnaz Safavian (2013) find that between 50 and 70% of female microcredit borrowers in Pakistan hand their loans over to male relatives, and when men are unable to take out loans, they force their wives to borrow on their behalf." Table 6.2 provides a snapshot of some access indicators such as number of depositors and borrowers based on gender in different financial institutions.

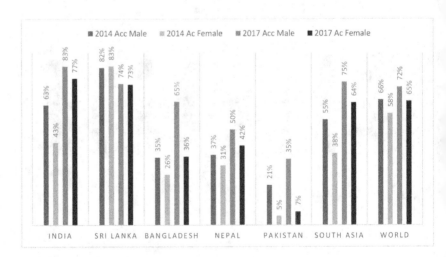

Figure 6.2 Account ownership based on gender.

Source: Global Findex Database, World Bank.

Table 6.2 Financial access indicators based on gender

Item	Countries	2015	2016	2017	2018	2019
Number of male depositors of the household sector with commercial banks per 1,000 male adults	Bangladesh	511.57	522.42	842.37	906.18	1,001.31
	Pakistan	351.84	351.09	331.49	399.03	446.75
Number of female depositors of household sector with commercial banks per 1,000 female adults	Bangladesh	214.56	242.94	392.49	470.36	499.61
	Pakistan	88.52	98.15	102.27	111.86	144.64
Number of male borrowers of the household sector from commercial banks per 1,000 male adults	Bangladesh	80.79	84.64	117.97	120.76	119.42
	Pakistan	38.53	37.85	36.61	24.09	25.19
Number of female borrowers of the household sector from commercial banks per 1,000 female adults	Bangladesh	18.24	9.01	13.91	14.14	14.38
	Pakistan	3.27	3.41	3.21	2.21	2.67
Number of male borrowers of household sector from all microfinance institutions per 1,000 male adults	Pakistan	–	–	–	41.10	40.75
Number of female borrowers of household sector from all microfinance institutions per 1,000 female adults	Pakistan	–	–	–	52.19	51.75

Source: Financial Access Survey, IMF, 2020.

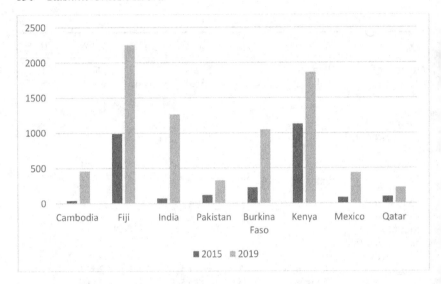

Figure 6.3 Number of registered money accounts per 1,000 adults.

Source: Financial Access Survey, IMF, 2020.

Among various data sources, IMF's Financial Access Survey launched in 2009 covering 189 countries provides data on mobile money accounts and other digital forms such as credit card, debit card and internet transactions for countries in the South Asian region mainly Bangladesh, India, Pakistan, and Nepal to a certain extent. According to FAS 2018, the number of mobile money accounts was more than twice the number of bank accounts per 1,000 people. Mobile money accounts have especially expanded in Sub Saharan Africa and Asia providing financial services to less banked or unbanked population. Figure 6.3 shows the number of registered money accounts per 1,000 adults. As this shows, the number of registered mobile money accounts increased sharply in Fiji and also India.

According to latest FAS data, the value of mobile money transactions grew especially faster in low and middle-income countries. For instance, in 2019 this was around 70% of GDP in Ghana and 90% in Cambodia (IMF, 2020). The Table 6.3 below shows some indicators for the year 2019 on the extent of digital financing in South Asia.

Globally mobile phone subscriptions were 6.686 billion as at end 2019 (World Bank indicators). Within this, the share of South Asia was 22.5% or 1.506 billion increasing from 20% in 2017. Mobile cellular phone subscriptions per 100 people was 87.36 in South Asia, in contrast to higher figure of 106.51 at the global level. This is also much lower compared to other regions. At the country level, this was 101.55 in Bangladesh, 84.27 in India, 139.45 in Nepal, and 142 in Sri Lanka and lowest in Pakistan at 76. In India wireless teledensity is much lower in the rural areas compared

Table 6.3 Digital financing in South Asia: Some indicators, 2019

Items	Bangladesh	India	Pakistan	Nepal
Number of registered mobile money accounts per 1,000 adults	517.14	1,264.79	327.79	188.67
Outstanding balances on active mobile money accounts (% of GDP)	18.63	0.02	0.01	0.08
Value of mobile money transactions (during the reference year) (% of GDP)	75.35	0.57	10.57	NA
Number of credit cards per 1,000 adults	12.06	37.99	11.08	5.36
Number of debit cards per 1,000 adults	165.22	872.69	228.44	283.66
Value of mobile and internet banking transactions (during reference yr) (% of GDP)	458.74	145.13	58.43	17.63

Note: Data for Sri Lanka was not available.
Source: Financial Access Survey, IMF (2020).

to urban areas. Wireless teledensity according to Telecom Regulatory Authority of India was 156.42 in the urban areas and just 56.68 in the rural areas (TRAI, 2019).

In terms of gender, according to a recent survey of GSMA (2018), on an average, women in low and middle-income countries are 10% less likely to own a phone compared to men (about 184 million fewer women than men own a mobile); in South Asia this figure increases to 26%. Besides ownership of phones, substantial gender gap exists also in its usage for instance, in low and middle-income countries over 1.2 billion women do not use mobile internet (measured as internet used at least once in past three months on a mobile) and in South Asia women are 70% less likely than men to use mobile internet (Arora, 2020). Thus, in South Asia the gender gap in the use of mobile internet is highest at 70% compared to the global gap of 26% reflecting high gender inequality in the region (GSMA, 2018). In India, for example, only 13% women had used mobile internet in the last three months compared to 31% men. In Pakistan, the figures are even lower where only 10% of women used mobile internet compared to 26% men. In contrast to above, the corresponding figures for China for the same period were 74% for women and 77% for men.

Significant disparity exists not only at the regional level, but within country too. For instance, at the sub-national level within India, significant disparity exists in the ownership of phones by women that they themselves use. As National Family Health Survey (NFHS) Survey, 2015–2016 shows ownership of phones among women varies widely from just 29% in the northern state, Madhya Pradesh (including both rural and urban areas) to

81% in Kerala (NFHS survey 2015–2016). While women in urban and rural areas in Kerala had an equal access to mobile phones, in some states such as Madhya Pradesh and Odisha the gap was more than 30%. In Pakistan, the gender gap in ownership of phones was around 40% and 49% in the urban and rural areas with internet usage gender gaps even much higher.

In terms of other digital usage indicators in South Asia, the increase in debit card ownership was mainly led by men in the region as their share in total rose from 10% to 36%. Overall, ownership of debit cards in the region increased from 7% in 2011 to 27% in 2017. At the country level, 31% of women owned debit cards in Sri Lanka followed by India (22%) and was much lower at 4%, 6% and 3% in Bangladesh, Nepal, and Pakistan. Credit card ownership was much lower for both men and women across all countries in the region. Payment through other digital means is also much higher for men than women. As World Bank's Global Findex database for 2017 shows, in Bangladesh 47% men made or received digital payments in contrast to 21% women. Similarly, in India, Sri Lanka and Nepal too large gender gap persists. In Pakistan this is much wider as 29% men made or received digital payments in contrast to 5% women.

6.4 Barriers in accessing digital services

Having discussed the gender divide in the previous paragraphs, a question emerges, why this digital gender divide exists and what constraints and challenges women face in accessing digital financial services?

The barriers can be broadly divided into two groups: cultural and non-cultural barriers. Various barriers can be observed from Figure 6.4.

Among non-cultural barriers for women in accessing digital financial services are primarily infrastructure, education, income, and employment. Within infrastructural barriers low internet connectivity and its usage is low specially in the South Asian countries. The percentage of people using

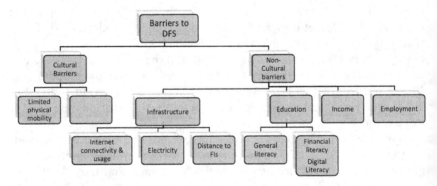

Figure 6.4 Barriers facing women in digital financial services.

Source: Author's development.

internet in 2019 was 20.1% in 2019 in South Asia. Within South Asia, the proportion of people using internet out of total population was considerably low at 13% in Bangladesh followed by Pakistan at 17%, India (20.1%), Nepal (21.4%), and Sri Lanka (34%). Interestingly, India's share declined from 32% in 2017 to 20% in 2019. These figures are considerably lower compared to other emerging and developing economies such as Brazil (70.4%); China (54%); Malaysia (84.2%); Russia (82.6); and South Africa (56%). Furthermore, digital divide persists even within the countries for instance, in India a large number of rural areas are deprived of internet connectivity (Agarwal & Panda, 2018; Rana et al., 2019). Nonetheless, according to GSMA (2020) in South Asia, the mobile internet gender gap is reducing and has narrowed from 67% in 2017 to 51% in 2019, which based on their estimates, has allowed internet facilities to another 78 million women. However, GSMA (2020) further observes, that despite positive outcomes as above, "the gender gap is still widest in South Asia at 51%, and remains fairly consistent in other regions such as Sub-Saharan Africa, which has the second largest gender gap at 37%." Among South Asian countries the gender gap is higher in Pakistan where women are 38% less likely than men to own a phone and 49% less likely to use mobile internet (GSMA, 2020). The gap further widens when ownership of smart phone is taken into account. Table 6.4 briefly shows the type of mobile phone ownership in different South Asian countries based on gender. The figures for South Asia also contrasts significantly with that of other countries such as Brazil in Latin America.

Various studies have also identified education as another barrier in the access of digital financial services especially for women. For instance, in a cross country study on factors impeding usage of internet in Bangladesh, Sri Lanka, and Nepal, Zhou et al. (2011) found that knowledge of English language was a specific barrier in accessing internet thereby implying that use of regional languages in internet apps would increase accessibility. Besides knowledge of english language, low levels of literacy in general for women in South Asia is another deterring factor in the uptake of digital financial

Table 6.4 Types of phone ownership in South Asia based on gender (%)

Countries	Men			Women		
	Smart phone	*Feature phone*	*Basic phone*	*Smart phone*	*Feature phone*	*Basic phone*
Bangladesh	36	31	19	21	26	13
India	37	9	29	14	6	31
Pakistan	37	7	39	20	6	23
Brazil	65	4	10	65	8	8
Algeria	68	2	20	55	2	26

Source: GSMA (2020).

services. In South Asia average literacy rate of women at 62.2 is much lower compared to world average of 82.6. Within the region, female literacy rate in Pakistan was just 46.5, 59.7 in Nepal, 65.8 in India, 71.9 in Bangladesh and much higher at 90.7 in Sri Lanka. The proportion of females with no schooling was highest in Pakistan at 59%, followed by Nepal (48%) and India (47%) with lowest in Sri Lanka at 6%. This educational gender gap is relatively large in South Asia compared to other regions. Various studies have also shown that discrimination against women in education impacts economic development and leads to winding of inequalities (Todaro & Smith, 2020).

Besides basic literacy, in our context financial literacy and digital literacy are also crucial factors in influencing uptake of financial services. The role of financial literacy and the ability to make informed financial decisions has been emphasised by several studies (Alessie et al., 2011; Cole et al., 2011; Hogarth & O'Donnell, 1999). In the OECD financial literacy index based on three dimensions: financial knowledge, financial behaviour, and financial attitudes, the average score for G20 countries was 12.7 and India's score was below average with scores in dimensions as 3.7 for financial knowledge, 5.6 for financial behaviour and 2.6 in financial attitude (OECD, 2018). Substantial gender gaps also persisted in financial literacy across the G20 countries. In the Indian case, interestingly, low financial literacy scores are irrespective of incomes with similarities across those with low and high incomes. Lacking a standard definition of digital financial literacy, Arora (2020) defined digital financial literacy (and literacy in general), "as the ability to send and receive text messages on phones." Acknowledging lack of clarity on the definition of digital financial literacy, FinDev Gateway (2020) defined it as a blended confluence of digital literacy and financial literacy. According to them, key enablers for women's digital financial literacy are literacy, consumer awareness (ability or awareness to make choices in digital financial products), numeracy, easy access to phones, design of products and above all social norms. Digital financial literacy is low within South Asia.

Lack of adequate income and geographic distance to financial institutions including ATMs are also cited other non-cultural barriers. For instance, in India with 66% of the rural population, the availability of ATMs is very low. Overall, ATMs per 100,000 adults in 2019 are currently abysmally low in South Asia at 16.45 comparing starkly with the world average (Table 6.5).

Above all, cultural barriers defined by deep social norms and attitudes towards women in South Asia persist in the region. As UNDP report (2020) observes:

Social norms are central to the understanding of these dynamics. For example, societies often tell their girls that they can become anything they want and are capable of, while investing in their education. But the same societies tend to block their access to power positions without giving them a fair chance.

These cultural barriers pervade every aspect of women's lives including their access to digital financial services as well. For instance, social norms such as family not approving owning phones is a significant factor impeding mobile internet use of women in South Asia mainly Bangladesh, Pakistan, India, and Sri Lanka (GSMA, 2017). Social norms are particularly stringent in Pakistan as GSMA (2020) reports that, "while disapproval by family members is not a top barrier in most markets, for women in Bangladesh and particularly in Pakistan, it is an extremely important factor grounded in conservative social norms that govern many women's choices and behaviour." Among the social norms, reputational risks to family due to internet use; limited decision-making power within households and less time available to women to learn new skills such as internet are the most cited factors constraining women's internet use in South Asia (Arora, 2020). In the South Asian context, GSMA (2017) observed that "expectations of married women were relatively consistent in all four countries. Women are typically expected to give up work outside the home, to devote most of their time to childcare and looking after the household, to acknowledge the authority of their husband (and parents-in-law) over where they go and how they spend their time, and to put the needs of their family before their own."

In South Asian societies which are highly patriarchal, the dividing line between cultural and non-cultural barriers is blurred as socio-cultural factors often influence various other aspects of women's lives including financial access. For instance, as FII Survey (2017) observes in Pakistan, "adherence to ultraconservative customs including the complete separation of men and women in all spheres of life and male guardianship have created barriers for women that cross income, age, geographic, and educational demographics." Even in India, financial decisions are mostly taken by men in the households. Thus, as the FII survey showed that in India 61% of men decide on how income of their wives is spent, in contrast to just 14% of women.

Table 6.5 Availability of ATMs (ATMs per 100,000, 2019)

Country	ATMs per 100,000 adults
South Asia	16.45
India	20.95
Bangladesh	8.86
Pakistan	10.84
Nepal	16.45
Sri Lanka	17.20$
Brazil	101.67
China	95.54
South Africa	65.31
World	49.61

Note: This only takes into account availability of physical ATMs. $: latest data is for 2015.
Source: World Bank indicators, World Bank.

6.5 Conclusion

This study examined the extent of gendered digital divide in South Asia. We focused on South Asia for a number of reasons. The region, specifically Bangladesh is the hub of microfinance services. In terms of socio-economic factors, poverty is very high in the region. Also, these countries have highly patriarchal societies and gender inequality is pervasive in the region. There are several similarities across the region historically, culturally, food, and even in terms of language. Access to finance is also quite low in the region. While several efforts have been taken to improve financial access in general, a large gender gap persists in accessing financial services. Our study employing cross-country data available from Global Findex database and other sources such IMF's Financial Access Survey examines two major research questions on the extent of digital divide in access to financial services to women and what are the barriers they face in accessing digital financial services. Findings indicate that although digital access although low for men as well, its access to women is even lesser. Furthermore, our study found that several cultural and non-cultural barriers prevent women from accessing digital financial services. These include low literacy including financial and digital literacy, poor access to mobile phones, low employment opportunities and above all strong cultural barriers which prevent women from accessing digital financial services.

In bridging this digital divide and enabling women to participate on an equal footing in economic growth, a concerted effort by all stakeholders such as government, mobile networks, and other development community is required (GSMA, 2020). This includes focus on girl's education, increased employment opportunities, raising awareness campaigns, and improved digital products to specifically meet women's needs. An important area to focus is also ensuring better data collection as currently data availability on women's access to financial services and digital in particular is quite sparse. For instance, data on age group access of financial services to women is not available limiting our understanding of which age group of women are more financially excluded. Interestingly, as GSMA (2020) showed while factors related to trust and security were found ranked very high for women (and men equally) particularly in Latin American countries such as Brazil, Guatemala and Mexico, in the South Asian countries, more so, in Pakistan family's disapproval of women using mobile phones (35%) was the major factor. Under these circumstances, technological solutions will also be of not much use unless these socio-cultural norms are directly addressed (Arora, 2020).

Notes

1. For an interesting account of the historical role played by women in finance see Maltby and Rutterford (2012).

2. Women's representation in executive committees in financial services in major countries shows that as in 2019 for instance, the proportion of women were as low as 4% in South Korea and 5% in Japan, in contrast to Israel (38%), Australia (34%), and Sweden (35%). Among South Asian countries data was only available for India, according to which the proportion of women on executive committees as in 2019 was 19% in India, this was an improved score by 8% compared to 2016 (Oliver Wyman 2020: Women in Financial Services Report 2020). Differences in women's representation are even more stark at the fintech level.
3. Several studies have however, found mixed evidence on the impact of micro-finance on women in South Asia (Hulme and Maitrot, 2014; Banerjee et al., 2015; Zulfiqar, 2017).

References

Agarwal, T., & Panda, P. K. (2018). Pattern of digital divide and convergence in access to ICT facilities among the Indian states. *Journal of Infrastructure Development, 10*(1–2), 37–51.

Agarwal, S., Shashwat, A., Ghosh, P., & Gupta, S. (2020). *Financial inclusion and alternate credit scoring for the millennials.* Role of Big Data and Machine Learning in Fintech.

Agyekum, F., Locke, S., & Hewa-Wellalage, N. (2016). Financial inclusion and digital financial services: Empirical evidence from Ghana. MPRA Paper No. 82885. Retrieved from https://mpra.ub.uni-muenchen.de/82885/. Accessed on July 28, 2019.

Aghion, P., & Bolton, P. (1997). A theory of trickle-down growth and development. *Review of Economic Studies, 64,* 151–172.

Aker, J., Boumnijel, R., McClelland, A., & Tierney, N. (2013). How do electronic transfers compare? Evidence from a mobile money cash transfer experiment in Niger. Retrieved from https://docplayer.net/53281481-How-do-electronictrans-fers-compare-evidence-from-a-mobile-money-cashtransfer-experiment-in-niger.html. Accessed on November 30, 2019.

Alessie, R., van Rooij, M., & Lusardi, A. (2011). Financial literacy and retirement preparation in the Netherlands. *Journal of Pension Economics and Finance, 10*(4), 527–545.

Aminuzzaman, S., Baldersheim, H., & Jamil, I. (2003). Talking back! Empowerment and mobile phones in rural Bangladesh: A study of the village phone scheme of grameen bank. *Contemporary South Asia, 12*(3), 327–348. doi: 10.1080/0958493032000175879.

Andrianaivo, M., & Kpodar, K. (2012). Mobile phones, financial inclusion and growth. *Review of Economics andn Institutions,* 3(2, Spring), 1–30.

Arora, R. U. (2014). Access to finance: An empirical analysis. *European Journal of Development Research, 26*(5), December, 798–814. doi: 10.1057/ejdr.2013.50.

Arora, R. U. (2020). *Gender bias and digital financial services in South Asia: Obstacles and opportunities on the road to equal access.* Emerald Publishers.

Asongu, S., Le Roux, S., Nwachukwu, J. C., & Pyke, C. (2019). The mobile phone as an argument for good governance in sub-Saharan Africa. *Information Technology & People, 32*(4), 897–920.

Bachas, P., Gertler, P., Higgins, S., & Seira, E. (2018). Digital financial services go a long way: Transaction costs and financial inclusion, *AEA Papers and Proceedings 2018,* 108: 444–448, https://doi.org/10.1257/pandp.20181013.

Banerjee, A., & Newman, A. (1993). "Occupational choice and the process of development". *Journal of Political Economy*, *101*, 274–298.

Banerjee, A., Breza, E., Duflo, E., & Kinnan, C. (2015). Do Credit Constraints Limit Entrepreneurship? Heterogeneity In The Returns To Microfinance accessed from https://pdfs.semanticscholar.org/12f2/16eca9e446f1a76011f24a40205f3c962587.pdf

Banks, E. (2001). *e-finance: The electronic revolution*, 1st ed. Wiley.

Bharadwaj, P., & Suri, T. (2020). Digital financial services in Africa: Improving financial inclusion through digital savings and credit, *AEA Papers and Proceedings 2020*, 110: 584–588, https://doi.org/10.1257/pandp.20201084

Beck, T., & de la Torre, A. (2006). The basic analytics of access to financial services (English). *Policy, research working paper; no. WPS 4026*. Washington, DC, World Bank.

Byder, J., Agudelo, D. A., & Arango, I. (2019). Gender matters most. The impact on short-term risk aversion following a financial crash. *Review of Financial Economics*, *37*(1), Special Issue on Behavioral Finance, January, 106–117.

Carlin, B., Olafsson, A., & Pagel, M. (2017). FinTech adoption across generations: Financial fitness in the information age. *NBER working paper no. 23798*. Cambridge, National Bureau of Economic Research.

Chava, S., Paradkar, N., & Zhang, Y. (2017). Winners and losers of marketplace lending: Evidence from borrower credit dynamics. Working paper.

Claessens, S., & Perotti, E. (2007). Finance and inequality: Channels and evidence. *Journal of Comparative Economics*, *35*, 748–773.

Cole, S., Sampson, T., & Zia, B. (2011, December). Prices or knowledge? What drives demand for financial services in emerging markets? *The Journal of Finance*, LXVI, 6.

Dollar, D., & Gatti, R. (1999). *Gender inequality, income, and growth: Are good times good for women?* (pp. 1–42). World Bank.

D'Acunto, F., Prabhala, N., & Rossi, A. G. (2019). The promises and pitfalls of robo-advising. *The Review of Financial Studies*, *32*(5), 1983–2020.

Demirguc-Kunt, A., & Levine, R. (2008). Finance, financial sector policies and long-run growth. *Washington DC, working paper no.11*, Commission on Growth and Development, World Bank.

Demirguc-Kunt, A., & Levine, R.. (2009). *Finance and inequality: Theory and evidence*. 1–52. Washington DC: World Bank.

Demirguc-Kunt, A., Klapper, L., Ansar, S., & Jagati, A. (2017). *Making it easier to apply for a bank account: A study of the Indian market policy research working paper*. Washington, DC: World Bank.

Demirguç-Kunt, A., Klapper, L., Singer, D., Ansar, S., & Hess, J. (2018). *The global findex database 2017: Measuring financial inclusion and the fintech revolution*. World Bank.

Docquier, F., Lowell, L., & Marfouk, A. (2009). "A gender assessment of highly skilled emigration. *Population and Development Review*, *35*(2), 297–321.

Duflo, E. (2012). Women empowerment and economic development. *Journal of Economic Literature*, *50*(4), 1051–1079.

Dupas, P., & Robinson, J. (2013). Savings constraints and microenterprise development: Evidence from a field experiment in Kenya. *American Economic Journal: Applied Economics*, *5*(1), 163–192.

FinDev Gateway (2020). Accessed from https://www.findevgateway.org/training-events/digital-financial-literacy

FII Survey (2017). *Pakistan 2017, wave 4 report FII tracker survey.* Financial Inclusion Insights Survey.

Fuster, A., Goldsmith-Pinkham, P., Ramadorai, T., & Walther, A. (2018). Predictably unequal? The effects of machine learning on credit markets. Working paper.

Fuster, A., Plosser, M., Schnabl, P., Vickery, J. (2019). The Role of Technology in Mortgage Lending, *The Review of Financial Studies*, Volume 32, Issue 5, May 2019, Pages 1854–1899, https://doi.org/10.1093/rfs/hhz018.

Galor, O., & Zeira, J. (1993). Income distribution and macroeconomics. *Review of Economic Studies, 60,* 35–52.

Gine, X., & Townsend, R. (2004). Evaluation of financial liberalization: A general equilibrium model with constrained occupation choice. *Journal of Development Economics, 74*(2), 269–307

Goetz, Anne-Marie and Sen R. Gupta. 1994. "Who Takes the Credit? Gender, Power and Control over Loan Use in Rural Credit Programmes in Bangladesh." *World Development* 24(1): 45–63.

Gomber, P., Koch, J.-A., & Siering, M. (2017). Digital finance and FinTech: Current research and future research directions. *Journal of Business Economics*, 87, 537–580. doi:10.1007/s11573-017-0852-x

GSMA. (2017). *Triggering mobile and internet use among men and women in South Asia. Global system for mobile communications association.* UK AiD.

GSMA. (2018). *Connected women: The mobile gender gap report 2018.* UK AiD.

GSMA (2020). Connected Women: The Mobile Gender Gap Report 2020.

Haider, H. (2018). *Innovative financial technologies to support livelihoods and economic outcomes. K4D helpdesk report.* Institute of Development Studies.

Haq, A. and Safavian, M. (2013). *Are Pakistan's Women Entrepreneurs Being Served by the Microfinance Sector?.* Washington, DC: World Bank. http://elibrary.worldbank.org/ doi/abs/10.1596/978-0-8213-9833-3#.

Hendriks, S. (2019). Banking on the Future of Women, Finance & Development, March.

Hogarth, J. M., & O'Donnell, K. H. (1999). Banking relationships of lower-income families and the governmental trend toward electronic payment. *Federal Reserve Bulletin, 85,* 459–473.

Hulme, D., & Maitrot, M., (2014). Has Microfinance Lost its Moral Compass? (November 20, 2014). Available at SSRN: https://ssrn.com/abstract=2560331

IMF (2020). Financial Access Survey, 2020: Trends and Developments, Statistics, International Monetary Fund.

Johnson, S. (2004). Gender norms in financial markets: Evidence from Kenya. *World Development, 32*(8), 1355–1374.

Ke, D. (2018). Cross-country differences in household stock market participation: The role of gender norms, gender norms and discrimination, AEA Papers and Proceedings 2018, 108: 159–162 https://doi.org/10.1257/pandp.20181097

Kusimba, S. (2018). It is easy for women to ask: Gender and digital finance in Kenya. *Economic Anthropology, 5*(2), 247–260. Special Issue Theme: Financialization.

Levine, R. (1997). Financial development and economic growth: Views and agenda. *Journal of Economic Literature, 35*(2), 688–726.

Maltby, J., & Rutterford, J. (2012). In Cetina, K. K. and Preda, A. (Eds.), *Gender and finance in the oxford handbook of the sociology of finance.* Online Publication Date: Jun 2013. DOI: 10.1093/oxfordhb/9780199590162.013.0027.

Morawczynski, O., & Pickens, M. (2009). *Poor people using mobile financial services: Observations on customer usage and impact from M-PESA.* Consultative Group to Assist the Poor.

OECD (2018). *Financial markets, insurance and private pensions: Digitalisation and finance.* Organisation for Economic Co-operation and Development.

Ozili, P. K. (2018). Impact of digital finance on financial inclusion and stability. *Borsa Istanbul Review, 18*(4), 329–340.

Piketty, T. (1997). "The dynamics of the wealth distribution and the interest rate with credit rationing". *Review of Economic Studies, 64*(2), 173–189.

Popov, A., & Zaharia, S. (2016). *"Credit market competition and the gender gap: Evidence from local labor markets. Mimeo.* European Central Bank.

Quisumbing, A., & Maluccio, J. A. (2003). Resources at marriage and intrahousehold allocation: Evidence from Bangladesh, Ethiopia, Indonesia, and South Africa. *Oxford Bulletin of Economics & Statistics, 65*(3), 283–327.

Rana, N., Luthra, S., & Rao, H. (2019). Key challenges to digital financial services in emerging economies: The Indian context. *Information Technology & People, 33*(1), 198–229.

Rossi, A., & Utkus, S. (2019). Who benefits from robo-advising. Working paper.

Sahay, R., Čihák, M., & Other IMF Staff (2018). Women in finance: A case for closing gaps, *IMF Staff Discussion Note,* SDN/18/05, International Monetary Fund.

Sassi, S., & Goaied, M. (2013). Financial development, ICT diffusion and economic growth: Lessons from MENA region. *Telecommunications Policy, 37*(4), 252–261.

Seguino, S., & Floro, M. S. (2003). Does gender have any effect on aggregate saving? An empirical analysis. *International Review of Applied Economics, 17,* 147–166.

Stiglitz, J. (1989). Financial markets and development. *Oxford Review of Economic Policy, 5*(4), 55–68.

Stotsky, J. G. (2006). Gender and its relevance to macroeconomic policy: A survey. *IMF working paper.* Washington, DC: Fiscal Affairs Department, International Monetary Fund.

Todaro, M. P., & Smith, S. (2020). *Economic development* (13th ed.), Pearson.

TRAI (2019). *Highlights of telecom subscription data as on 30th June, 2019.* Press Release No. 59/2019. New Delhi, Telecom Regulatory Authority of India.

UNDP (2020). Tackling social norms: A game changer for gender inequalities. 2020 Human Development Perspectives, UNDP.

Van der Spuy, A., & Souter, D. (2020). *Women's digital inclusion, background paper for the G20.* Internet Society and the Association for Progressive Communications.

Yiming, W., & Clark C. (n.d.). Driving Poverty Alleviation through Digital Financial Inclusion accessed from https://cdrf.org.cn/jjh/pdf/shuzipuhuijinrongtuopin-gongjian.pdf

Zhou, Y., Singh, N., & Kaushik, P. D. (2011). The digital divide in rural South Asia: Survey evidence from Bangladesh, Nepal and Sri Lanka. *IIMB Management Review, 23,* 15–29.

Zulfiqar, G. (2017). Does microfinance enhance gender equity in access to finance? Evidence from Pakistan. *Feminist Economics, 23*(1), 160–185. doi: 10.1080/13545701.2016.1193213.

7 Intraday price reaction to filing bankruptcy and restructuring proceedings – the evidence from Poland

Błażej Prusak and Marcin Potrykus

7.1 Introduction

Already at the end of the 20th century and the beginning of the 21st century, research was conducted showing that Information and Communication Technologies (ICT) tools can reduce information asymmetry and support market efficiency. In particular, the development of the Internet contributed to this (Antweiler & Frank, 2004; Wysocki, 1998). Lee et al. (2019) distinguished two ICT diffusion on stock market efficiency effects. On the one hand, it can support the flow of information, which has a positive impact on market efficiency. On the other hand, it may spread false information and contribute to reducing market efficiency. These authors undertook research aimed at determining the impact of ICT diffusion on the market efficiency and verifying which of the above-mentioned effects prevails. Their research shows that stock markets in countries with high ICT diffusion are efficient while stock markets in countries with low or medium ICT diffusion are not all efficient. Moreover, the effect of ICT diffusion in reducing market noises was more significant than its effect on magnifying the noises (Lee et al., 2019).

The doubts about whether the Internet, will significantly reduce the cost of obtaining capital through public or quasi-public offering can be also found in Black (1998). The author states that the most important single barrier standing between small companies and capital providers is information asymmetry. The Internet is not a solution/tool for potential investors for verifying, the quality of the information that a company provides. What is more, it was also showed that the level of the digitalization does not affect profitability (Niemand et al., 2020). This research was prepared on data from the banking sector. The weak role of ICT diffusion in improving economic growth in middle and low-income countries is also shown in Cheng et al. (2021). But the authors also state that in high-income countries ICT diffusion can improve economic growth. Very similar conclusions, presented above, can be found in Yartey (2008). In that article also is emphasized that for countries with underdeveloped financial markets ICT diffusion can give negative results. In Poland, the Electronic System for Information Transmission (ESPI) system is an ICT system, certain tool

DOI: 10.4324/9781003199076-7

facilitating the transfer of digitalization information in a standardized form between companies listed on the Warsaw Stock Exchange and investors. As part of this system, the companies present all relevant information on an ongoing basis, including data on filed bankruptcy applications or the introduction of restructuring proceedings. The purpose of this chapter is to analyse the reaction of share prices to the information provided in the ICT system called ESPI about filing applications for bankruptcy or restructuring proceedings against companies listed on the Warsaw Stock Exchange. We anticipate that the functioning of such ICT system should contribute to reducing the asymmetry of information between investors and, at the same time, increasing market efficiency. Event analysis was used as a research method and it was carried out in an ultra-short period, i.e., within 120 minutes after such information appeared in ESPI, taking into account minute data. For the purposes of this chapter, it was assumed that ultra-short time applies to minute data and a period shorter than one session day. In some publications, the term intraday is used, and this one is used in this publication as well. Few similar studies have been reported so far, mainly for the US market, but only using daily or longer data. For example, Schatzberg and Reiber (1992) noted a short-term effect of the share prices reverse of American companies for which Chapter 11 was claimed, i.e., after significant price drop during the application period, a surplus return rate was generated. An analogous effect was achieved by Datta and Iskander-Datta (1995) and Dawkins et al. (2007). Coelho and Taffler (2009) examined the long-term effect for US companies applying for Chapter 11. As for the analysis of events in minute intervals, the ones examined included, among others, the impact of the following events on share prices: publishing information about new share issues (Barclay & Litzenberger, 1988), the occurrence of price shocks (Zawadowski et al., 2006), submitting of stock market recommendations (Bradley et al., 2014), the publication of macroeconomic data (Hanousek et al., 2009). Depending on the research periods and the types of events and markets, the adjustment of prices to the emerging information usually took place within a few minutes (Patell & Wolfson, 1984; Robertson et al., 2007). Busse and Green (2002) proved even that this adjustment could be made faster, because within seconds after the positive information is revealed. Reacting to negative data takes longer, up to 15 minutes. The research conducted in Poland has so far focused on the reaction of the Warsaw stock exchange indices WIG (Warsaw Stock Exchange Index) and WIG20 (Warsaw Stock Exchange Top 20 Index) to data on the macroeconomic situation in the United States (Będowska-Sójka, 2010; Gurgul et al., 2013; Suliga & Wójtowicz, 2013) and were conducted in 5-minute intervals. Price reactions to digital information about filed bankruptcy or restructuring applications were not analysed.

As it was shown at the beginning ICT developing has an impact on market efficiency. The market efficiency theory is associated with Fama (1965a,b, 1970) who was awarded the Nobel Prize in 2013. The foundations of this theory, however, can be found much earlier, at the beginning of the 20th century, when Bachelier (1900) developed the random walk theory. In the same period as Fama, also Samuelson proposed the efficient market hypothesis (Delcey, 2019). According to that theory, the prices of the securities reflect all information concerning them. Fama (1970) formalized the assumptions of this theory, presenting three forms of information efficiency, i.e., weak (historical information is included in the price), semi-strong (both historical and publicly available information is included in the price) and strong (all information, both publicly available and available to selected groups, e.g., investors, management board, is reflected in the price). This theory, although still alive, is subject to criticism, and there are still disputes regarding its assumptions and verifiability (Malkiel, 2003; Schwert, 2003; Fama & Thaler, 2016). There have been many studies showing anomalies that allow achieving the so-called above-average rates of return (Dimson [Ed.], 1988; Latif et al., 2011). The concepts of price overreaction and underreaction were proposed, undermining the assumptions of market efficiency hypothesis (Dreman, 1982; De Bondt and Thaler, 1985; Howe, 1986). The noisy trading theory was also created by Black (1986), which was later developed by Trueman (1988) and De Long et al. (1990). The latter proposed a division into noise traders and sophisticated investors. Noise traders behave irrationally and believe they have additional information that affects the value of the shares. This information may come from various sources, e.g., technical analysts, investment advisors. They are also often characterised by excessive subjective confidence in making investment decisions. This results in a situation in which share prices significantly differ from their internal value. Sophisticated traders are perceived as persons who make rational investment decisions taking into account accurate information. Therefore, in their case, the price adjusts quickly to the emerging relevant information and reflects the intrinsic value of the share. Depending on which group dominates the stock market, it is more or less effective.

Apart from the introduction that shows the theoretical framework and background, the chapter structure is as follows. The next section presents the research methodology. The results are included in Section 7.3. The last part is devoted to discussing the findings and implications of our research.

7.2 Materials and methods

The selection of observations for the sample was carried out as follows. First, all current digital reports from the ESPI system submitted by companies listed on the Polish stock market in the period 6.10.2004 to 31.12.2019 and available at http://biznes.pap.pl/pl/reports/espi/company/82,2018,0,0,1 were analysed. Out of 367,365 reports, those concerning the filing of bankruptcy applications or restructuring proceedings by companies from the Warsaw Stock Exchange listed in the continuous system were selected. The observations, which were disrupted during the research period were omitted.

144   *Błażej Prusak and Marcin Potrykus*

Table 7.1 Test sample characteristics

	Bankruptcy	Restructuring	Sum
Before and after session	10	22	**32**
During session	5	14	**19**
Sum	**15**	**36**	**51**

Source: Own study.

Ultimately, data for 51 applications were obtained. The sample was also divided into several categories:

•   type of application submitted (restructuring – first group, bankruptcy – second group),
•   time of publication of information about the submitted application (during the session – the first group, before or after the session – second group).

The breakdown into the above groups is shown in Table 7.1.

To evaluate the reaction of share prices to the information presented above, an event study was applied, which can be used to assess market efficiency and at the same time allows to estimate above-average rates of return during the period of the event (Konchitchki & O'Leary, 2011; Kothari & Warner, 2007). The calculations were carried out in program R, based on the event study package by Schimmer et al. (2015), which was adapted for a minute analysis.

The basis for the assessment of the examined effect will be the following interest rates, determined based on logarithmic rates of return for the analysed companies and the benchmark (WIG index):

$$AR_{i,t} = R_{i,t} - (\alpha_i + \beta_i * R_{m,t})$$

$$AAR = \frac{1}{N}\sum_{i=1}^{N} AR_{i,t}$$

$$CAR(t_1,t_2) = \sum_{t=t_1}^{t_2} AR_{i,t}$$

$$CAAR = \frac{1}{N}\sum_{i=1}^{N} CAR(t_1,t_2)$$

where

• $R_{i,t}$ – the rate of return for company "i" on day "t."
• $R_{m,t}$ – the rate of return for the WIG index on day "t."
• α_i, β_i – the estimated market-based model parameters.
•   AR – abnormal return.

- AAR – average abnormal return.
- N – number of analysed event in each group (for example 15 for liquidation bankruptcy proceedings).
- CAR – cumulative abnormal return.
- t_1 – the beginning of the research window (in this study always 5 minutes before the event).
- t_2 – the ending of the research window (in this study always 120 minutes after the event).
- CAAR – cumulative average abnormal return.

Data on prices of particular assets and the benchmark, which were used to determine the logarithmic rates of return of the surveyed companies were obtained from the website https://info.bossa.pl/notowania/pliki/intraday.

Additionally, a market model was used to determine the abnormal return (AR) rate. Due to low market liquidity, the models for the AR rate were determined based on the daily data from 110 observations seven days before the information was published. The study window, however, ranges from 5 minutes before the event to 120 minutes after the event (the 10, 5, and 1-minute intervals after the event were used).

Statistical tests that were used to assess whether the submission of the analysed applications has a statistically significant impact on share prices are (the literature source for the test is given after the colon):

- for rates AR and CAR:
- T-test, Gurgul (2019).
- for rates AAR and CAAR:
- Kolari and Pynnönen adjusted Patell or Standardized Residual Test (Adj. Patell Z), Kolari and Pynnönen (2010).

The above methodology together with the created breakdowns of the applications from Table 7.1 allows assessing whether the type of application (restructuring, bankruptcy) has an impact on the emergence of above-average rates of return on the market that would be statistically significant. Moreover, the second breakdown (applications submitted during the session or outside the session) allows the assessment not only whether the above rates are present, but also with what average delay the market reacts to the publication of information about insolvency, and thus how much time investors need to respond to the emergence of new information using the available information and technology tools.

7.3 Results

7.3.1 Analysis of data for a 10-minute interval

The results for all surveyed companies, without division into groups presented in Table 7.1, are presented in Figure 7.1 and Table 7.2.

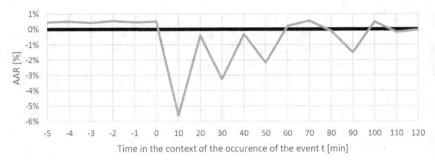

Figure 7.1 The value of the AAR rate for the sample of companies n = 51, for a
10-minute interval.

Source: Own study.

Figure 7.1 shows how AAR rates developed in 10-minute intervals after the event.

Based on the data presented in Figure 7.1, it can be concluded that, up to 5 minutes before the occurrence of an event, the surveyed companies had an above-average positive (although low) rate of return. On the other hand, after 10 minutes from the occurrence of an event, the highest negative rate of return was recorded at a level exceeding –5%, further significant drops are visible after 30 and 50 minutes after the occurrence of an event. However, the last drop not exceeding –2% was observed 90 minutes after the event. Table 7.2 presents the results of the statistical test for the tested 10-minute intervals.

The applied statistical test did not show the occurrence of above-average statistically significant rates of return in the time before the event, therefore, for the sake of clarity, these data are not presented in the table above. The results of the testing performed are consistent with the previous graphical data analysis. It turned out that above-average negative and statistically significant rates of return were recorded 10, 30, 50, and 90 minutes after the event occurred. However, for the first three mentioned moments, statistical significance was observed at the level of $\alpha = 0.01$, while in the 90th minute it was at the level of $\alpha = 0.05$. In the remaining analysed periods, it was not found that the value of above-average rates of return was statistically significant.

Based on the above results, Table 7.3 presents the value of basic descriptive statistics and T-test results for AR and CAR rates at the previously indicated statistically significant points of the study.

The data in Table 7.3 are the basis for the following conclusions:

•   The above-average negative rates of return appear already in the first examined moment after the event, i.e., after 10 minutes. The reaction to the release of information about the submitted application is the strongest at the time of its release, and the subsequent drops are smaller and appear after longer periods. This suggests that the market is adapting the share price to new information that has emerged.

Table 7.2 Statistical test results for the surveyed sample of companies n = 51

Test	AAR											
	(10)	*(20)*	*(30)*	*(40)*	*(50)*	*(60)*	*(70)*	*(80)*	*(90)*	*(100)*	*(110)*	*(120)*
Adj. Patell Z	−7.291 (***)	−1.041	−4.266 (***)	0.09	−4.367 (***)	0.329	0.316	0.18	−2.148 (*)	0.93	−0.196	0.05

Note: If the significance was at α = 0.01 then the symbol (***) was used, for α = 0.05 (**), for α = 0.1 (*).
Source: Own study.

Table 7.3 Descriptive statistics value for statistically significant 10-minute
intervals and CAR rate

Descriptive statistic	AR(10)	AR(30)	AR(50)	AR(90)	CAR
Mean	−5.6%	−3.3%	−2.2%	−1.5%	−9.5% (CAAR value)
Median	−1.1%	0.0%	0.3%	0.2%	−8.2%
Standard deviation	12.7%	12.0%	9.3%	9.0%	22.1%
Kurtosis	17.1	19.2	23.6	43.2	0.0
Skewness	−3.6	−4.2	−4.3	−6.3	−0.5
Range	82.0%	74.4%	67.1%	67.2%	93.4%
Minimum	−74.4%	−68.6%	−56.3%	−62.4%	−65.9%
Maximum	7.5%	5.9%	10.8%	4.8%	27.6%
Number of negative AR's[a]	32 (8)	26 (4)	25 (5)	22 (2)	x
Number of positive AR's[a]	19 (0)	25 (0)	26 (0)	29 (0)	x
Number of negative CAR's[a]	x	X	x	x	33 (6)
Number of positive CAR's[a]	x	X	x	x	18 (0)

[a] The number of AR and CAR rates that were statistically significant at least at $\alpha = 0.05$, is
presented in brackets.

Source: Own study.

- The average value of the cumulative rates of return for all analysed events is −9.5%, which clearly indicates that the appearance of information about the submitted application causes, on average, a significant discount of shares of such a company within the examined 120 minutes.
- Moreover, the shorter the time from the appearance of the information, the greater the variability of the obtained return rates within the examined sample, which is evidenced by the decreasing value of the standard deviation.
- In the analysed sample, significant differences were also observed between the minimum and maximum values of the tested rates of return. The lowest rates of return are also several times higher than the observed maximum rates of return. The value of the presented range also proves that the rates of return are highly diversified.
- The number of all above-average negative rates of return is higher than the number of above-average positive rates of return for the surveyed companies in the first two distinguished moments of the survey. After 50 and 90 minutes after the occurrence of the event, there were more companies for which above-average positive rates of return were recorded, however, as indicated earlier, the values of these positive rates of return are much lower than of the negative ones. It is worth mentioning here that, after the T-test was carried out, no above-average positive

and statistically significant rate of return was recorded in the sample, as evidenced by the values presented in brackets.

• Moreover, in the analysed period, 33 companies achieved negative cumulative values of above-average return rates, and for eighteen companies, submission of the application was not associated with obtaining a negative, above-average cumulative return rate.

Also, the value of the test for the CAAR rate turned out to be statistically significant at the significance level of $\alpha = 0.01$. This means that, on average, the companies examined had an above-average negative cumulative rate of return in the examined period of 5 minutes before and 120 minutes after the announcement of an event.

The following figures – Figures 7.2 and 7.3 show the value of the AAR rate in successive 10-minute intervals, but these values apply to companies broken down by type of submitted application and it is a restructuring application and a bankruptcy application, respectively. Each figure also shows whether the value of the calculated test statistic was statistically significant, and the following rule was adopted for the determinations used in the graphs: If the significance was at the level of $\alpha = 0.01$, then the symbol (***) was adopted, for $\alpha = 0.05$ (**), for $\alpha = 0.1$ (*), statistically insignificant results were marked with the symbol (), only if they were previously identified as statistically significant moments for the entire study sample.

In the case of applications for restructuring, in the first examined time interval, as for all of the analysed applications, there was the biggest drop in the quotations of the companies in question, which was close to -6%. It was

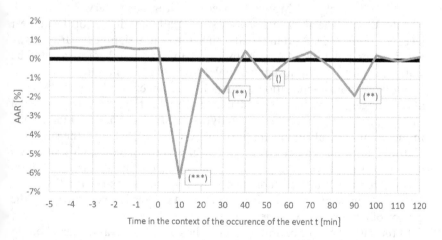

Figure 7.2 Value of the AAR rate for restructuring applications n = 36, for a 10-minute interval.

Source: Own study.

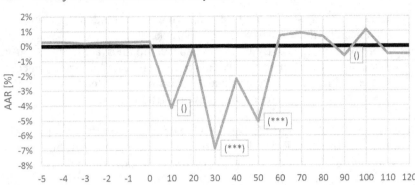

Figure 7.3 Value of the AAR rate for bankruptcy applications n = 15, for a 10-minute
interval.

Source: Own study.

a drop with the highest considered significance level. In the 30th and 90th
minutes, statistically significant (for α = 0.05) above-average return rates
were also recorded, but the considered declines amounted to nearly –2%. In
the 50th minute, there was also a drop in quotations, but it amounted to less
than –1% and turned out to be statistically insignificant. In the remaining
time intervals, no statistically significant above-average rates of return were
recorded either.

For bankruptcy applications, it can be noticed that the lowest rate of
return appears in the 30th minute after the announcement of the event,
which is a drop of –7%. Moreover, over –5% drop was observed in the 50th
minute. Both of the above drops were statistically significant for the highest
level of significance. Also in the first time interval, a significant drop of the
listed shares, reaching –4%, was observed. However, it did not turn out to be
statistically significant, just like a slight drop in the 90th minute.

For bankruptcy applications, therefore, a stronger effect can be observed
after a longer period than for restructuring applications. It can be assumed
that despite the use of numerous analytical tools, investors need more time
in the event of bankruptcy applications to thoroughly assess the situation
and take appropriate actions related to the sale of shares. This situation
is also consistent with the previously presented conclusions that investors
need more time to include more negative information in the valuation.

Table 7.4 presents the values related to CAAR rates, broken down into the
groups of companies examined above.

In the case of both examined groups, the CAAR rate value turned out to
be statistically significant, for α = 0.05. It should be noted that in the case
of bankruptcy applications, the average value of above-average cumulated
drop was more than twice as high as in the case of restructuring applications.

Table 7.4 Test statistics value for CAAR rate by type of application submitted

Grouping variable	CAAR value	pos:neg CAR	Number of CARs considered	Adjusted Patell Z
Restructuring	−7.1%	14:22	36	−1.98 (**)
Bankruptcy	−15.2%	04:11	15	−2.12 (**)

Source: Own study.

What is more, both analysed groups also show a significant advantage of negative CAR rates over positive CAR rates, for the surveyed companies.

In the next step, AAR rates for the surveyed companies are presented, but broken down by the moment of announcing the application.

The data presented in Figure 7.4 are the basis for the conclusion that if the information about the submitted application appears at a time when there is no active session (late afternoon, night, or morning hours), then immediately after the opening of the next session there is a sharp sale of shares of such companies. The value of the AAR rate after 10 minutes is close to 8%, which is influenced by the accumulation of orders placed at the opening of the session. To verify whether the analysed drops occur earlier, research was also carried out for 5-minute and 1-minute intervals, which is presented later in this chapter. In subsequent moments analysed, statistically significant, above-average negative return rates with the highest level of significance were recorded. For the remaining 10-minute intervals, there were no above-average rates of return that would be statistically significant. It can also be observed that the given values of AAR rates for applications submitted outside a session are characterised by considerable

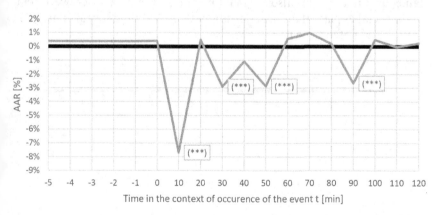

Figure 7.4 Value of the AAR rate for applications submitted outside the session n = 32, for a 10-minute interval.

Source: Own study.

variability. Twenty minutes after the application, for example, the value of AAR rate is positive.

From the results shown in the Figure 7.5 it can be observed that a different course of the AAR rates can be seen for the applications emerging during the session. Apart from the previously identified test moments as statistically significant, there is also a statistically significant value (for $\alpha = 0.05$) at the 20th minute. For these applications, it can be seen that although the first decline occurs immediately, it is almost four times smaller than in the case of applications submitted outside the session. There is no effect of the accumulation of orders, which was visible in the second group of applications, submitted outside the session. For the applications submitted during the session, one can see a gradual reduction in the price of the shares for 30 minutes after the event is announced. In the 10th and 20th minute, the drops are close to –2%, and in the 30th minute, there is the largest one-off drop of nearly –4%. Importantly, the latter drop is statistically significant at the level of $\alpha = 0.01$, and the other two previously mentioned at the level of $\alpha = 0.05$. There was no statistically significant above-average negative rate of return at the 50th minute, and there was a slight but positive rate of return at the 90th minute. Importantly, for applications submitted during the session, after 30 minutes, a comparable drop in the value of shares is observed (–7.8%), as for applications submitted outside the session at the first 10-minute measurement (–7.7%). It can therefore be concluded that the market needs additional 20 minutes for applications submitted during the session to reach the level of drop adequate to that observed for requests submitted outside the session. Besides, for applications submitted during the session, the observed drops are less pronounced, as there are no longer statistically significant drops in the 50th and 90th minute.

This is also confirmed by the data for the CAAR rate, which are contained in Table 7.5. It is also a signal for companies that a lower overpricing of shares takes place if information about the proceedings occurs during the session and not outside it.

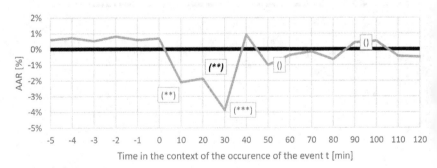

Figure 7.5 Value of the AAR rate for applications submitted during the session n = 19, for a 10-minute interval.

Source: Own study.

Table 7.5 Test statistics value for CAAR rate due to the time of application

Grouping variable	CAAR value	pos:neg CAR	Number of CARs considered	Adjusted Patell Z
Outside the session	–12.0%	11:21	32	–2.88 (***)
During the session	–5.2%	07:12	19	–1.46 ()

Source: Own study.

The average value of drops for applications submitted outside the session is more than twice as high as the average value of drops for applications submitted during the session. Moreover, the calculated value of the test statistics does not constitute a basis for stating that the cumulative drops obtained for applications submitted during the session are statistically significant. However, for the second group of applications, there are no doubts as to the statistical significance of the obtained results.

7.3.2 Analysis of data for a 5-minute interval

The research carried out in the 10-minute interval allowed to identify key moments for the researched groups of companies, which are important for the conducted analysis. In the next step, a 5-minute and 1-minute interval study was carried out to obtain in-depth information on the previously indicated moments after the event. Figure 7.6 shows the cumulative results for the tested sample for a 5-minute interval.

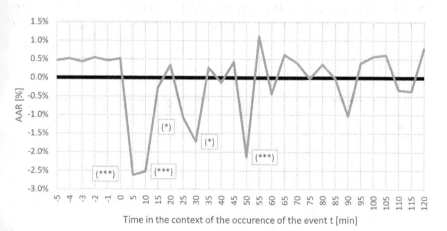

Figure 7.6 The value of the AAR rate for the examined sample of companies n = 51, for the 5-minute interval.

Source: Own study.

The data presented in Figure 7.6 corresponds to the data presented in Figure 7.1. It turns out that the highest drops recorded in the first 10-minute interval are a consequence of cumulative drops in the 5th and then in the 10th minute after the event occurred. In both of these moments, the drops amounted to over –2.5%, which resulted in such significant drops in the first interval in Figure 7.1. This means that the reaction of investors to the occurrence of an event is even faster for some companies, as a statistically significant overestimation takes place already in the 5th minute after the event and continues in the next 5-minute interval. A similar situation occurs 30 minutes after the event. In Figure 7.1, a statistically significant negative rate of return of α = 0.01 was observed at this point. The 5-minute interval study shows that the 30-minute discount is the cumulative value of negative returns from 25 and 30 minutes. Both these rates were statistically significant at α = 0.1 level. The situation of the 50-minute study remained unchanged. Both for the 10-minute and 5-minute intervals, above-average negative rates of return were observed at this point. Also, no statistically significant negative return rate was observed after 45 minutes for the 5-minute interval, which indicates that the negative drops from the 50th minute (in a test with a 10-minute interval) are not due to an accumulation of negative return rates from the 45th and 50th minute of the test. The rate obtained in the 90th-minute window was also not statistically significant, as the other rates determined for the remaining moments in the 120th-minute window.

As shown in Figure 7.7, in the case of the 5-minute interval, only the drops for the first two intervals, after 5 and 10 minutes from the occurrence of the event, are statistically significant. Both of these drops are statistically significant at α = 0.01. The remaining moments, previously identified as key moments, i.e., the 30th and 50th minute, do not show return rates that would be above-average and statistically significant. It can be seen that the earlier (in the test with the 10-minute interval) diagnosed drops from the 30th

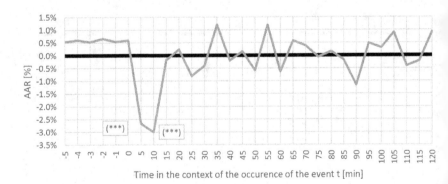

Time in the context of the occurence of the event t [min]

Figure 7.7 Value of the AAR rate for restructuring applications n = 36, for a 5-minute interval.

Source: Own study.

minute are preceded by stronger discounts from the 25th minute. On the other hand, for the 50th minute, a negative above-average rate of return was observed (–0.5%), but it is preceded by an average positive rate of return in the 45th minute. Moreover, it can be seen that for the 5-minute interval in the case of restructuring applications, there is no significant differentiation in the achieved rates of return. Most of the results are in the range (–1%, 1%). A greater variability was noted for bankruptcy applications, as shown by the data in Figure 7.8.

As shown by the course of the AAR curve, it can be seen that in the case of bankruptcy applications, there are two moments with above-average negative rates of return, and these are the 30th and 50th minutes after the occurrence of the event. The negative impulse from the 50th minute is located in the vicinity of two moments with above-average positive rates of return. Interestingly, a 5-minute interval study indicates a certain pattern. Before the event, the companies recorded slight positive rates of return, the occurrence of the event contributes to the appearance of an above-average negative rate of return in the 5th minute, and this rate is not statistically significant. However, the drops are not continued with such strength in the following minutes of the test, i.e., 10th and 15th minute. In the 20th minute, there is a positive rate of return, followed by significant discounts of the 20th and 30th minute. A similar situation occurs at another important point of the test. After a positive 45th minute return rate, a significant negative above-average rate of return occurs. Such a course indicates that the appearance of a positive return rate encourages investors to sell off their shares and avoid companies for which unfavourable information appears. And such a positive

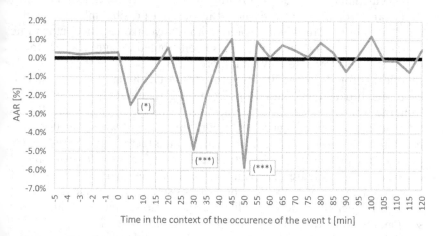

Figure 7.8 Value of the AAR rate for bankruptcy applications n = 15, for a 5-minute interval.

Source: Own study.

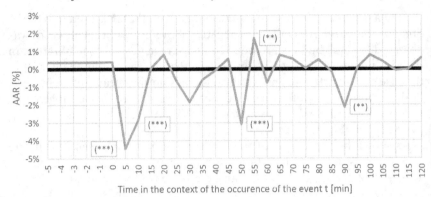

Figure 7.9 Value of the AAR rate for applications submitted outside the session n = 32, for a 5-minute interval.

Source: Own study.

rate of return allows compensating for at least a small part of the losses previously incurred as a result of the event.

Also, the second division made for the test, grouping the applications into those submitted during the session and outside the session in a 5-minute interval, leads to new conclusions and is the basis for maintaining the previously diagnosed regularities based on the test with a 10-minute interval. The results of the test for the 5-minute interval for applications submitted outside the session are presented in Figure 7.9.

Figure 7.9 and the data contained therein are the basis for the conclusion that the declines for applications submitted outside the session are sudden and occur immediately at the opening of the following session. The most significant drops were already noted in the first possible interval for this test that is in the 5th minute. Another above-average negative return rate appears in the 10th minute, which also contributed to significant drops in the 10-minute interval test. What is more, it can be seen that the statistically significant drops from the 30th minute in the test with the 10-minute interval have been broken down into drops from the 25th minute of –1% and drops from the 30th minute of –2%. Another above-average and a statistically significant rate of return occurs at the 50th minute, and what the 10-minute interval study did not show, in the 55th minute there is an above-average positive rate of return, which is statistically significant for $\alpha = 0.05$. Based on the data from Figure 7.9, it can also be concluded that the variability of the obtained rates of return for applications submitted outside the session is much greater than the variability for applications submitted during the session, for which the AAR value is presented in Figure 7.10.

Importantly, applications that appear during the quotation process are subject to a delay of at least 5 minutes in the reaction of investors to the event. Figure 7.10 shows that the occurrence of an event has practically

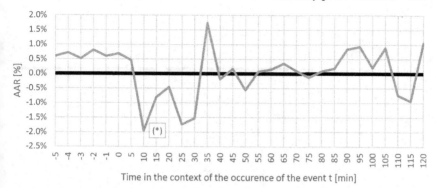

Figure 7.10 Value of the AAR rate for applications submitted during the session n = 19, for a 5-minute interval.

Source: Own study.

no impact on the quotations of the surveyed companies. The value of the AAR rate in the 5th minute does not deviate from the level that can be observed 5 minutes before the event. Only in the 10th minute, one can see an above-average negative rate of return, reaching nearly 2%. At no other time of the study, with the use of the 5-minute interval for this group of companies, was the statistically significant above-average rate of return. Importantly, the drops that started in the 10th minute last continuously until the 30th minute, and it is only in the 35th minute that an above-average positive return rate exceeding the level of 1.5% can be observed. The use of research with a 5-minute interval allows therefore to identify a certain "time gap," which consists in the fact that an investor looking for above-average profits should take a short position on the market in less than 5 minutes after being informed of the company's bankruptcy or restructuring. Such above-average profits will appear if the application is made during the session and investor behave as described above. The key to the success of such an operation may be the use of an automated transaction system that will interpret and properly use the occurring event. Such a short position should be closed at the latest within the 30th minute after the event.

7.3.3 Analysis of data for a minute interval

In the next step of the study, an analysis for the minute interval was performed. Due to the previously obtained results, the results presented below range from 5 minutes before the event to 12 minutes after the event. Such an analysis should allow for capturing the key differences between the examined groups of companies in the first moments after the publication of information on the application and even better to identify the previously found time gap.

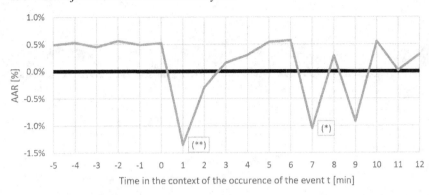

Figure 7.11 The value of the AAR rate for the examined sample of companies n = 51, for the 1-minute interval.

Source: Own study.

As shown in Figure 7.11, the tested companies are characterized by a statistically significant, above-average return rate in the first minute after the occurrence of the event. These drops reach almost 1.5%. Also in the 7th and 9th minute, there are revaluations of these actions reaching almost –1%, with the first drop being statistically significant for $\alpha = 0.1$, while for the second one no statistical significance was observed at the studied levels. It is the drops from the 1st, 7th, and 9th minutes that are the reason for the statistically significant drops in the 5th and 10th minutes for the 5-minute interval, and in the 10th minute for the 10-minute interval.

Figure 7.12 shows the values of the AAR rate for the published information on the restructuring applications. The data in Figure 7.12 are the same as those in Figure 7.11. Also in the 1st, 7th, and 9th minute, the most significant drops were recorded. At the first two mentioned moments, the

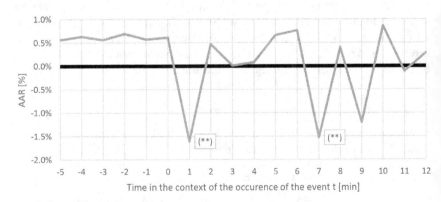

Figure 7.12 Value of the AAR rate for restructuring applications n = 36, for a 1-minute interval.

Source: Own study.

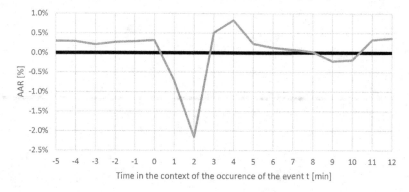

Figure 7.13 Value of the AAR rate for bankruptcy applications n =15, for a 1-minute interval.

Source: Own study.

above-average negative rates of return were statistically significant at the level of α = 0.05. Moreover, the drops for restructuring applications are slightly higher than for all the companies surveyed.

In the analysed window shown in Figure 7.13, there were no statistically significant rates. The situation was similar for this group of companies in the test with the 5-minute and 10-minute intervals. However, in the case of publication of information about bankruptcy, drops can be observed in both the 1st and 2nd minute of analysis. They are at the level of –1% and –2%, respectively, which indicates a significant downward correction of the shares of these companies in the first 2 minutes after the information appeared. In the subsequent minutes of the study, the course of quotations with little volatility can be observed, different from that for restructuring application or for all surveyed companies.

The results presented in the Figure 7.14 show that for the group of applications that were submitted outside the session, statistically significant drops

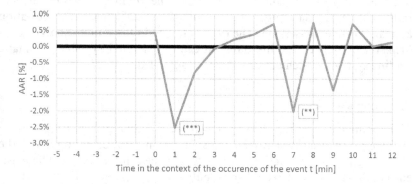

Figure 7.14 Value of the AAR rate for applications submitted outside the session n = 32, for a 1-minute interval.

Source: Own study.

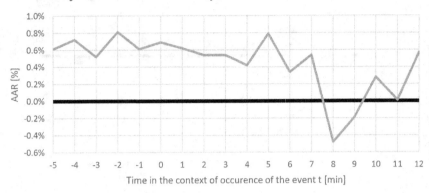

Figure 7.15 Value of the AAR rate for applications submitted during the session
n = 19, for a 1-minute interval.

Source: Own study.

in the first (for $\alpha = 0.01$) and 7th minute (for $\alpha = 0.05$) can be observed in the first 12 minutes after the resumption of quotations. A significant drop in the tested sample also appears in the 9th minute, but it is not statistically significant, despite its value close to –1.5%. Moreover, it was also observed that the sudden reaction in the first minute was accompanied by another negative rate of return in the 2nd minute of the quotation. These four drops in the 1st, 2nd, 7th, and 9th minute amount together to nearly 7%, which affects the previously presented results for 5-minute and 10-minute intervals.

The data presented in Figure 7.15 are the basis for the statement that the previously identified time gap in the study with a 5-minute interval is even longer and amounts to an average of 7 minutes. The minute analysis shows that the first drops for companies for which information appears during quotation occur in the 8th and 9th minutes. Importantly, these declines are not statistically significant, and their size is nearly five times smaller than in the case of the data presented for companies for which the information appears outside the session. The data obtained in the minute analysis confirms the existence of a time gap that can be exploited by using automatic trading systems, which has already been signalled.

7.4 Conclusions

The conducted research showed that there is a time gap of 7 minutes on average on the market between the submission of information about the application and the reaction of investors to such information. The existence of this gap has been confirmed only for applications published during an ongoing trading session, as if information about the submitted application appears outside the duration of the trading session, then there is no such gap. Then investors' immediate reaction to the opening of the following session is observed, which manifests itself in significant drops in quotations:

* –2.5% in the first minute of the 1-minute interval study.
* –4% and –3% in the first two 5-minute intervals, i.e., in the 5th and 10th minute.
* –7.5% in the first 10-minute interval.

All of the above-mentioned drops are statistically significant at the highest significance level assumed in the study, equal to $\alpha = 0.01$.

The fact that there is an identified time gap on the market may be used by investors who, using automated trading systems, will take a short position on the relevant assets in advance of traditional investors. Moreover, it has been shown that the depth of the drops for applications made during an ongoing session is much lower than for events that occur outside the ongoing session. It turned out that if the digital information about the submitted application appears during a session, then on average, such a company records an above-average drop in the value of its shares by nearly 5%, but it is not a statistically significant drop and covers the range from 5 minutes before the event to 120 minutes after the event. On the other hand, if the information about the submitted application appears outside the ongoing session, the transfer of investors' reactions to the session on the next working day results in a significantly higher average overpricing of shares of such companies, which is 12% and is statistically significant. Paradoxically, it turned out that it is more advantageous for the owners of companies information about the application for insolvency proceedings to be disclosed during the session because then the average above-average declines are not only lower but also have a less volatile course.

The second part of the study, which divided the conclusions drawn into those concerning bankruptcy and restructuring, leads to the following conclusions. First, bankruptcy applications have more than double the above-average cumulative rate of return, which is over –15%. Meanwhile, for restructuring applications, this figure was –7.1%. For both groups, the calculated cumulative values were statistically significant for $\alpha = 0.05$. These values were observed in the examined window, i.e., from 5 minutes before the event to 120 minutes after the event with a 10-minute interval. Second, applications for restructuring have the most significant drops in the first 10 minutes after the occurrence of the event, while bankruptcy applications have the highest drops in the 30th and 50th minutes. Such results were obtained for the test with a 10-minute and 5-minute interval. In addition, in the first 12 minutes after the occurrence of the event, with a 1-minute interval test, it was observed that restructuring applications were characterised by higher volatility of above-average return rates than bankruptcy applications.

All this conclusion shows that digitalization gives a great opportunity for incorporating new investments strategies. The accessible of data is here a positive side of developing ICT.

Further studies on the diagnosed time gap should assess whether it is shortening over time and with the development of information technology and transactional systems. For the time being, such a study could give a distorted picture of the actual situation due to a small number of cases in such groups.

References

Antweiler, W., & Frank, M. Z. (2004). Is all that talk just noise? The information content of internet stock message boards. *Journal of Finance, 59*(3), 1259–1294.

Bachelier, L. (1900). Théorie de la spéculation. *Annales scientifiques de l'É.N.S. 3e série, tome, 17*(1900), 21–86.

Barclay, M. J., & Litzenberger, R. H. (1988). Announcement effects of new equity issues and the use of intraday price data. *Journal of Financial Economics, 21*(1), 71–99.

Będowska-Sójka, B. (2010). Intraday CAC40, DAX and WIG20 returns when the American macro news is announced. *Bank and Credit, 41*(2), 7–20.

Black, F. (1986). Noise. *Journal of Finance, XLI*, (3), 529–43.

Black, B. S. (1998). Information asymmetry, the internet, and securities offerings. *SSRN Electronic Journal.* doi: 10.2139/ssrn.84489.

Bradley, D., Clarke, J., Lee, S., & Ornthanalai, C. (2014). Are analysts' recommendations informative? Intraday evidence on the impact of time stamp delays. *Journal of Finance, 69*(2), 645–673.

Busse, J. A., & Green, T. C. (2002). Market efficiency in real time. *Journal of Financial Economics, 65*, 415–437.

Cheng, C., Chien, M., & Lee, C. (2021). ICT diffusion, financial development, and economic growth: An international cross-country analysis. *Economic Modelling, 94*, 662–671. doi:10.1016/j.econmod.2020.02.008.

Coelho, L., & Taffler, R. J. (2009). Market Underreaction to Bad News: The Case of Bankruptcy Filings. Available at SSRN: https://ssrn.com/abstract=1364413.

Datta, S., & Iskander-Datta, M. E. (1995). The information content of bankruptcy filing on securityholders of the bankrupt firm: An empirical investigation. *Journal of Banking & Finance, 19*, 903–919.

Dawkins, M., Bhattacharya, N., & Bamber, L. (2007). Systematic share price fluctuations after bankruptcy filings and the investors who drive them. *Journal of Financial and Quantitative Analysis, 42*, 399–420.

De Bondt, W. F. M., & Thaler, R. H. (1985). Does the stock market overreact? *Journal of Finance, 40*(3), 793–808.

Delcey, T. (2019). Samuelson vs Fama on the efficient market hypothesis: the point of view of expertise. *Œconomia – History/Methodology/Philosophy, 9*(1), 37–58.

De Long, J. B., Shleifer, A., Summers, L. H., & Waldmann, R. J. (1990). Noise trader risk in financial markets. *Journal of Political Economy, 98*(4), 703–738.

Dimson, E. (Ed.) (1988). *Stock market anomalies.* Cambridge University Press.

Dreman, D. (1982). *The new contrarian investment strategy.* Random House.

Fama, E. (1965a). The behavior of stock market prices. *Journal of Business, 38,* 34–105.

Fama, E. (1965b). Random walks in stock market prices. *Financial Analysts Journal, 21,* 55–9.

Fama, E. (1970). Efficient capital markets: A review of theory and empirical work. *Journal of Finance, 25,* 383–417.

Fama, E., & Thaler, R. (2016). Are markets efficient? Interview with Eugene Fama and Robert Thaler, 30 June 2016, https://review.chicagobooth.edu/economics/2016/video/are-markets-efficient (20.03.2020).

Gurgul, H., Suliga, M., & Wójtowicz, T. (2013). The reaction of intraday WIG returns to the U.S. Macroeconomic news announcements. *Quantitative Methods in Economics, XIV*(1), 150–159.

Gurgul, H. (2019). *Analiza zdarzeń na rynkach akcji: Wpływ informacji na ceny papierów wartościowych.* Wydawnictwo Nieoczywiste.

Hanousek, J., Kocenda, E., & Kutan, A. M. (2009). The reaction of asset prices to macroeconomic announcements in new EU markets: Evidence from intraday data. *Journal of Financial Stability, 5*(2), 199–219.

Howe, J. S. (1986). Evidence on stock market overreaction. *Financial Analyst Journal, 42*(4), 74–77.

Kolari, J. W., & Pynnönen, S. (2010). Event study testing with cross-sectional correlation of abnormal returns. *Review of Financial Studies, 23*(11), 3996–4025. doi: 10.1093/rfs/hhq072.

Konchitchki, Y., & O'Leary, D. E. (2011). Event study methodologies in information systems research. *International Journal of Accounting Information Systems, 12*(2), 99–115.

Kothari, S. P., & Warner, J. B. (2007). Econometrics of event studies. In B. E. Eckbo (Ed.), *Handbook of corporate finance: Empirical corporate finance* (Vol. *1*, pp. 3–32). Elsevier.

Latif, M., Arshad, S., Fatima, M., & Farooq, S. (2011). market efficiency, market anomalies, causes, evidences, and some behavioral aspects of market anomalies. *Research Journal of Finance and Accounting, 2*(9/10), 1–13.

Lee, M. H., Tsai, T. C., Chen, J., & Lio, M. C. (2019). Can information and and communication technology improve stock market efficiency? A cross-country study. *Bulletin of Economic Research, 71*(2), 113–135.

Malkiel, B. G. (2003). The efficient market hypothesis and its critics. *Journal of Economic Perspective, 17*(1), 59–82.

Niemand, T., Rigtering, J. C., Kallmünzer, A., Kraus, S., & Maalaoui, A. (2020). Digitalization in the financial industry: A contingency approach of entrepreneurial orientation and strategic vision on digitalization. *European Management Journal.* doi: 10.1016/j.emj.2020.04.008.

Patell, J. M., & Wolfson, M. A. (1984). The intraday speed of adjustment of stock prices to earnings and dividend announcements. *Journal of Financial Economics, 13*(2), 223–252.

Robertson, C., Geva, S., & Wolff, R. (2007). Predicting the short-term market reaction to asset specific news: Is time against us? In Huang, J.Z., and Ye, Y. (Eds.) *Proceedings industry track workshop, 11th pacific-asia conference on knowledge discovery and data mining (PAKDD 2007),* pp. 1–13, Nanjing, China.

Schatzberg, J., & Reiber, R. (1992). Extreme negative information and the market adjustment process: The case of corporate bankruptcy. *Quaterely Journal of Business and Economics, 31*, 3–21.

Schimmer, M., Levchenko, A., & Müller, S. (2015). EventStudyTools (Research Apps). Retrieved 23 March 2020, from http://www.eventstudytools.com

Schwert, G. W. (2003). Anomalies and market efficiency. In Constantinides, G.M., Harris, M., Stulz, R. (Eds.) *Handbook of the economics and finance,,* Vol. 1, Part B, 939–974.

Suliga, M., & Wójtowicz, T. (2013). The reaction of the WSE to U.S. Employment news announcements. *Managerial Economics, 14*, 165–176.

Trueman, B. (1988). A theory of noise trading in securities markets. *Journal of Finance, XLIII*(1), 83–95.

Wysocki, P. (1998). Cheap talk on the web: The determinants of postings on stock message boards, *Working paper no. 98025*. University of Michigan Business School.

Yartey, C. A. (2008). Financial development, the structure of capital markets, and the global digital divide. *Information Economics and Policy, 20*(2), 208–227. doi: 10.1016/j.infoecopol.2008.02.002.

Zawadowski, A. G., Andor, G., & Kertesz, J. (2006). Short-term market reaction after extreme price changes of liquid stocks. *Quantitative Finance, 6*(4), 283–295.

8 Money market digitization consequences on financial inclusion of businesses at the base of the pyramid in Nigeria

Oluwafemi Michael Olagunju and Samuel C. Avemaria Utulu

8.1 Introduction

This work addresses four key concepts central to development discourses in the 21st Century: microfinance banks, digitization, inclusion, and the base of the pyramid economy (Akingunola et al., 2018; Dismas et al., 2018; Prahalad, 2005; Young, 2002). Given the importance of money, finance, and investment in the 21st-Century development discourse, the financial market is critical to programs initiated to promote development. According to Fabozzi et al. (2002), financial markets are the markets that provide access to funds required by businesses to run. The money market is an integral part of the financial market. It offers short loans that are repayable between six months and one year and does this through financial institutions such as microfinance banks. Microfinance banks are critical to meeting individuals' financial needs and small business in rural (and excluded) areas where people and businesses do not have easy access to financial services provided by other types of banks (Adu et al., 2019; Akingunola et al., 2018). In a simple term, digitization is computerization and can be done either through automation or digital augmentation. Automation denotes the transformation of all the processes required to achieve tasks, for instance, opening accounts with microfinance banks, maintaining the accounts and providing money and other services to account owners, into forms where they can only be completed using information and communication technology (ICT) (Dismas et al., 2018). An excellent example is the automated teller machine which banks use to provide access to the opening of accounts, withdrawals, account statements and money transfer and payment services (Fashoto et al., 2017). Digital augmentation has to do with transforming a part of the processes required to complete tasks, in this case, tasks related to accessing microfinance bank products and services, into forms where they can be accomplished using both manual systems and ICT based systems (Mhlanga, 2020).

The third term that is of concern to scholars that study development in the 21st Century is inclusion (Young & Wigdor, 2021). The term has become very popular in the extant literature of different academic disciplines including,

DOI: 10.4324/9781003199076-8

education, information technology, ICT for development, economics, and other academic disciplines (Mader, 2018; Silver, 2015). The term derives its essence from democratic principles and philosophies (Young, 2002). It advocates the importance of allowing stakeholders, irrespective of their social and economic standing, to participate in the processes leading to the development and implementation of strategies used to tackle issues that directly or indirectly impact their lives (Young, 2002). The fourth term, the base of the pyramid economic development ideology was propounded by Prahalad and popularized by many other scholars (Kramer & Belz, 2017; Prahalad, 2005). Arguments in the works of notable scholars propose that meaningful development can only be achieved across the globe if poor people are factored into not-for-profit development initiatives championed by multinational corporations. Multinational corporations make not-for-profit investments in poor people as their corporate contributions to eradicate poverty across the globe (Prahalad, 2005). The four concepts discussed so far point to the complex and multidisciplinary nature of contemporary discourses on development in developing countries (Mader, 2018; World Bank Institute, 2005). They also provide grounds for questioning the assumption that digitization can automatically promote the level of financial inclusion required to stimulate development at the base of the pyramid economy.

The aim of ongoing digitization of microfinance banks in Nigeria is to promote financial inclusion at the base of the pyramid economy. However, we observed that most businesses within the base of the pyramid economy are not yet financially included. We, therefore, investigated why ongoing microfinance bank digitization did not lead to financial inclusion at the base of the pyramid economy in Nigeria. We studied petty traders between March and August 2020 through interviews and observation to assess their experiences with ongoing financial digitization of microfinance banks and its impact on the extent to which they experience financial inclusion. Petty traders constitute the largest population of businesses in rural settlements in Nigeria. The remaining part of the work consist of literature review carried out on digitization and inclusion, microfinance bank and financial inclusion, microfinance banks and base of the pyramid economy, methodology, study findings, and analyses of the findings and conclusion.

8.2 Literature review

8.2.1 Digitization and inclusion

Digitization and inclusion are concepts that have always been jointly used either explicitly or implicitly in ICT related disciplines such as software engineering and information systems. Software engineering has to do with systematically structuring and modelling software development processes (Pressman, 2005). Software engineering has become crucial in contemporary times because of the role software applications play in the effective and efficient digitization of business processes. In software engineering, team-work, and a proper understanding of individual and team roles are very crucial. The software development team coordinator's main objective is to get the team to clearly understand individual and team roles as may be spelt out in the software development processes. Many software process management normative frameworks have been developed to help software engineers effectively and efficiently complete software development processes. The main ideas underlying existing normative software process improvement methodologies revolve around spelling out processes and dividing the processes into easily understood and easy-to-complete sub-processes. Doing this also spells out cooperative teamwork along differentiated software design responsibilities (Ngwenyama & Nielsen, 2003; Utulu et al., 2013). Software process management is essential because it is driven by the notion that each stakeholder involved in software development is crucial to successful software engineering. Invariably, software engineering starts with needs analyses. Needs analyses have to do with finding out why the software to be designed is required; that is how the software applications can be made the closest digital representation of social and technical realities in real life. Software process management is essential because factors that determine successful digitization go beyond the needs of software engineers and the organizations and/or individuals that commission them to develop software applications that are used for digitization. The reason is that stakeholders that determine successful digitization include a wide range of human entities and non-human entities (Latour, 2013). Human entities may consist of software engineers, groups and individuals that commission them, digital platform implementers, and digital platform users. Non-human actors include ICT, social realities and processes, organizations, and rules and regulations.

In information systems, systems design, analysis and implementation pay close attention to how teamwork can be enforced when meeting systems design, analysis and implementation objectives (Coronel & Morris, 2016). Systems design has to do with developing models that spell out systems modules, architecture, components, data requirements and interfaces (Coronel & Morris, 2016; Kearsley, 1988). It ensures proper implementation digital platforms in real-life contexts. The purpose of systems design is to provide enough data and information about systems requirements. It is assumed that this ensures consistency with entities spelt out in models and views of the system. Also, systems analysis has to do with identifying and understanding business and related social processes around individuals, groups, and inter-groups. It enables systems developers to develop digital platforms that can effectively and efficiently accomplish identified business and related social processes. Systems implementation entails the social and technical processes that will allow prospective and actual digital platform users to understand, accept and use information systems (Nielsen, 2014). The idea that motivates these bodies of literature is that every stakeholder namely, designers, analysts, implementers, and users, is essential to achieving digital platform design, analysis, implementation, and use objectives (Freeman et al., 2010). Microfinance banks digitization is therefore problematic. It has to do with the design, analysis, and implementation of digital platforms to facilitate the automation and digital augmentation of the processes that make up microfinance banks' financial products and services development and use. What then is inclusion? In its simplest form, inclusion means involving someone in some events. Between the middle and the turn of the 20th Century, inclusion started to take a new meaning (Thomas & Mefalopulos, 2009; Young, 2002). The new meaning was brought about by social realities that showed that some people are excluded from participating in social and economic activities essential to their wellbeing. Consequently, the word, inclusion began to be used to denote enabling people that are considered excluded from taking part in the activities that directly affect their wellbeing to start to take part in the activities (Thomas & Mefalopulos, 2009). During this period countries in the United Kingdom enacted laws that mandated the establishment of institutional frameworks that were considered helpful in promoting inclusion (Young, 2002). The gaps between the extent to which the rich and poor, citizens and immigrants, white and black, abled and disabled, sick and healthy, government and governed, etc. were allowed to participate in social and economic activities that directly or indirectly affected their lives resulted to this. Freire's (1972) postulation on the need for participatory education provided the grounds for the evolution of theoretical insights that formed the basis of the principles of inclusion. Freire's concern was the need to address the extent to which the education provided by oppressive colonial and apartheid governments aligned with the people's socio-economic and educational needs. So, he advocated for participatory development of educational philosophies and ideologies, and contents taught in classrooms. By participation, he meant that those to receive the education are to be included in the processes through which the kinds and ranges of education they received were determined (Freire, 1972). Over the years, Ferrier's ideas evolved into other concepts: participatory communication and inclusion (Gupta & Vegelin, 2016; Thomas & Mefalopulos, 2009; Young, 2002). It evolved into inclusive education, inclusive development, inclusive ICT design and implementation, and financial inclusion (Mbutor & Uba, 2013; Rowe et al., 2020; Slee, 2011). Ideas embedded into participation and inclusion promote the notion that philosophies of education, development approaches, ICT design and implementation and financial services should be developed and implemented in ways that enable all stakeholders to participate in their design and implementation. It is believed that this will facilitate meeting stakeholders' expectations given their involvement. However, the ways inclusion is conceptualized in the extant literature and operationalized in real-life situations in the recent past remain questionable. Financial inclusion, for instance, is defined as increasing the number of people that have accounts in banks and access to savings, credits and other financial services (e.g., Asongu & Odhiambo, 2019; Mbutor & Uba, 2013; Rasheed et al., 2019). According to the Nigerian Financial Inclusion Strategy quoted in Mbutor and Uba (2013, p. 319) "...financial inclusion is achieved when adult Nigerians have easy access to a broad range of formal financial services that meet their needs at an affordable cost." This definition is inadequate given notions in the traditional definition of inclusion. The definition neglects stakeholders' participation in the processes that lead to the development and implementation of financial inclusion strategies. It only emphasized "easy access to a broad range of formal financial services" without given credence to the need to include adult Nigerians in the processes of developing and implementing policies and frameworks where what constitutes easy access to formal financial services is laid out.

Our claim in this work is not that the notions promoted in existing definitions are incorrect. However, our claim is that the notions are inadequate because they exclude the need to allow people financially excluded to partake in the processes leading to developing and implementing financial inclusion policies and strategies. We argue that this aspect is crucial if microfinance bank digitization is to be used to achieve acceptable level of financial inclusion. For instance, Kenya Bankers Association (KBA) (2014) quoting G20 Financial Inclusion Experts Group's nine principles on innovative financial inclusion argue that encouraging "partnerships and direct consultation across government, business and other stakeholders (p. 4)" is crucial to attaining financial inclusion. KBA's position is similar to the notion we proposed in this work. We presumed that direct consultation with businesses and other stakeholders includes consulting with businesses and stakeholders at the base of the pyramid economy. Consulting with them will enable them to participate in the development and implementation of policies and frameworks that will positively impact their financial inclusion. Thakur's (2015) position that access to markets, local knowledge and acceptance through community trust is crucial to community marketing also justifies our claim. Our argument is that microfinance bank digitization can spur financial inclusion if implemented in two phases: first, the phase where microfinance digitization and financial inclusion policies and frameworks are developed in consultation with people at the base of the pyramid economy. Second, the phase where microfinance digitization and financial inclusion are implemented jointly with people at the base of the pyramid economy.

Making microfinance bank digitization inclusive is crucial because of the wide of range people and businesses that are involved in the creation of the social and technical systems that necessitate the digitization. Inclusion is also important to microfinance digitization because of the number of people and businesses whose needs must be identified, and adequately and appropriately embedded into the desired digital systems. This is to say that two realities determine the adequacy of the principles and philosophies necessary for driving microfinance bank digitization that can promote adequate

170 Oluwafemi Michael Olagunju and Samuel C. Avemaria Utulu

financial inclusion at the base of the pyramid economy. First, are the social realities that are created by diverse human and non-human entities that make the digitization of microfinance banks necessary for attaining financial inclusion. Second, is the diverse human and non-human entities that are required to be consulted in order to design and implement microfinance banks' digitization that promote productive financial inclusion. These two factors make providing answers to the following questions necessary: who are the human and non-human entities that create the social realities that make the digitization of microfinance banks necessary for facilitating financial inclusion at the base of the pyramid economy? How can all the human and non-human entities that create the social realities that make the digitization of microfinance banks necessary for facilitating financial inclusion at the base of the pyramid economy be included in the financial inclusion processes? Adequate and appropriate answers to these questions require that stakeholders should rethink the ways the term inclusion has been conceptualized over the years.

8.2.2 Microfinance banks and financial inclusion

The money market consists of financial institutions such as commercial, mortgage, microfinance and other forms of banks. Money markets perform five crucial functions namely, trade financing, investment, supporting commercial banks' self-efficacy and lubricating central banks' policies (Acha Ikechukwu, 2012; Agrawal & Sen, 2017). Microfinance banks are regarded as financial institutions for the poor. The primary responsibility of microfinance banks is to help poor people have access to the financial products and services they need for livelihood and to get out of the poverty line (Barman et al., 2009). They are also instrumental to lubricating central banks' policies on poverty eradication at the base of the pyramid and were first established in Bangladesh in the 1970s (Acha Ikechukwu, 2012; Agrawal & Sen, 2017). It follows that microfinance banks have been established in all most all countries across the globe to serve as platforms for including people and businesses that are usually socially and geographically marginalized and isolated from formal financial institutions. People are regarded as socially marginalized because they stay in rural areas where there are no commercial banks given the cost of setting up and maintaining commercial banks. They are also regarded as geographically isolated because they are unable to access the products and services of commercial banks situated in urban areas. Globally, rural areas constitute the majority of settlements that are characterized by limited or total lack of social amenities that are necessary for siting and running commercial banks (Olubiyo & Hill, 2002).

Microfinance banks can be categorized, based on ownership, into three types namely, government owned, individually owned, and private organization owned. Model for managing loans include loans provided to individuals and groups (Self Help Group and Grameen Group models) (Barman et al., 2009). In some countries governments establish microfinance banks with the aim of using them to promote financial inclusion of rural populace and small businesses and in effect, promote the development of base of the pyramid economy. This category of microfinance bank existed in Nigeria in the 1990s when the People's Bank was established by the Military Junta headed by General Ibrahim Gbadamosi Babangida through Decree No. 22 of 1990. The function of the bank as stated in the decree is:

a The provision of basic credit requirements for under-privileged Nigerians who are involved in legitimate economic activities (e.g. roadside mechanics, petty traders, small scale farmers) in both urban and rural areas and who cannot normally benefit from the services of orthodox banking system due to their inability to provide collateral security.

b The acceptance of savings from the same group of customers and make repayments of such savings together with any interests thereon after placing the money, in bulk sums, or short term deposits with commercial and merchant banks. (People's Bank of Nigeria Act No. 22, 1990).

The Bank of Agriculture, Nigeria which was established in year 2000 was another form of microfinance bank that was established and funded by government. The bank was established to provide credit facilities to both small and large scale farmers and small businesses in rural areas that lack to capacity to provide collateral required to get loans from commercial banks (Olubiyo & Hill, 2002). Consequently, Bank of Agriculture branches were mainly sited in rural and sub-rural areas. Microfinance banks established by an individual or groups of individuals are normally situated in urban areas to service the financial needs of people and organization that do not have ready access to financial services provided by commercial banks.

There is a deluge of research studies that have been done in Nigeria and other countries across the globe on microfinance banks. A couple of the studies underscored the challenges and prospects of microfinance banks (e.g., Acha Ikechukwu, 2012; Taiwo et al., 2016). These studies argue that microfinance banks were established in Nigeria to promote financial inclusion of the poor, provide employment, engender rural development, and reduce poverty (e.g., Acha Ikechukwu, 2012). Most of the studies, as expected, focused on assessing the role microfinance banks play in the eradicating poverty in rural areas and spurring economic and social development there. Microfinance banks were consequently, conceptualized from the point of view of financial institutions that serve as links between development program of the government and rural and poor people (Yahaya & Osemene, 2011). Conversely, most of these studies reported inadequate infrastructure, social misconception, poor legal and regulatory frameworks, unbridled competition from other financial institutions, abandonment of core values, and lack of qualified manpower as the challenges microfinance banks face (e.g., Acha Ikechukwu, 2012; Taiwo et al., 2016; Yahaya & Osemene, 2011). Like with other organizations, microfinance banks are involved in digitization. They digitize their financial products and services because of the need to ensure efficiency and effectiveness (Agrawal & Sen, 2017). Accountability and efficiency drive microfinance banks' digitization in most parts of the globe. Accountability has to do with ensuring that corrupt practices are eliminated from microfinance banks, while efficiency has to do with ensuring that microfinance banks are able to effectively ensure the inclusion of those they are meant to serve.

Microfinance bank digitization could be in the forms of automation and digital augmentation (Agrawal & Sen, 2017; Ratan et al., 2010). Automation of microfinance banks involves activities that center around digitizing major components of microfinance banks' work processes, products and services. Digital augmentation occurs mainly in situations where microfinance banks are unable to fully automate their processes, products and services. This is common where microfinance bank customers still use paper based forms to register for services and apply for financial products that will be delivered using ICT based systems (Ratan et al., 2010). The proliferation of ICT led to the inclination to digitize microfinance banks across the globe. It follows that digitization makes products and services provided by microfinance banks to become information related. This is to say that money becomes computer digits and product and services become digitized webpages that can only be assessed using ICT. It is therefore argued that digitization enables efficient and effective production and access to microfinance bank products and services over large geographical spaces and with minimal time and effort. In Kenya, reports provided by the UN shows that the One Acre Fund helped to cut repayment collection by 46%, and costs by 80% (UNSGSA, 2018). This is the reason why the assumption that digitization has the potential to promote easy access to microfinance bank services and products and in effect, eliminate financial exclusion has become widespread. In its current state, literature that report the impact of microfinance bank digitization on financial inclusion of the base of the pyramid economy promote the notion that digitization is deterministic (e.g., Rasheed et al., 2019). This category of literature conceptualize financial inclusion as efforts made to enable adults have access to, and use commercial bank products and services. The category of literature did not see the inclusion of adults in the processes of developing policies and frameworks guiding digitization as critical to financial inclusion. The implication of this ideology is that it jettisoned basic principles as expressed in Freire's (1972) theory of participation. The fact that there are still obvious financial exclusion of adults despite ongoing digitization of microfinance banks (e.g., De la Torre et al., 2017; Harigaya, 2017), serve as pointer to the need to rethink how financial inclusion is conceptualized.

8.2.3 The base of the pyramid economy and financial inclusion

Base of the pyramid economy was identified by Prahalad at the beginning of the 21th Century. Scholars started to develop new theoretical insights into the phenomenon and termed it new marketing and wealth creating theory (Kramer & Belz, 2017; Prahalad, 2005). Although Prahalad and his colleagues were disposed to a business logic that was driven by multinational corporations, soon after, other scholars started to see that the base of the base of the pyramid economy can be profitably harnessed without multinational corporations (Thakur, 2015; Vachani & Smith, 2007). Most people living in rural and sub-urban areas in Africa, South America, and Asia where poverty is endemic, fall under the category of those that live and operate in the base of the pyramid economy. Apart from these set of people, most immigrants and refugees living in secluded areas in rich regions such as North America and Western Europe also fall into the category of people operating at the base of the pyramid economic. These group of people are characterized by low earnings, petty businesses, exclusion from social and economic amenities, general lack of ability to acquire and use digital financial facilities and other forms of negative characteristics. Prahalad (2014) suggests that investors and scholars should understand that the base of the pyramid economy has distinct characteristics and that they should incorporate these discrete characteristics into their thinking whenever they are dealing with issues concerning the base of the pyramid economy. In fact, there are several distinguishable groups that live and operate within the base of the pyramid economy. These discrete characteristics make it very difficult to study and develop understanding on how financial inclusion can be implemented at the base of the pyramid economy.

Traders, artisans, farmers and people and businesses rendering services in the educational, health, entertainment, and tourism sectors all constitute part of the base of the pyramid economy. The factor common to these groups is that they mainly operate in rural areas and need community marketing strategies for their needs to be well identified and provided for (Thakur, 2015; Yaacoub & Alouini, 2020). This is not to say that there are no businesses and people that operate at the base of the pyramid in sub-urban and urban areas. There are evidences of petty trending and other forms of base of the pyramid businesses in sub-urban and urban areas in developing countries (Yaacoub & Alouini, 2020). The issue of discrete characteristics of businesses and people operating and living in the base of economy is made more profound because they exist in rural, sub-urban and urban areas that are characterized by different socio-economic, political, and technological realities. There is also the issues of the discreteness of businesses that are characterized as small business, one man businesses and petty trading. While some small businesses are formally registered by government, most one man businesses and petty trades are not. This is the reason why most of them are categorized as informal businesses. Our observation during the cause of the study reported in this work indicates that businesses in the base of the pyramid that are categorized as informal sector businesses have ways to raise the funds they need for businesses and rarely use microfinance banks due to financial inclusion challenges. This is consistent with Mas' (2010) study that showed that traditional saving and credit systems done through hiding cash at home, loans to friends and relatives, deposit collectors livestock and physical assets are mainly the sources of finances and credits for business in the informal sector. Rasheed's et al. (2019) study also shows that in Pakistan only 58% of the small and medium scale enterprises (SMEs) own and use bank accounts in formal financial institutions. The study however, covers SMEs that have been formally registered and not the deluge of SMEs that run within the Pakistan informal sector. In Nigeria, statistics provided by the CBN (2018) indicate that in 2016 48.6% of adult in Nigeria are formally included in the financial inclusion bracket while 9.8% are informally included. This position seems to portend that ongoing financial inclusion efforts still have a lot to deal with. This situation is likely to be worsened if accurate data on the full range of people and businesses rural areas that still suffer lack of access to microfinance banks are factored into current statistics.

The nature of the base of the pyramid economy makes issues regarding financial inclusion to be very complex. The socio-physical nature of the base of the pyramid economy require that the sector be looked at and addressed vis-à-vis the differentiated categories of people, businesses, settlements, technologies, policies and regulations, and social realities. Stakeholders seem to have reached consensus that financial inclusion refers to a state in which people are able to get access to the formal financial institutions' products and services (Rasheed et al., 2019; CBN, 2018). While this definition seems accurate, there are many fluid and subjective views and issues that are peculiar to the base of the pyramid economy that this definition did not cater for. The Nigerian financial inclusion strategy refresh for instance, acknowledges seven different stakeholders that are likely to determine the success or failure of financial inclusion in the country. They are namely, financial services providers, other financial institutions, users (made up of consumers and advocacy groups), development players, public sector institutions, distribution actors (super agents, inter-bank settlement providers, and mobile network providers), and regulators (CBN, 2018). The ways these stakeholders were defined in the document were not explicit. Also, the ways the document categorized people and business at the base of the pyramid where financial exclusion is endemic was not explicit. The role of ICT organizations and other important non-human entities that are crucial to successful financial inclusion at the base of the pyramid was not also well explicated in the document. Another crucial omission in the document is the non-participation of people and businesses in the base of the pyramid economy in the formulation of policies and frameworks used to push financial inclusion. It follows that the document is not base of the pyramid friendly.

8.3 Methodology and research participants' demography

The methods used to collect data for the study are observation and short unstructured interviews. We also did extensive literature review did not follow specific systematic procedures (Avgerou, 2010). It is unlike the systematic literature review or grounded theory literature review that require systematic procedures (Okoli & Schabram, 2010; Utulu et al., 2013; Wolfswinkel et al., 2013). However, the extensive literature review provided avenue to access insights in the extant literature on the digitization of microfinance bank and financial inclusion at the base of the pyramid economy. Two broad types of literature were reviewed: grey literature-government publications and position work s and scholarly literature-journal articles and textbooks. Grey literature are materials produced outside of formal scholarly publishing cycles (Garousi et al., 2019; Schöpfel, 2010). They were got online by search through google scholar and from library shelves. The observation was done for about six months. We observed in real-time events connected to petty traders' awareness and experiences of financial inclusion and microfinance banks digitization. Findings derived through observations were documented in field notes and formed a part of the qualitative data used for the study. The interview sessions lasted between fifteen to twenty minutes each and were recorded using an electronic device. The language used for the interviews is the Yoruba Language. Interviews were transcribed and translated into the English Language. The data were collected in six rural communities (Moniya, Ajibode, Idi-Ose, and Ede, Ode-Omu and Gbongan) in Oyo and Osun States, Nigeria. The four concepts addressed in the study were used as key terms for determining the publication used for the research, interview questions and the events observed. Thirty petty traders were interviewed. Ten of them were male, while twenty were female. Their ages were between the age range of twenty to forty five years. They were involved in different forms of petty trading: sales of retail products, foods products and fruits, drinks and cooked food. The petty traders had their products displayed on tables or containers purposely built to serve as petty trade shops. Their daily income ranges between two thousand five hundred naira and twelve thousand naira. Although most of the petty traders run their trades alone, in some cases, members of their immediate families also help them. The helpers include their children or relatives living with them.

8.4 Study findings

8.4.1 Awareness of microfinance bank digitization

An important finding in the study is that most of the petty traders were not aware of ongoing microfinance bank digitization and financial inclusion programs in Nigeria. Only a quarter of them had dealings with microfinance banks. They had a popular metaphor they used to describe microfinance banks: "gbomule lanta"; which literarily translates to "put your body on burning lantern." The metaphor signifies the high risks associated with the loans provided by microfinance banks. Three of the petty traders who seem to be aware of microfinance bank digitization used to the word "computer" to describe digitization of microfinance banks. They claimed that since microfinance banks started using computers that assessing their services has become more complex. They also noted that digitization requires them to go physically to microfinance banks if they need to access any their financial services. This claim however, alludes to registration requirements put in place by microfinance banks for customers to be able to benefit from their financial services. These realities show that petty traders are not clear about microfinance bank digitization.

8.4.2 Awareness of financial inclusion programs

The study revealed that petty traders are not aware of the financial inclusion programs in Nigeria and the role of microfinance banks in implementing the program. All of them equated financial inclusion programs of microfinance banks to new ways of making them open accounts to keep their monies in microfinance banks. They had this feeling because the primary service microfinance banks advertised to them was opening and owning personal or business accounts. They noted that the microfinance banks they have dealt with do not talk much about providing access to loans to support their livelihood and businesses. Two of them opined that when microfinance banks talk about loans that their loans are normally too expensive and difficult to get. The two petty traders further alluded that since microfinance banks started to use "computers" that getting loans from them have become more stringent.

8.4.3 Availability of microfinance banks in research contexts

Through observation we found out that there are no microfinance banks in the rural settlements that we studied. Most microfinance banks were situated in urban settlements and sub-urban settlements that were close the capital cities of the two states studied. However, some microfinance banks are about one to two kilometres close to rural settlements that are close to sub-urban and urban areas. We also observed that the microfinance banks that were available to be used by the petty traders understudy do not have automatic teller machines (ATMs). This implies that microfinance banks have done very little to create access to cash to the petty traders. Consequently, most of the petty traders studied had the feeling that microfinance banks are not meant for them. The nonexistence of microfinance banks and ATMs in the rural settlements understudy impacts negatively on the extent to which petty traders were aware of financial inclusion programs and microfinance bank digitization.

8.4.4 Microfinance banks' financial inclusion strategies

A striking revelation in the study is that microfinance banks adopt traditional daily contribution system that was the hallmark of money management in rural settlements in South Western Nigeria. We observed that microfinance bank employees go to the six rural settlements that we studied to encourage petty traders to participate in daily contributions. The incentive for participating includes having access to short-time small loans payable within the month. Daily contribution services were also provided by local daily-contribution-collectors. Like microfinance bank employees, the daily-contribution-collectors go to petty traders to collect their contributions everyday. The difference between traditional daily-contribution-collectors and microfinance banks is that petty traders' contributions are paid into the accounts they opened with microfinance banks. So it serves as motivation for opening and owning accounts with microfinance banks. However, all the petty traders indicated that the financial benefits accrued to daily contributions with microfinance banks is not comparable to those accrued to traditional daily-contribution-collectors. Petty traders opined that they prefer the informal business relationship that they have with traditional daily-contribution-collectors to the more formalized relationship they have with microfinance banks. Petty traders noted that they have not had any reason to be afraid of losing their money given that daily-contribution-collectors were residences· in their neighbourhood and had close social ties with petty traders. Some petty traders also indicated that the daily contribution collectors they deal with are their relatives.

8.4.5 Government contributions and ICT environments of the research contexts

We observed that the only level of government that is visible in the research contexts is the local government, given that they are all rural settlements. Apart from Police Posts and Stations, every other government owned institutions-mainly primary schools and primary healthcare centers- in the research contexts are owned by local governments. Unfortunately, the local governments where the research contexts are situated do not show much concern about issues relating to financial inclusion of rural settlements. They also do not have programs for promoting the establishment of microfinance banks in rural settlements. A popular financial inclusion program in the research contexts is the use of point of sale (POS) machines for withdrawals and deposits. The program is however, private sector driven given that it is promoted by commercial banks and individuals that establish POS outlets as means of participating in the financial service value chain. The research contexts also do not have a favourable ICT environment. Aside outlets where mobile phones and mobile phone accessories are sold, there are no outlets where ICT facilities and equipments are sold in the research contexts. There are also no business organizations that provide ICT based services such as repair, installation, and maintenance of ICT facilities and equipment in the research contexts. These two scenarios negatively impact the establishment of microfinance banks and other financial inclusion initiatives in the research contexts.

8.5 Rethinking microfinance bank digitization and financial inclusion at the base of the pyramid economy

The study was prompted by the need to know why ongoing microfinance bank digitization did not lead to desirable level of financial inclusion at the base of the pyramid economy in Nigeria. Revelations in the work show that the ways financial inclusion was conceptualized (Asongu & Odhiambo, 2019; Mbutor & Uba, 2013; Rasheed et al., 2019) influence its implementation at the base of the pyramid economy. Findings in the work further show how the ways financial services rendered by microfinance banks were determined by the ways stakeholders view financial inclusion and how it hampered the financial inclusion of petty traders in the research contexts (Acha Ikechukwu, 2012; Agrawal & Sen, 2017; CBN, 2018). The work reveals critical social realities-*awareness of microfinance bank digitization; awareness of financial inclusion programs; availability of microfinance banks in rural settlements; microfinance banks' financial inclusion strategies; government contributions and ICT environments in rural settlements*- that evolved at the base of the pyramid economy due to the ways financial inclusion was conceptualized. These social realities made it impossible for the digitization of microfinance banks to promote financial inclusion at the base of the pyramid economy.

Stakeholders need to understand these social realities and manage them to promote financial inclusion at the base of the pyramid economy. The work shows that it is necessary for stakeholders to rethink existing social realities if financial inclusion objectives are to be attained. Microfinance banks, government and other stakeholders, particularly rural settlement dwellers, have to acknowledge that financial inclusion has to do with two needs that must be well articulated and understood. First, is the need for them to collaboratively develop well-articulated financial inclusion frameworks. Second, is for them to collaboratively implement financial inclusion programs using the scaling-up strategy. Appropriate financial inclusion program implementation is important because as revealed in the work, the social realities that determine successful use of microfinance bank digitization to induce financial inclusion at the base of the pyramid economy do not only evolve due to events going on in rural settlements. Events going on in sub-urban and urban areas also trigger the social realities that determine successful financial inclusion. Our work shows that the following entities: people, businesses, microfinance banks, ICT organizations, ICT facilities, governments, and policies and regulations put in place by different organizations lead to the events that promote the evolution of the social realities that hamper the use of microfinance bank digitization to attain financial inclusion. Most microfinance banks in Nigeria are domiciled in sub-urban and urban settlements whereas petty traders and businesses in the base of the pyramid economy operate in rural settlements.

Although the study reported in this work was carried out in six rural settlements in two states in Western Nigeria, revelations in the work point to the fact that the extant literature is still lacking studies that appropriately assessed the state of microfinance banks in rural settlements (Acha Ikechukwu, 2012; Olubiyo & Hill, 2002; Taiwo et al., 2016). Given that most microfinance banks are situated either in urban or sub-urban areas, the insights propagated in the extant literature may not be accurate enough to help stakeholders to understand why microfinance bank digitization is not able to promote financial inclusion. The reality is that there are very few microfinance banks in rural settlements in Nigeria. This reality may also be hampering ongoing efforts made to reduce rural-urban migration through social and economic development. The study also revealed the problem that has to do with the fact that microfinance banks in Nigeria run with only one branch; with majority of them not having automatic teller machines (ATMs). By not having ATMs, microfinance bank customers can only access their monies within banking halls. Unfortunately, most microfinance banks' banking halls are physically far from rural settlements. Our work shows the divide between microfinance bank customers that resides in rural settlements, and those that resides in sub-urban and urban settlements. The revelation is important because it shows that there are differences in the ways microfinance bank digitization and financial inclusion is playing out in rural settlements where poverty and lack of access to ICT is endemic and in sub-urban and urban settlement. Our work shows that Prahalad's (2014) advice that governments and organizations that want to deal with businesses at the base of the pyramid should put into cognizance the unique socio-economic contexts where they operate is relevant to microfinance bank digitization and financial inclusion.

8.6 Conclusion

This work deals with how the ways financial inclusion is conceptualized determine the extent to which microfinance banks digitization promotes financial inclusion at the base of the pyramid economy in Nigeria. It chose to address base of the pyramid economy because the sector is crucial to poverty eradication given that majority of poor people and petty traders that are financial excluded are domiciled there. The work treats four concepts namely, digitization, microfinance banks, inclusion and base of the pyramid economy. It argues that the ways financial inclusion is conceptualized by scholars is problematic. Stakeholders that are involved in implementing financial inclusion through digitization of microfinance banks see inclusion only from the point of view of using digitized systems to create access to money. They exclude the inclusion of those expected to patronize digitized microfinance banks in the processes followed to come up with policies, regulations and assumptions that drive microfinance bank digitization and financial inclusion. The work therefore proposes the rethinking of how financial inclusion should be conceptualized. The work exposes critical social realities that constitute challenges to microfinance bank and financial inclusion at the base of the pyramid. It exposes how these social realities evolve due to the events going on in rural, sub-urban and urban settlements and how they impact the extent to which microfinance bank digitization was able to positively impact financial inclusion at the base of the pyramid economy in Nigeria. The work consequently extends insights in existing studies on how microfinance banks impact financial inclusion at the base of the pyramid economy. The work argues for the improvement of the knowledge available on the impact of microfinance banks digitization on financial inclusion of the base of the pyramid economy. The work concludes that achieving financial inclusion through microfinance banks digitization requires: re-conceptualizing financial inclusion and understanding and redressing the social realities in rural settlements that determine microfinance bank digitization and financial inclusion.

References

Acha Ikechukwu, A. (2012). Microfinance banking in Nigeria: Problems and prospects. *International Journal of Finance and Accounting, 1*(5), 106–111.

Adu, C., Owualah, I., & Babajide, A. (2019). Microfinance banks' loan size and default in some selected microfinance banks in Lagos State, Nigeria. Proceedings of INTCESSS 2019-6th International Conference on Education and Social Sciences.

Agrawal, P., & Sen, S. (2017). Digital economy and microfinance. *PARIDNYA: The MIBM Research Journal, 5*(1), 27–35.

Akingunola, R., Olowofela, E., & Yunusa, L. (2018). Impact of microfinance banks on micro and small enterprises in Ogun state, Nigeria. *Binus Business Review, 9*(2), 163–169.

Asongu, S., & Odhiambo, N. (2019). Inequality thresholds, governance and gender economic inclusion in sub-Saharan Africa. AGDI Working Work, No. WP/19/033, African Governance and Development Institute (AGDI), Younde. Available at: http://hdl.handle.net/10419/205003 Accessed on 25 September 2020.

Avgerou, C. (2010). Discourses on ICT and development. *Information Technologies and International Development, 6*(3), 1–18.

Barman, D., Mathur, H., & Kaira, V. (2009). Role of microfinance interventions in financial inclusion: A comparative study of microfinance models. *The Journal of Business Perspectives, 13*(3), 51–59.

Central Bank of Nigeria (CBN) (2018). *Exposure draft of the national financial inclusion strategy refresh.* CBN.

Coronel, C., & Morris, S. (2016). *Database systems: Design, implementation, & management.* Cengage Learning.

De la Torre, A., Gozzi, J., & Schumukler, S. (2017). *Innovation experiences in access to finance: Market-friendly roles for the visible hand?* The World Bank.

Dismas, N., Baptiste, M., & Francois, M. (2018). Assessing the effectiveness of business automation in micro-finance institutions: Customers' perspective. *International Journal of Information Engineering and Applications, 1*(3), 145–149.

Fabozzi, F., Mann, S., & Choudhry, M. (2002). *The global money markets.* Wiley & Sons Publishers.

Fashoto, S., Ogunleye, G., Okullu, P., Shonubi, A., & Mashwama, P. (2017). Development of a multilingual system to improved automated teller machine functionalities in Uganda. *JOIV: International Journal on Informatics Visualization, 1*(4), 135–142.

Freire, P. (1972). *Pedagogy of the oppressed.* Trans. Myra Bergman Ramos. Herder.

Freeman, R, Harrison, J., Wicks, A., Parmar, B., & de Colle, S., (2010). *Stakeholder Theory: The State of the Art.* Cambridge University Press. https://doi.org/10.1002/9781405164771.ch0

Garousi, V., Felderer, M., & Mäntylä, M. (2019). Guidelines for including grey literature and conducting multivocal literature reviews in software engineering. *Information and Software Technology, 106*, 101–121.

Gupta, J., & Vegelin, C. (2016). Sustainable development goals and inclusive development. *International Environmental Agreements: Politics, Law and Economics, 16*(3), 433–448.

Harigaya, T. (2017). Effects of digitization on financial behaviours: experimental evidence form the Philippines. Available at: http://scholar.harvard.edu Accessed on 20 October 2020.

Kearsley, G. (1988). *Online help systems: Design and implementation.* Vol. 12. Intellect Books.

Kramer, A., & Belz, F. (2017). Consumer integration into innovation process: A new approach for creating and enhancing innovation for the base of the pyramid. In *Sustainability challenges and solutions at the base of the pyramid*, pp. 214–241, Routledge.

Latour, B. (2013). Reassembling the social. An introduction to actor-network-theory. *Journal of Economic Sociology, 14*(2), 73–87.

Mader, P. (2018). Contesting Financial Inclusion. Article *in* Development and Change Available at: https://www.researchgate.net/publication/320226228 Accessed on 10 January 2021.

Mas, I. (2010). Saving for the poor: banking on mobile phones. *World Economics, 11*(4).

Mbutor, M., & Uba, I. (2013). The impact of financial inclusion on monetary policy in Nigeria. *Journal of Economics and International Finance, 5*(8), 318–326.

Mhlanga, D. (2020). Industry 4.0 in finance: The impact of artificial intelligence (AI) on digital financial inclusion. *International Journal of Financial Studies, 8*(3), 45.

Ngwenyama, O., & Nielsen, P. (2003). Competing values in software process improvement: An assumption analysis of CMM from an organizational culture perspective. *IEEE Transactions on Engineering Management, 50*(1), 100–112.

Nielsen, N. (2014). Processes to overcome IS implementation barriers. *European Journal of Information Systems, 232*, 205–222.

Okoli, C., & Schabram, K. (2010). A guide to conducting a systematic literature review of information systems research. Working Work s on Information Systems. Available at: http://sprouts,aisnet.org/10-26 Accessed on 20 October 2020.

Olubiyo, S., & Hill, G. (2002). Beyond the risk factor: Bank lending to small scale peasant farms in Nigeria. *African Review of Money, Finance and Banking,* 5–22.

People's Bank of Nigeria Act (1990). Available at: http://nlipw.com/peoplesbankof-nigeria Accessed on 19 October 2020.

Prahalad, C. (2005). *The fortune at the base of the pyramid: Eradicating poverty through profits.* Wharton Publishing.

Prahalad, C. (2014). *The fortune at the base of the pyramid: Eradicating poverty through profits.* (Revised and Updated 5th Anniversary Edition), Anniversary Edition. Prentice Hall.

Pressman, R. (2005). *Software engineering: A practitioner's approach.* Palgrave Macmillan.

Rasheed, R., Siddiqui, S., Mahmood, I., & Khan, S. (2019). Financial inclusion for SMEs: Role of digital micro-financial services. *Review of Economics and Development Studies, 5*(3), 571–580.

Ratan, A. L., Chakraborty, S., Chitnis, P. V., Toyama, K., Ooi, K. S., Phiong, M., Koenig, M. (2010). Managing microfinance with work, pen and digital slate. In proceedings of the 4th ACM/IEEE International Conference on Information and Communication Technologies and Development, pp. 1–11.

Rowe, F., Ngwenyama, O., & Richet, J. (2020). Contact-tracing apps and alienation in the age of COVID-19. *European Journal of Information Systems,* 1–18.

Schöpfel, J. (2010). Towards a Prague definition of grey literature. In Twelfth International Conference on Grey Literature: Transparency in Grey Literature. Grey Tech Approaches to High Tech Issues. Prague, 6–7 December 2010 (pp. 11–26).

Silver, H. (2015). The contexts of social inclusion. Department of Economic & Social Affairs DESA Working Paper No. 144 ST/ESA/2015/DWP/144.

Slee, R. (2011). *The irregular school: Exclusion, schooling and inclusive education.* Taylor & Francis.

Taiwo, J., Agwu, P., & Benson, K. (2016). The role of microfinance institutions in financing small businesses. *JIBC, 21*(1).

Thakur, R. (2015). Community marketing: Serving the base of the economic pyramid sustainability. *Journal of Business Strategy, 36*(4), 40–47.

Thomas, T., & Mefalopulos, P. (2009). *Participatory communication: A practice guide.* The World Bank.

UNSGSA (2018). *Igniting SDG progress through digital financial inclusion.* United Nations Secretary-General's Special Advocate for Inclusive Financial Development.

Utulu, S., Sewchurran, K., & Dwolatzky, B. (2013). Systematic and grounded theory literature reviews of software process improvement phenomena: implications for IS research. Proceedings of the information science and information technology education Conference, pp. 249–279.

Vachani, S., & Smith, N. (2007). Socially responsible distribution: Distribution strategies for reaching the Bottom of the pyramid. INSEAD Business School Research Work, (2008/21).

Wolfswinkel, J. F., Furtmueller, E., & Wilderom, C. P. (2013). Using grounded theory as a method for rigorously reviewing literature. *European journal of information systems, 22*(1), 45–55.

World Bank Institute (2005). Summary Report: E-conference on building inclusive financial sectors for development: widening access, enhancing growth and alleviating poverty, March 28 to April, 2013.

Yaacoub, E., & Alouini, M. (2020). A key 6G challenge and opportunity-correcting the base of he pyramid: A survey on rural connectivity. *Proceedings of the IEEE 180.4, 108*(4), 533–582.

Yahaya, K., & Osemene, O. (2011). Effectiveness of microfinance banks in alleviating poverty in Kwara state, Nigeria. *Global Journal of Management and Business Research*, 11(4).

Young, A., & Wigdor, A. (2021). "Ideal Speech" on Wikipedia: Balancing Social Marginalization Risks and Social Inclusion Benefits for Individuals and Groups. Proceedings of the 54th Hawaii International Conference on System Sciences.

Young, I. (2002). *Inclusion and democracy*. Oxford University Press.

Index

Note: *Italic* and **Bold** page numbers refer to figures and tables. Page numbers followed by 'n' refer to notes.

Printed in the United States
by Baker & Taylor Publisher Services